MERCHANTMAN REARMED

Sir David W. Bone, Kt., C.B.E., LL.D., Master Mariner

MERCHANTMAN REARMED

By
DAVID W. BONE

With drawings by
MUIRHEAD BONE

1949
CHATTO & WINDUS
LONDON

PUBLISHED BY

Chatto & Windus

London

★

Clarke, Irwin & Co. Ltd.

Toronto

To My Son

DAVID

(Lieut. Commander David D. Bone, D.S.C., R.N.)

INTRODUCTION

SOMEWHERE in the great City of London, within a Chancellery where high decisions upon Shipping Control are made, there are—as I am informed—these words of a carved inscription set out above the central fireplace in the boardroom.

As concerning ships, it is that which everyone knoweth and can say, they are our armaments, they are our weapons, they are our strength, they are our pleasures, they are our defence, they are our profits: the subject by them is made rich, the Kingdom through them strong, the Prince in them is mighty: in a word, by them in a manner, we live, the Kingdom is, the King reigneth.

My informant, himself a seaman, was greatly impressed by the sequence in the attributes to ships—all leading up to the final sentence 'the Kingdom is, the King reigneth'. First, the ship as armament and weapon, strong and powerful upon the seas: then, the ship as affording pleasure to hand and to the eye. Defence precedes profit. It seems clear that the author knew his ships and the sea in about the seventeenth century when there was no great difference between a King's Ship and a merchant's ship, between merchantman and bluejacket, in importance to the realm. Under the protection and guidance of the King's ships, the Merchant Navy of to-day has had to take to arms again as armament and weapon, in strength too and not wholly without satisfaction. Of profit, it is perhaps too early yet to write, but still the Kingdom is and the King reigneth.

On the morning of November 20th, 1918, and from the navigation bridge of H.M.S. *Melampus*, I witnessed the surrender of the German U-boats off the port of Harwich. It was a grave quiet day, typical of settled weather in the North Sea. There were sunlit threads on the calm grey surface of it, the sun just peering over banks of low vapour—the pride of the morning—that shrouded the eastern horizon. Growing to the eye in that point of the compass, light cruisers of our Channel Force appeared and, in their almost unruffled wake—for the convoy was proceeding at slow speed—the submarines of the enemy followed in irregular formations. They numbered thirty-seven. At the destroyer rendezvous where the act of surrender took place there was no particular ceremony to mark this Victory. It was almost a routine proceeding familiar to the sailor—changing pilots, just one command 'taking over' from another. But I did notice one incident that had, for me, a very special significance. The destroyer in which I was an accredited observer had the duty of placing naval armed guards and personnel in the captured U-boats as they arrived off the harbour booms. Several of the German commanders did not—or would not—comply with instructions and urged their craft beyond the limits of the swept channel. It was necessary to halt them quickly. The signal used by the yeoman in *Melampus* to arrest them was the mercantile two-flag hoist of the urgent group, International Code, flags 'M.N.'—meaning 'Stop instantly!'

The International Code is designed for use at sea between ships of different nationality. Its phrases are short and one can only become loquacious by expenditure of considerable arm strain in hoist and re-hoist of the flags. But the brief seamanlike phrases in it cover almost all the business of sailors—from enquiry into the cost of bunker coal at Antofagasta or the strength of the nor'east trades, to a comforting assurance addressed to a crippled ship 'we shall stand by until the weather moderates'. Be ye English or Turkish or Esthonian, a hoist of International Code flags can speak for you to a stranger at sea.

This circumstance, the significance of the flags used to bring the beaten German submarine flotillas to a halt, prompted me to write of it in the concluding chapter of *Merchantmen-at-Arms*. That book was published in 1919.

' "M.N." The old flags out again after discard in four years of bitter sea warfare; the old flags of the days when there was peace on the seas, when the German commercial ensign was familiar and respected in all the seas and all the seaports of the World. How many of the Germans in their submarines would appreciate the full significance of the tradesman's signal that brought them to a standstill at the prison gates? The day had long passed since they had used this urgent signal to justify a procedure in sea law and order. No "M.N." to the great *Lusitania* before littering the Irish Sea with her wreckage; no such signal to *Arabic* or *Persia*; no warning to *Belgian Prince*, to *California*, to all the long list; no summons to the Hospital Ships—alight, and indeed specially blazoned, to advertise their presence and humane mission at sea. And now ... their ensign dishonoured, their name as seamen condemned to a tale of infamy, their once-proud commercial seafaring destroyed ... to come into custody ... to render and submit ... all at the beckoning of an International signal!

' "M.N." *Stop instantly*. Disobey at your peril!

'At last, at long last, the Freedom of the Seas, the security of the merchant ships, the safety of all who pass at sea on their lawful occasions, completely re-established by the flutter of old remembered flags!'

There are perhaps too many marks of exclamation in the passages I have quoted from an earlier book. I would agree now that I was emotional when I wrote these lines and that my vaunt had not the substance of long and serious reflection. But, at the date it was written, it was sincere and perhaps even justified by contemporary and better informed opinion. Was it not largely upon the issue I have stressed that the United States entered the War beside us in 1917? Not again, was the current of opinion then, not again would the merchant seaman become a combatant in sea warfare. There was to be a powerful League of Nations to see to that by upholding International Law. The trading seaman could go about his business, he could plan for normal days at sea again, for the only Nation then known to be devoted to savagery at sea had been rendered powerless.

For normal days at sea? I can recall the substance of my thought of that as I stood on the navigation bridge of *Melampus* on that November day off Harwich. Certainly I was elated by the character of the day and my sanguine mood was maybe fortified by an instruction I had, that morning, received: as a result, I saw my sea horizon again in rosy prospect. I was to return to peacetime duty in command of a transatlantic liner.

I had been promoted to my first permanent command during war service and had perhaps my own bright vision of what such a post could be in a world at peace and quiet. The great war was over. I was in good standing, approaching middle age and healthy. My lines would be cast in pleasant places. Transatlantic Ferry? A week at home in Scotland, a week westbound in the Atlantic: a few days amongst friends in Boston and New York. Then return again, and again, and again, . . . but ever sailing with the wise reminder that comes in wind and sea to save me from the rut of over-confidence. No. There would be anxious days too; days of high endeavour in testing seas, in impenetrable fog,—in ice areas with the incidence of low visibility, and always the responsibility for lives and property in trust. But these would be sea days, to be met by vigilance and prudent seamanship. And surely there would be gracious days too, gracious days in which there would be no need for sudden vicious orders to the man at the wheel . . . days when I would have no hurt in my eyes through scanning again and with apprehension the last inch of darkling sea ahead. Would peacetime at sea give me back the hours of ease when I might, with confidence, step down from the bridge and take observant interest in the pleasant rounds of ship-life?

There was a stir on the deck below that recalled me from my thought of peacetime voyaging. A group of German submarine commanders—disembarked from their surrendered U-boats—had been ferried on board *Melampus*. Just tolerated perhaps as they climbed the pilot ladder and stood at the gangway, they seemed disinclined to go towards the place allotted to them on deck. They were speaking loudly, one to the other, and I gathered that they had not expected to be treated in the coldly formal manner that seemed the order in the British destroyer; something was said too about the shame—*das scham*—of carrying in hand their own personal belongings: there might even have been a reference to the Rules of War that, for so long, they had ignored. To my imperfect ear, the German language has its peculiar stridency in protest. It appeared that the U-boat officers objected to being grouped with their own seamen on the decks of a man o' war: it was *nicht wurdevoll*. A young Lieutenant of

Royal Marines, acting as interpreter, restored quiet on the deck below me. He waved them over towards a part of the deck where German seamen were standing about or seated on the bundles of their kit. I remarked that, when the Lieutenant spoke to the U-boat commanders, he did not use the term *Offizieren*. He said *leute*, which means all, everybody. As I remember it, he said '*Alles deutsches leute muss dahin stehen*'. But he said it politely enough.

As the enemy officers obeyed and moved over towards their compatriots I had opportunity to observe them at close hand. It may be that my happy mood yet persisted for I could not see any particular villainy in the faces of the defeated enemy. All were young, most were not unhandsome, and some—even on this historic day of reckoning seemed not seriously disheartened. I had known German prisoners of war before, having trooped them out of Salonica the year before. But these men were not the dispirited weaklings that we had embarked on that occasion. These were sailors. I thought of other German sailors I had seen in the war. At New York in 1915. They too were prisoners, but prisoners self-detained and free to come and go whilst the United States was neutral—the merchant crews of *Furst Bismark, Kaiser Wilhelm die Grosse, Kronprinzessen Cecily,* held to their piers there by the distant majesty of the Grand Fleet.

My train of thought led me back to sailing days in square rig, to days when—as Mate in a full-rigged ship—it was my business to mark my 'crowd', to assess ability and character in the man 'before the mast' upon whose *willingness* we could perhaps count upon making a good passage. It was my experience that the north Germans in our manning—we were truly international when it came to signing on a crew then—were not ill-intentioned and always did their best when the best was something seriously required: the alternative being extinction. I would admit that, in the comfortable feeling I had on that victory day off Harwich, I pondered the prospect of the German merchant seaman without bitterness. I could see nothing but heavy storm ahead for him. Was not his proud commercial seafaring destroyed when no longer could he sail confidently, relying upon the rules of the Nations? It was thought that, never again, would Germany proceed on Naval occasions. How wrong was that confident assumption, and how terribly we were awakened!

In the years between the Wars my dream of gracious days was no illusion. My plan worked out without serious divergence from the course I had considered whilst watching the surrender of the submarines off Harwich in 1918. The chilling blast of the shipping depression in 1930–34 gave me and many others our moments of anxiety—but one can lose canvas and still make port. I had twenty years of complete happiness at sea. I could not even count my blessings. The cross-atlantic service is prodigal of friendships and I was always the fortunate recipient. In 1938, my plan for days at sea was drawing towards a not unhappy conclusion. It was on my calendar that I was due to retire from active service a year later upon reaching the date when commanding sailors are expected to sit down and ask themselves a few questions. I had the answers all ready. In prospect of retirement, I had my plan. That was to re-engage in an employment that had already afforded me great interest and a modest profit. Of books having to do with matters of seafaring, I had written five. What better could I do than to continue this congenial enterprise? Yes. When someone other—my hope, my second in command—would be treading the deck planks of the bridge in the ship I had urged for so long, I would be writing up my personal Log of remembered days.

But, no. I was to be denied that. The Second Great War came. I was again to see *Merchantmen-at-Arms* engaged in many far seas and to take my part with them in proving the inscription set up above that central fireplace.

*   *   *

Merchantman Rearmed is a personal record of experiences in the War and is largely an exercise in recollection. It can be said that almost every civilian workman employed within the United Kingdom during hostilities was in possession of some information not in itself important, but forming part of a secret which the enemy was at pains to uncover. At home and abroad, the merchant seaman was in a position shrewdly to assess and determine the purpose and direction of his voyages and was thus to be particularly courted by enemy informers, out abroad and in his neighbourly haunts when on home leave. On the outbreak of War, a special censorship was imposed on all ships. Amongst the measures put into effect for this purpose of Security was the prohibition enjoined on all sailors against the keeping of Diaries or personal records. Even the ship's Deck, Engine, and Wireless Log Books (so important for reference in the common event of claims and litigations, and normally deposited with the vessel's Owners on the termination of a voyage), were forwarded to a Naval Authority at Blackpool, of all places, and were there retained—it is hoped in careful custody.

I was thus deprived of such useful aid in re-constructing my days at sea and in port throughout the conflict. But there were other sources from which my recollections could be prompted and encouraged. My letters home, although guardedly conforming with the rules, were of value. Often, I wonder if the sight of one's own handwriting does not reflect the mood in which it was written and there springs out of the creased and crinkled sheet of paper a thought that transcribes an apparently senseless phrase into vivid remembrance of the day and its incident. There was also the official channel of communications. 'BY SAFE HAND OF PILOT' was the inscription on the envelopes containing my Report of Proceedings. The pilot was an air-pilot of the R.A.F. and the often bulky envelope was addressed to The Director of Sea Transport at London. Within, I had enclosed a copy of my report together with a request that it be forwarded to my Owners in due course. To the kindness of The Anchor Line I am indebted for access to these formal records.

* * *

My brother's drawings which he has, so generously, allowed me to use in illustration of my text were, for the most part, made during the War while he was Official Artist to the Admiralty. The original drawings are in various public collections, chiefly the National Maritime Museum at Greenwich and the Imperial War Museum in London. I have to thank the Trustees and Directors for kind co-operation in making the pictures available for my book.

I would also wish to thank the Editor and Proprietors of *Life* magazine and their Staff Photographer, Mr. Carl Mydans, for permission to reproduce the photograph that forms the outer cover of the book. Carl Mydans sailed with me in the *Circassia* on the landing in the South of France and his plate reflects my mood of worried conjecture on that important D Day, . . . Then too, I would be remiss indeed if I did not set down my high regard for my friend Robert Eadie, R.S.W., who made the drawing that brings my war text and my long seafaring to its conclusion.

1949   DAVID W. BONE

LIST OF CONTENTS

LIST OF CONTENTS

LIST OF PLATES

LIST OF PLATES

The Frontispiece, and Plates 7, 8, 9, 11 and 12 are Crown Copyright
Plates 3, 4, 10 are reproduced by courtesy of the Trustees
of the National Maritime Museum
Plate 15 Crown Copyright, by courtesy of the
Trustees of the Tate Gallery

LIST OF HEADPIECES

LIST OF HEADPIECES

Chapter I

1918–1939

In the Merchant Navy we were not quite unprepared for action when war came in 1939, and certainly we were not as ill-briefed for hostilities as in 1914. The Admiralty's interest in us, stimulated by our conduct in the earlier World War, had not been allowed to fade entirely in the years between.

Although the sailing of merchant convoys during war at sea is an old resort well-documented in naval annals it was not until all else had been tried the Admiralty again adopted it in June, 1917, when our fortunes in ocean transport were desperately low. Convoy had not before been practised by merchant *steamships* and many important sailors, including at least one high Admiral, predicted failure. There was no failure. By the time that war came to an end it was fully demonstrated that the merchant seaman had proved his ability to keep station in any group of ships, difficult as that sometimes was in the early stages when inter-ship signalling was unfamiliar and even such a necessity as a speaking tube to the engine-room was not always fitted. That My Lords were wishful to continue, and indeed to expand, the good relations between the two great sea services was expressed in this public Signal of late November, 1918.

On the occasion of the first Meeting of the Board of Admiralty after the signing of the German Armistice, their Lordships desire, on behalf of the Royal Navy, to express their admiration and thanks to the Owners, Masters, Officers and crews of the British Mercantile Marine, and to those engaged in the Fishing Industry, for the incomparable services they have rendered during the War, making possible and complete the Victory which is now being celebrated. . . . The Merchant Service and the Royal Navy have never been so closely brought together as during this War. In the interests of our glorious Empire this connexion must prove a lasting one.

The sweetening of public relations between Departments was not, in 1919, the recognised business it has since become. It is possible that the first effort in this direction was the appointment of Naval Liaison Officers at that date to encourage friendly feelings between the personnel of the Royal and Merchant Navies. These officers were posted to unusual duty in the great seaports and seafaring districts of the United Kingdom. They would probably be listed under the Trade Division and they would have duties in that department of Admiralty, but they are chiefly remembered by the merchantmen as welcome visitors to the trading ships in port. Through them, matters of joint interest were communicated to some higher naval authority and by them we were encouraged to express our views on points of seafaring. I recall a long discussion and some good papers on the best method of weathering a heavy gale in convoy: whether to 'heave to' with the wind and sea on the bow, or slow down and keep the gale astern: the 'Star and Scatter' diagrams providing for emergency dispersal of a convoy under heavy attack —that we had to memorise in 1940—were curiously reminiscent of the plans I heard argued with the N.L.O. appointed to the Clyde (now Commodore E. G. Jukes-Hughes). We got along very well together, but this association did not last for long. It seems likely that the Geddes axe fell with swift decision upon such an ornamental if useful branch of the Naval Service. It was discontinued in 1922. Subsequently, our acquaintanceship was remote, if not quite forgotten.

There was a period of prosperity in shipping when the first World War had ended. The scarcity of tonnage, due to our serious losses, and the urgency of cargo transport combined to establish high freights. Emigration too was abnormal, particularly to the United States. There were crowded passages westward to American ports and the homeward voyage was made with the passenger fittings taken down and the resultant spaces stowed tightly with great bulk of express cargo. For a time we did well. Many new ships were laid down; others were acquired at high cost from abroad. Some German ships were taken over as reparations. (We did not think then of the new and more

The *Queen Elizabeth* ready for launching in 1938; the *Transylvania* outward bound towards New York

economical tonnage that Teutonic ingenuity could later build in their place.)

But the sea and the commerce it serves are not static for long. Labour difficulties prevented the completion of much of the new tonnage before advantage could be taken of the boom in shipping freights. There was a slump in commodity exchange and the ships, that are its servants, fell upon evil days. Inevitably, the waterside streets of the seaports became crowded with unemployed seamen and the docks and harbours packed closely with idle ships. But storm blows out in time and the tide does not always ebb. In 1936, there were better prospects and three years later we were well built and reasonably employed.

From amongst my now unimportant papers I have taken a card headed 'Merchant Navy Defence Course'. It records my attendance at lectures on Shipping Defence in September, 1937 —two years before the outbreak of war. At that date the Merchant Navy had again become an interest of the Admiralty. All masters and officers were brought into the scheme of instruction as a necessity for continued employment at sea. Shipowners too were advised to put the ships in order against the requirements of convoy practice. We were warned in time.

The classes at Glasgow were conducted at the R.N.V.R. Headquarters—that had seen the merchantmen prepared in the war of 1914–18. The lecturer in charge was Lieut.-Commander R. A. Cassidi. It was obvious that he had been specially selected for the post for he was lucid and fluent and possessed a turn of humour that did much to enliven the sober substance of his text. I think it likely that his sea service included escort duties with convoys in the earlier war for his comment on our endeavours and many mistakes showed an intimate acquaintance with life under the Red Ensign. International Law as it affected the merchant seaman was the subject of the first lecture and it seemed curious to learn that there was still an insistence on our non-combatant status. Many who sat to listen had been shot at on sight on the high and international seas and put up embarrassing questions . . . that were not answered. It was not known with certainty, the lecturer went on, that the enemy would resort to 'sink at sight' when hostilities were opened. In the strict ruling of International Law, we could only defend our ships when directly attacked. Procedure then was to turn the ship's stern towards the enemy and emit smoke. Our guns would be so fitted that they could only be trained on a stern-ward bearing, and fire must not be opened except upon the direct order of the Master or—in his absence—of the next senior officer. It seemed incredible that the lessons of the last war had been so soon forgotten. But there *was* a derisive grin on the speaker's face as he noted the ill reception of such a *pro-nunciamento*. . . . He hoped he had our assurance that Counsel's opinion on the matters of ship defence would be given due attention.

From law to literature was a short step and the care and custody of confidential books and documents was next con-sidered. At this date (1937), the lecturer said, it would not be advisable to list and detail the many publications that would be held on signature in the merchant ships if war should come. But security would not be compromised by some suggestions regarding the safe-keeping of these important secret papers and the manner of their destruction in the imminence of capture or grave casualty. It was in respect of the latter the speaker cap-tured our interest, as so often he did, by relating an incident in point. Destruction by fire was, of course, the safest and most satisfactory method of disposal and as far as possible the books and papers would be of an easily inflammable quality. But there was not always time for that and the quickest way would be to dump the consignment overboard. A weighted and eyeletted bag would be provided for this purpose to ensure its immediate sinking. He added that we would have to give thought to the depth of water in which the jettison was made and instanced the case of a great 'find' in Channel waters in 1915, a Brixham trawler having dredged up a set of German codes and plans that had been thrown over by a surfaced submarine when hopeless under attack by our destroyers.

Convoy would be put into operation at the earliest possible date after the outbreak of war. Merchant ships had not sailed in such formations for twenty years and the new generation of watchkeepers had no practical experience of keeping station. But the younger men were much more expert at quick inter-ship signalling than we elders had ever been. The ships were better fitted for the work. We were no longer dependent on home-made 'Heath Robinson' contraptions for contact with the engine-room. There would not be that difficulty in acquiring the knack of station-keeping in convoy. But the lecturer had to keep to his text. It was thought that not all merchant seamen were convinced of the advantage and safety of voyaging in convoy and some might be loath to relinquish their independence. So it was doubtless to counter this feeling the lecturer emphasised the significant figures of merchant ship losses in the war of 1914–18. He said that 16% was the casualty figure for ships sailing independently and 0.5% when voyaging in convoy —a statement as challenging to the doubtful as reassuring to those long since convinced.

Attendance at the Defence Course was not necessarily a day to day obligation. Ships had still to be sailed on their voyages and one could interrupt the series to conform with sea duty. I note that it was nearly a year later when I returned to the Headquarters in Whitefield Road to be instructed against sea mines and refreshed in gunnery. It seemed then (1938) that we were on the brink of war and D.E.M.S. (the department for Defensively Equipped Merchant Ships) was already in occupation of the R.N.V.R. Gunnery Sheds, intensively employed in drilling merchant crews. I found it strange to be back again, alongside what I think was the same Vickers 4″ gun at which I learned a little in 1917. But the years having taken their toll, I was not expected to sweat at every number in the gun's crew as I did then. It was enough that I could still order the correct sequence of a probing bracket and leave its execution to more agile sailormen with nimbler fingers.

It seemed odd that the course should open with a text on International Law and end on a note that envisaged a breach of it. We were told that the Germans would possibly use poison gas from the air against us and an exhibit of the garb in which we might have to navigate and fight, worn by a stalwart navy rating, was paraded in front of the class. He wore an oilskin suit and hefty rubber boots, tied up by rope-yarns at wrist and waist and ankles; he was mittened in special gloves that had fore-finger and thumb loosely knotted for trigger work. His head was protected by a steel helmet and his face by a fearsome gas mask of Navy pattern. A startling apparition! I wondered how we could be expected to stand up in such encumbrances when quick seamanlike duty was to be undertaken. The class looked on, gravely.

The lecturer had said it was not certain that gas would be used by any combatant if war came and it was doubted if it could be released from the air in lethal concentrations against shipping. It was known that the Germans and possibly the Italians held stocks and had made experimental flights. When asked if we too 'were in the trade', he admitted that we were not quite with-out our form of retaliatory *schrecklichkeit*. He said we had made experiments at sea, but not always with success. In one case where a corps of scientific observers, suitably garbed like the leading seaman we had just seen, were embarked in a trawler off the Orkneys, matters did not go well. The co-operating aircraft had hurriedly to be ordered back to base and the tests cancelled. It was a day of brisk wind and sea. In the minutiae of arrangements the claims of Father Neptune had been over-looked. It was found impossible to combat sea-sickness . . . in a gas mask!

Chapter II

EVERYTHING FOR THE
BALLROOM

I WOULD set my date of serious apprehension as late in August, for that was when I had to seek out a shipchandler in the port of New York who could supply me with thick black paper cut to patterns of many sizes. The *Transylvania* was a large ship of 17,000 tons. In the 575 feet length of her hull there were many windows and circular ports or scuttles: on the upper decks were hundreds of larger windows that included the highly decorative frames of the lounges and public rooms. For a complete 'blackout' in the ship a great quantity of paper would be required and the cutting of it to fitting sizes so that no chinks would emit a beam of light at night-time was a considerable undertaking not anywhere laid down in a seaman's manual. Yes, 28th August, 1939, that was the day I journeyed from my ship together with Felix McGlennon in search of protection for her. It appeared to me quite definite that war would break upon us on the passage home. It was time to 'take all precautions' as laid down in our Defence Course instructions.

That we, in the ships, had not already done so requires explanation. The great business of passenger traffic in the North Atlantic is peculiarly sensitive to the shades of publicity and particularly to newspaper comment. Whilst favourable report is eagerly welcomed, another shade might arouse disquiet in the intending voyager. There was the state of emergency on this date but war had not yet been declared. It was still a possibility that we could reach the Clyde before the lights went out at sea. Almost hourly editions of the New York papers blazed conflicting headlines. In search of 'copy' the ship news reporters were eagerly alert on the waterfront. It would not do to assume the worst and make preparation for war at sea at too early a date; already the fact that we and other British liners in the port had raised and were maintaining steam for a sudden sailing had been given a few capital lines in an 'extra' and even the simple precautionary measure of placing special crew watchmen in the ship's cargo holds was cue for half a column on the probabilities of sabotage.

But, if we in *Transylvania* had our minor irritations over such undue attention, we were in good content as compared with the tribulations of the *Bremen* of the Norddeutscher Lloyd that lay upstream from us. To her at Pier 88 there was a path well trodden by United States Officers, Customs Investigators, the Coast Guard, even ordnance surveyors of the U.S. Navy. That their greater attention was paid to the German vessel was in no way a hint of preference in the imminent struggle at sea. The United States was very strictly neutral. But the *Bremen* was of a special class that called for investigation. She had high speed and could be converted at sea without difficulty to become a formidable commerce raider. The fact that, apparently, she carried no weapons on her entry into the port of New York remained to be proved and the Customs, Coast Guard, and naval experts were detailed to examine her and report. It was said that the spaces of the ship were taped and measured in search of a hidden compartment in which armament could be concealed. When it was established that the *Bremen* carried no artillery the text of comment in the newspapers drifted to ingenious conjecture. An unidentified steamship was rumoured to be held offshore, would rendezvous with the *Bremen* on sailing and transfer to her all the men, weapons and ammunition needed to harry the Allied trade routes. A sinister prospect; it would be as well to acquire all that was necessary for complete blackout.

In general, ships' stores laden abroad are of standard quality and pattern: in quantity they are governed by the season of the year and the estimates of passenger booking. Felix, who was the Company's purchasing agent, was nothing if not efficient. He had been known to have an incoming ship's drystores stacked up on the dockside ready to be hoisted on board before the ship for which they were intended had passed inward at Sandy Hook. It was a rare occasion when he was faced by demands that taxed his experience and uncommon knowledge of the resources of the port. But the novel indent that I submitted to him was quite beyond his range of former purchases.

'One thousand filled sandbags, each half-hundredweight size,' he read—wondering. 'You goin' inta th' building trade, Captain?' 'Shovels—eight feet shafts attached.' . . . 'A long way from th' job at that.' . . . 'Bleachin' powder, eh? Never heard o' them goods in a ship. . . .an' rubber hoods 'n' forty suits oil-skins! *Jeez!* Th' clothin' trade too. . . . Ye'll be in cloaks an' suits nex'. What's th' big idea?'

Explanation followed; that the sandbags were required for protection of the bridge and wheelhouse and the engine-room skylight, that the shovels were long-handled to keep the operator at distance when dealing with incendiary bombs. The hoods and oilskins were to protect a working party against gas attack from the air. Felix's kind old face clouded at this mention of peril in a ship he knew. He agreed to get busy on the orders and I could almost see his left hand curving in anxiety to grasp a telephone receiver. But it was the larger item of 'thick black paper, cut to the pattern of sizes following' that brought an incredulous whistle from his lips. 'Sizes following' comprised three sheets of foolscap, looking somewhat like an examination paper in advanced mathematics. Perplexed, he studied the requisition, then his face cleared as his active memory of former unusual requests occurred to him.

'Max Fertigs,' he shouted, rubbing his hands confidently, 'Max Fertigs. Everything f'r th' Ballroom. . . . Masks an' faces. . . . Paper hats. . . . Fertigs kin do it, Captain. Can ye come downtown wit' me now? . . . Might, they'd be some difficulty about them sizes.' Felix was on his mettle. He seemed excited as he led me down the gangway.

Transylvania, in the winter season, had been largely employed as a cruising liner, sailing out of New York on glamorous schedules and having 'giant' programmes of festival activities on board and on shore. 'Rudy Valee Orchestras' . . . 'Bridge Tuition by Experts' . . . 'Crime Club Sessions conducted by Famous International Detectives' . . . 'Visit the Jai Alai Games at Havana' . . . 'Dance in the Moonlit Patio at Sans Souci' . . . 'Hear the Voodoo Drums in Darkness at Port au Prince'.

All these, and other arresting 'slogans' occurred to me as I sat with Felix in the staff car bound downtown to Messrs. Fertig in quest of war equipment. We turned south on Greenwich Avenue and purred on to the lesser and West Broadway, then drew up at a wide doorway. If the outer aspect of the establishment was somewhat dingy and colourless, the great windows made up for that; they blazed with gaudy tinselled emblems of communal excitement. Over all, a huge stripbanner was displayed. The lettering upon it was—just as Felix had exclaimed—MAX FERTIG, INC. . . . EVERYTHING FOR THE BALLROOM. We alighted and turned into the doorway. Felix asked for Mr. Guttekunst. Very much to my astonishment, Mr. Guttekunst expressed no surprise at our unusual requirements. Yes . . . cut to the required sizes too . . . but that would be expensive . . . and would take time. I mentioned a date for delivery and left Felix to arrange details with our quick efficient friend whilst I had a look around the showrooms.

It was a curious place from which to sail out towards the likelihood of savage warfare at sea. Not all the exhibits were of tinsel and coloured paper. A large showcase in which silken flags were displayed interested me. The insignia embroidered on them showed a catholicity of patronage that ranged from the brilliant banner of a Lithuanian Brotherly Society to the modest blue emblem of the Daughters of St. Madan. The pennants of schools and colleges formed a considerable part of the display; masonic sashes and aprons were there too. But I saw no 'swastika' included. I had the thought to enquire, but another glance at Mr. Guttekunst seated in his office led me to consider such a query not at all tactful. Arrangements concluded, we said good-bye and left the warehouse. Felix was in high spirit and, naturally, proud of his acumen in solving the unusual problem of supply—'cut to sizes'. On return to the ship I had my moment of doubt and expressed a fear that Mr. Guttekunst was maybe somewhat sanguine. We had given him only two days: there might be delay in delivery of the goods.

'He kin do it all right,' said Felix. '. . . tol' me he knew all about fittin' black paper t' ship window sizes. . . . said Max Fertigs had just filled a big order . . . f'r th' *Bremen*.'

*　　*　　*

It would have been more in keeping with the mood of dread expectancy, or recurrent rumour and alarm, that marked the dying days of that momentous August of 1939, had we been permitted to sail in the quiet of the night—to slip from Pier 45 with no undue advertisement and head out on our voyage without uncertainties. But the State Department at Washington was at pains to insist that every stop and comma in the outward manifest (of cargo for overseas) was rightly placed. These were not the days for liberal admission of a corrective post-entry, an amendment that pre-supposed the ship's early return to a port in the United States. (It was not unlikely that the sudden night flight from New York of the German raider, *Kronprinz Wilhelm*, was recalled from the files of 3rd August, 1914.) Washington was adamant; the ship's clearance would only be granted upon rigid inspection of documents and we must put to sea in the broad of day.

So, on sailing day, I had ample opportunity to study the painted murals in the great central hall of the Custom House downtown. It was not that they were unfamiliar to me for I had seen the artists at work on them in the days of the great depression, Indeed, was I myself not one of Uncle Sam's oldest customers in the matter of sea traffic that is registered there? For a period of about twenty-four years, inward and outward bound, I had made oath to 'the truth of the entries' at the desk of many Deputy Collectors. Certainly, I had known delays before, but these were not often of serious moment. There would be a brief session at the desk telephone, the Company's clerk would perhaps bounce out of the Hall for a few minutes ... then hurry back, waving a missing docket or a voucher for the Light Dues. A simple matter, quickly concluded.

But not on that day of sailing. It was with an apologetic but friendly smile Mr. Farrell, the Deputy, asked me to stay around for a while. There were some export items under scrutiny. He hoped word would come through soon ... from Washington. Nor was I the only shipmaster thus detained for further confirmations. The hall was crowded as I had rarely seen it in midweek. Perspiring clerks, shippers, forwarders, agents, scurried about from desk to desk in quest of documents: long queues formed up here and there—where harassed officials were poring over bulky files. Standing apart from the active crowd in the central rotunda were many shipmasters, pursers and seafaring men, attendant but alien to the clerical issues involved. We were all, of course, in shore attire—some were dandy in light summer clothes for it was a steaming hot day and it was not yet that the uniform of the Merchant Navy could be worn with propriety on the sidewalks of New York. We waited long, and I had opportunity to reflect upon an earlier prelude to warfare at sea, to recall the days of 1914 when I had awaited rectification of export items in the ship's papers, idling about on the same tiled squares and in thought of a sombre prospect at sea. The hall of the Custom House had undergone its changes in the many years, in some way dictated by the W.P.A. mural paintings, but it was the character of the busy throng crowding it that held my chiefest interest; all were so feverishly intent upon affairs, the coming and the going was abrupt, tense, regardless—one man of the other; the matters seemed so serious. Serious business was there too—in 1914—but oddmen were included in the congregation then, casual negociants come in from the streets to seek friendly contact with the sailor just newly in from sea. A waiting period then could be made bearable in such company.

I recalled the dapper figure of a shipchandler's runner with his display of opulent cigars peeping from the edge of an upper waistcoat pocket, all a-ready to be drawn with a flourish and proffered to a likely seafaring customer; and the well-dressed boarding masters, exuding a benevolent interest in manning difficulties and able to supply 'prime' seamen at a moment's notice—and at a price; laundrywomen, tailors and outfitters, slop-chest suppliers, bootmakers—the tattoo artist with his book of fanciful designs (who also peddled invisible inks), the racing tipster who held fortune in his hands; there was too the constant servitor, the old Italian shoeblack who could conjure time away by quaint and friendly comment on the doings of the day, the while he roused a polish that no one other could outshine. Where? Not here any more. Nor were the 'camp' followers of the war in Europe, the inventors, the share promoters, the earnest and doubtless well-meaning students in the science of war who had each his plan for us to prosecute and achieve immediate victory. At that date, wireless was not in universal use, the Atlantic telephone was not known: letter mails and the use of the telegraph had come under censorship. It seemed to the hopeful visitant that, in the rotunda of the Custom House, great plans could be disclosed to the voyaging sailor, plans that they thought in all innocence could later be submitted by him to high authority in the British Isles. I remembered Mr. Lindley, an inventor who had devised a self-controlled projectile for use against the hostile aircraft of the day. It was designed to minimise casualties within our own lines and was fitted in some way with a tumbler 'cut-off' and could only explode on *upward* flight. We were to make our fortune together—if only I could contact the British Minister of Munitions! Nor did I forget the keen-faced stranger—doubtless blown in from the nearby Curb

Exchange—who endeavoured to sell me shares in an Alabama coal seam by assurance that the British Navy had acquired a controlling interest in it. . . . But the oddmen were gone now, perhaps by reason of the vigilant Customs guards that I remarked in attendance.

The great clock above the southern entrance showed three of the afternoon when I was called to sign the papers and make oath to the truth of them. Mr. Farrell bade me 'a good voyage' and I thought the warmth of his handshake comforting. To the ship then, quickly—and fingering my warrant to depart. At the street entrance to Pier 45 all the activities of embarkation were proceeding normally. The lading of cargo from the lower area of the dock had ceased but some miscellaneous packages were being carried by the dockers from trucks towards the passenger gangways. This was perhaps unusual . . . but so were the packages. It was evident that Mr. Guttekunst had not had time to wrap the large consignment of his goods in the customary containers for shipment. Certainly they were well and sufficiently protected by rolls of outer coverage but the black content was exposed on two sides. Stepping politely amongst the gaily-dressed passengers—for the embarkation squad of dockers are picked for special duty—the labouring men and their burdens seemed to strike a sombre note: the black paper peeped out beside the white outer covers, uncommonly like certificates of mourning.

But that funebral note had been relieved by Mr. Guttekunst's bright idea of reiterated advertisement. Prominently stencilled on each one of the many packages was the 'slogan' of the house, MAX FERTIG, INC. . . . EVERYTHING FOR THE BALLROOM. And the inscription was printed in a shade of red . . . which is the colour of warfare.

Chapter III

ENVELOPE 'Z'

ENVELOPE 'Z' which had lain in my safe for over a year had not the appearance of containing an important message. It was of insignificant size and, handling it, one could guess that it held no more than a single flimsy sheet. In such an investigation, care had to be taken not to crack the imposing Admiralty seal on the back of it for at the end of a voyage it had often to be produced for examination by the waterguard of His Majesty's Customs. It was addressed to The Master, S.S. *Transylvania*, and was inscribed—'Not to be opened until instructed by wireless message'. It was kept inviolate amongst the confidential pamphlets and circulars that the threat of war had addressed to shipboard. Often when consulting the others I had turned it over and weighed it in my hand, wondering in what circumstances I would be told to open it, and what would be my state of mind when the seal was broken. In the earlier World War I had gained knowledge of the skill and resource of the enemy in sea operations, my ship—the first *Cameronia*—having been torpedoed and sunk in the Mediterranean in 1917. What new weapons would be employed and how far would our defences prevail? To the menace of attack by surface raider and submarine would now be added the new offensive from the skies. The booklets that lay beside the fateful envelope made horrendous reading. Most had to do with the treatment of wounds and illness caused by gas or incendiary attack from the air: the protective measures advised inspired little confidence. I was always glad to turn the key in the safe again, trusting that my alarms could be controlled . . . if the time came.

We were four days out from New York when the time came. Mr. Macdonald, the senior wireless officer, marked it himself at seven in the morning of Sunday, 3rd September. A glance at his face gave me at once the text of the message that he held out without comment. It was typed carefully on the same printed IMMR form that had so often conveyed birthday greetings or other home reminders to me at sea. It was from the Admiralty and read simply that war against Germany was declared and that Envelope 'Z' was to be opened.

I suppose the long year of uncertainty since Munich had bred a state of mind that welcomed a final decision, however frightful that decision appeared. We would have to get it over and done with now. There is a relief in action, but for a brief moment I was reluctant to open the envelope. Its lettered title seemed so final. 'Z', the last barking character of the alphabet! The terminator of all reasoned argument!

But Mr. Macdonald was waiting. Rightly, he had concluded that there would be orders to put into operation the long prepared plans for restriction of his 'sparks'. There was nothing very new in the message. It conformed with the instructions of the Defence Course we had both attended but—of interest to his department—there was given the secret call sign by which the *Transylvania* would now be known. Except in emergency, all forms of wireless transmission were forbidden. But the receivers would be continuously manned and we were warned to act instantly on the text of any subsequent message that included our new call sign in the preamble. All privately-owned wireless sets within the ship were to be impounded. We had already anticipated such an order, having maintained a discreet wireless silence since sailing from New York, not without arousing considerable complaint amongst passengers who could see no harm in their plainly-worded cablegrams. And we had had our difficulty in rounding up the many private sets, now so compactly-fashioned as to need no visible aerials. . . . When the officer had gone, I turned to the other matters regarding the navigation. On clearing from Sandy Hook I had taken the northern route as the shortest way home, but now it was in orders to avoid frequented Atlantic tracks and it would be necessary to swing far north towards the crown of a great circle that would lead me into lone waters west of the Hebrides. The weather at the moment was clear. There was little wind and the sea was calm. I had not thought that I would ever wish a clement day put off my sea calendar, but mist or fog was what we wanted now to screen us from gunsight and that, as I considered, we were likely to experience in the north.

I had misgivings of the manner in which the ill-news that it was now my duty to announce would be received. Four days out, fine weather, and the ship obviously making her best speed, had encouraged the belief that we would succeed in making port before war was declared. It was known that Poland had been attacked and in part overwhelmed, but the hope of another Munich was doubtless held by many on board. We were a very crowded ship. The great World's Fair in New York had been an attraction for Scottish people, largely of the scholastic classes, for whom modest fares had been quoted and who were now returning. There was also a considerable number of American citizens, for the most part medical students sailing over to resume study at our universities. Being Sunday, I thought the most conformable opportunity to make the dire news known would be when at Morning Prayer, for there is always an element of comfort in such a gathering together during grave emergency. As we did not include a chaplain amongst our passengers, it fell to me to conduct the service.

I was not at my ease nor was my mind disengaged from the many problems that crowded up for settlement. I felt that my proper place was now at my post on the bridge even although all necessary orders had been passed. The news was accepted in silence. It was possibly discounted by prior knowledge, as not all the private broadcast receivers had been gathered in and the 'galley wireless' is swift on shipboard. I learned later that there was a group demanding immediate return to New York, mostly confined to the American students, but they did not directly present that view to me. Perhaps the recital of the Sailors' Prayer that followed in the course of the service may have done something to allay all fears, as always it had disburdened mine.

'Correct us in our judgment, O Lord, and incline us always towards our duty: that we may be a security and a safeguard to all who pass at sea upon their lawful occasions.'

★   ★   ★

The intention of the enemy in respect of International Law at sea was quickly disclosed. There was not to be, as in 1914, a period of suspense and political exchanges before 'sink at sight' became the German rule. In the early hours of the 4th September we learned that the *Athenia* had been torpedoed without warning in the Atlantic and grievous loss of life was reported. We were then far distant from the position given but it seemed near, for it was out of the same quiet sea this first blow had come. In the morning when passengers were astir the news of the disaster was made public on the bulletin board in an effort to forestall the sensational rumours that could be expected, for there was still a 'cat's whisker' undetected and already it had bombed Berlin and sunk the German fleet. Gloom there was, but if fear and apprehension was aroused by the grim news there was no panic sign of it amongst the passengers when they came on deck. Only there was a resigned gravity in expression as they surveyed our preparations against entry into the danger zone that then I estimated to extend to 40° W.

From the upper decks the ship looked strangely larger and broader because of the lifeboats, transferred from their inboard chocks and now outswung and overhanging the water in readiness for any sudden lowering away. There, and with the covers unrolled, they made a long sinister array—a constant reminder of the last resort. It can be confessed that a ship's boats are rarely the exhibits of which a crew can be proud and ours were no exception. Promotion is not often earned by any pristine appearance of their inboard planking, although service-ability is assured by frequent inspection. They are grim and grey and perhaps not overclean: the bulk of necessary but diverse gear and equipment makes stowage difficult and with an awkward appearance of congestion and disorder. But that disorder is more apparent than real and as I surveyed them from

Outbound shipping in the Hudson River

the bridge I had the confidence that they were in working order and ready for use. I did not care to study their new positioning overlong for the thought of the survivors of a ship we knew well adrift on the Atlantic in just such small unsheltered craft was not stimulating.

I had not known the Atlantic so empty of ships as on the passage. Had the weather been grey and misty—as I had hoped —the absence of shipping would not have been noticed, but day succeeded day with the sea calm and the visibility exceptional. Since Nantucket Lightship had dipped in the sea line astern, we had sighted only one distant fisherman on the Banks. It seemed almost as though the threats of war had cleared the Northern Atlantic. Zig-zagging all day and in the moonlight of the short summer nights robbed us of the swift and direct progress I had hoped to make and it was the morning of the 7th September when we sighted the lone pinnacle of Rockall.

No wireless signals from the Admiralty with our war tally in the preamble had come through, but our receiving ear in the radio cabin had its full of news that we studied long in the effort to gain knowledge of operations at sea. Not only what was signalled, but what was not, was taken into account. The discontinuance of Atlantic weather reports at a late date in August was significant of impending action, but one could take assurance that the enemy's air force had not yet extended operations far at sea by the continued signals of commercial aircraft flying between Botwood and Foynes. That the Trade Division of the Admiralty had sprung busily into action could be gathered from the long signals directing, recalling, and re-routeing British ships in all the seas of the world. Signals of distress were not infrequent. They were mostly from positions in the Channel and in the waters around the British Isles. From such items it could be taken that the U-boats had not yet advanced far into the Atlantic, but that hope was abandoned when the American liner *Washington* reported that she had picked up the crew of the torpedoed *Olivegrove* in 15° W. In all the flood of signals there was none to indicate a change of interest in *Transylvania* and we augured well from that. On sailing, we were scheduled to call at Moville in Lough Foyle to land passengers there before proceeding to the Clyde. But Moville was now a neutral port and I had abandoned the intention of going there.

I had not thought I would ever see Rockall on my voyaging. It is a small lone pinnacle far out in the Atlantic and few sailors other than the Iceland fisherman on their trawler passages sight it. No ocean sea route goes near it and with shipping tracks to be avoided in wartime it seemed a fitting point of landfall. It is distant about 350 miles from the Clyde—a day's run—and it was in prospect of traversing the more dangerous waters of the Western Approaches between Scotland and Ireland in night time I had elected to steer so far north. There was too another consideration. Our course would take us near to the position in which the *Athenia* was sunk and that I judged would be a most unhealthy spot for a cruising U-boat. The barometer had fallen steeply and it was apparent that the long spell of fine weather was at an end. The overcast sky had the hard indigo appearance that presaged rain and, later, low visibility that would be welcomed now—as so often it had been condemned when making the land. But at daybreak it was still clear and the blue peak of Rockall stood out on the horizon in uncommon clarity.

All day we zig-zagged in a south-east course towards the mainland, carving out a fantastic pattern on the flat of the leaden sea. We had many eyes. Lookout had been fortified by volunteers from amongst the passengers, but, during the clear period, there had been only the smoke of distant ships to reward their keen acceptance of the posts. Perhaps we were over-impatient to see some sign of life and action outboard the ship and it had been thought that an escort might now have been sent to meet us in this particularly dangerous zone. A crowded ship . . . and unarmed. I recalled the practice of the earlier war and the relief when a rendezvous had been made with an armed supporter. . . . Rendezvous? That was it. How could a rendezvous be made when we had not yet been supplied with a secret wireless code? . . . In late afternoon the rain came; not suddenly in squalls or heavy downpour, but growing in persistence from a wet mist to the steady drizzle of south-easterly weather.

24

We had just turned on an angle of the zig-zag when a small craft was sighted about two miles distant. Its relative bearing did not seem to change and I thought of a fisherman at his nets. But we were still far seaward of the 'hundred fathom' line and a cast in such deep waters could only be fruitless. As we drew on, the long telescope revealed her as a ship's lifeboat, apparently un-manned and adrift. Perhaps I was incautious to alter helm and steer to close her, for I remembered only too well that the Hun had his habit of penalising any motive of humanity at sea. But there might well be occupants, unable to stand up and signal their distress. We circled the little craft at close range but there was no one in her. From the established fact that the mast and sails were still lashed to the thwarts and a few discarded garments were strewn on the bottom boards it could be guessed that the occupants had been taken up from her. She had not been long in the water for the outside paintwork was fresh and clean. We could not distinguish any name or port for the customary lettering had been painted over. . . . We were not hardened to sea warfare then and the incident, that passed so swiftly, aroused anxiety that was not confined to the passengers on board.

In contrast with the empty waste of the Atlantic, the North Channel appeared to have more than its normal stream of traffic when we had sighted the dimmed glow of Oronsay at midnight. I was in doubt of the measures that would be taken thus early in the conflict and half-expected the coastwise lights to be extinguished (as many were) and it was a great relief to know that the more important were still exhibited, even if at diminished powers. The avoidance of collision was now the immediate task. The lights of shipping had gone out at sea on the 3rd September and without that aid there were elements of disaster. The night was darkly overcast and the rain persisted. One could not see very far ahead and an alteration of course, when it became necessary, had to be accompanied by dis-tinguishing blast or blasts of the steam whistle. The sounding of the powerful Willett-Bruce in this way, however accustomed the ship's seamen were to its note, was not as fully understood by the passengers. At frequent boat drills they had been told that six blasts of the whistle was the signal of alarm, on hearing which they must assemble at their boat stations with lifebelts firmly adjusted. But only the mariner counts the periods of a whistle, and the very first roar of the escaping steam brought everyone on deck in panic and confusion. It took long to explain and to quieten their alarms and it can be doubted if any went below again until daylight came in.

The Clyde when in mist or under dull rainy skies is often depressing, but surely the grey sight of it was never more inviting than when we crept up to anchorage at the Tail of the Bank. I felt that. We had been fortunate and had made the Atlantic passage safely. But passive defence had been an unconscionable burden that had worn me. It had been a long spell of physical effort in lookout but now, with opportunity to rest, sleep would not come. My mind was overactive and already expanding—strangely, with confidence—on measures to be taken on the next voyage abroad. The *Transylvania* had proved herself. Armed and better equipped for the new conditions at sea, we might do great things in her in the vital business of sea transport. I had a good and responsive ship and a willing and efficient crew. All seemed well again. But I had thought too of the lifeboat we had passed, empty and adrift. . . . How, yet buoyant, she had made her curtseys of good-bye in the wash of our displacement as we swept on and left her.

Chapter IV

SHIP'S HUSBAND

IN the dictionary there are ugly words whose sounds require a distortion of the facial muscles. Of them all 'redundant' is the worst. It has something of the crack of doom in the ferocious dental effort needed to say it. 'Surplus to requirements' is milder and has in it a slight concession to amity, even a hint of apology. But no conjury of word or phrase brought content to me when, after safe arrival in the Clyde from a first war-time passage, I learned that I would not sail out again in the *Transylvania*. I was redundant—and there was war at sea. My ship, upon which I had expended so much thought for her performance and safety in war voyaging, was to pass from me. Upon arrival alongside, she had immediately been requisitioned for Admiralty service as an armed merchant cruiser, would wear the White Ensign in that commission, and would be commanded by a naval captain. There was the slight solace in the news broken to me that most of the officers and men who had served with me so well and for so long were to continue in her; but, at sixty-five, I was advanced in years: there would not be a place for me in her manning.

I must admit I had bitter thoughts when the matters were resolved. It was not, in this communion, that I had any special pride in my own competence to sail her. Other sailors could handle her, humour her tricks, and master her sea behaviour, but only I could know her as one may know a child from birth. I had seen her plans before she was laid down at Fairfield, had watched her growth from a gaunt skeleton framing to the setting of her plates and a joyous launch into the waters of the Clyde; she would know my tread on the bridge from the day of her trials and throughout fourteen happy years of my command in her.

I had long known that I was slated to retire from active service at sea at the end of 1939. But this war would take all hands. Surely, as I thought, the slate would be washed clean in the torrent of it. My dismay upon receipt of the news was in no way a concern in respect of further employment, but rather a misgiving of the character of that employment. I had no liking for an office job ashore, however comfortable and gilded, that would doubtless be considered suitable for a mariner retired. Perhaps by native wit and observant method I might acquire a sufficiency of business knowledge in some routine of ship control; but maybe I was too set in my sea ways to pick up these unfamiliar threads. My only competence, as I saw it, was to sail a ship. That . . . I was determined to do.

Instructed to attend to the interest of the Owners in the immediate conversion of the ship, I had employment enough to banish sickly thought and in the busy scene of Clydeside find myself not out of date in hastening the effort to get her equipped and off to sea again. Back in the same shipyard, the same basin in which when new she was polished up for her maiden voyage, I attended to the dismantlement and removal of stores fittings, and furniture that were considered unnecessary in war service. In the haste of emergency that could not be done gently or with the regard due to fine furniture or fabric and I was not happy in recalling the care with which these were originally installed and the pride we had in them throughout the years. But speed in wartime is the urgent need and I had to let the pickaxe, jackscrew and crowbar undo all the interior fitments and panelling once so tenderly built up by prideful craftsmen. Many large liners were undergoing similar ruthless treatment in the shipyards and at berths on the river-side. They looked grim and important as they took on the appearance of fighting ships. But even the naval officers appointed to command them could be in no doubt of their unsuitability for the duty they had now to assume. Specially designed to be conspicuous in her trade, the ocean liner presents a large target on the sea, however cunningly the dazzle painter may have camouflaged her. She has, in her construction, a great mass of inflammable material that renders fire hazard an ever-present menace. Carrying no cargo on war service, she must needs be ballasted for stability: and that stability can rarely be obtained without increasing her 'rolling moment' to such a degree as to make the accuracy of gunfire an element of chance. Most of the large ships thus converted were intended for ocean patrol—to enforce the right of visit and search. To 'visit' a ship on the high seas, sea boats require to be manned, lowered, and sent away. The high side of a modern merchant liner, imposing at the dockside, has its own fearsome hazards in any sea, and a rolling ship—that she would be in her new condition—would make a pendulum of the lowered boat that could not easily be fended from its crash on the plating in such a long descent. A merchantman must always be an indifferent fighting ship, however gallant the fighting spirit of the men who man her.

H.M.S. *Transylvania* sailed from the Clyde in October, 1939, being 'in all respects ready for sea' as the initial phrase of her sailing orders would have it. I was loath to let her go and sailed in her to the Tail of the Bank at the invitation of her naval captain. On passage down the River Clyde I had opportunity to indulge my memories of her in a manner that my pre-occupations with her fitting out had, for the time, effaced. Despite the great changes and the gaunt altered outlook, I could re-people the same decks with the many friends I had known in her and pose them there just where the grey guns were mounted and the clips for ready-use shell obstructed the run of promenade. But a stormy winter evening on Clydeside, with driving rain lashing the river in creamy drifts had its reminder of the actuality of dismal circumstance and the futility of recollection.

I was to visit her but once again, as the guest of Captain Miles, when she returned from her first war voyage as a cruiser. She had been employed on the northern patrol. I did not learn of any stirring incident in the course of her long sea-keeping. The captain said he found her a little difficult in heavy weather and there was a list of substantial deck damages to be attended to before she was ordered to sea again. Strangely, I was not greatly moved by my visit, as I thought I might well be. It was not that I had forgotten her in the stresses of other employment; it seemed rather, that she herself had cast me adrift. She had adopted a curiously new character that I did not quite recognise. She appeared a grey ghost to me, there, in the King George Fifth Dock.

For a time I met many of my former shipmates uptown in the city, for the ship was based on the Clyde. At sight of her name on a cap ribbon I was always eager to hail the wearer and pass a word with him. I noted quickly that it was not of his new naval employment these old hands were wishful to talk. It was my impression that they were not happily interested in the rounds of duty in a warship. There was doubtless the monotony of long sea-keeping on patrol, lightened only by occasional incident—the sighting of a stranger, the chase, the summons to 'heave to' and be examined. Sometimes a German ship was brought-to and promptly scuttled herself, leaving the duty of picking up and succouring her mariners to the British warship. No. They were not enthusiastic. It was in recollection of former days they brightened up. 'D'ye mind', (which is Scots for 'Do you remember?') was the opening for the more agreeable confidences.

It was understandable that the position of our merchantmen in the requisitioned cruisers was difficult. They were perhaps grudgingly accepted by the Royal Navy in a form of engagement known as T.124. Under this agreement, they continued to receive pay of Merchant Navy scale which was higher than that of the regularly enlisted navyman. It can be surmised that this was productive of argument and disunion on the lower deck. Other than the navigating officers, not many of the sailors and deck hands had been recruited in the conversion of the ship. For the most part, the men transferred to the Navy were victualling and stokehold ratings, neither of whom are renowned for attachment to a ship's disciplinary regulation.

On the 10th of August, 1940, my old ship sailed on her occasions ... and did not return. She was torpedoed and sunk off Barra Head that same night. In the circumstances, the casualties were considered light, but many of my friends and former shipmates were lost in her.

Following upon the departure of my old ship towards northern waters and being in no mood for holiday, I sought active employment to dispel the feeling of frustration that burdened me, and it may have been as a kindly quittance of my importunity the Owners found a temporary post for me. Together with other senior officers similarly displaced by the requisition of their ships, I was sent to duty that recalled the common practice of my early days in square sail. When, after far voyages, a barque arrived at her home port, it was the custom of thoughtful Owners to send a 'Ship's Husband' to relieve the Master while in port and to conduct the affairs of the vessel. Usually he was a retired shipmaster. He might not be greatly endowed with worldly goods and so welcomed the opportunity to earn a competence, but more often he was of the breed that cannot keep out of the water—or, at least, away from the decks of a ship. There are such men.

Even at that early date in the long struggle it had become evident that the rigour of watch-keeping was imposing a strain on officers and men; and the load could only be unburdened by liberal shore leave whilst in port. There was too the need to relieve the regular crew from ship duty so that they could attend the many drills and instructional classes so necessary for the operation of the new devices that were rapidly being mounted in merchant ships. I found it a good commission on which to be engaged, for it carried with it a prospect of sea employment when opportunity should serve. Once I had climbed (not without difficulty) the pilot ladder on the high side of an incoming ship at the Tail of the Bank, I was in confidence that my physical powers would be no further extended. With a small but sufficient staff to assist, we could take over the duties, often irksome after a long voyage, of the inward bound. Some might have found the term at the anchorage tedious but I did not. The Clyde had already become the principal area from which ocean convoys were despatched and there was always wealth of incident in the assembly and departure of the ships to hold a sailor's interest. But there were days too when one could wish the press of shipping reduced, for the holding at the anchorage allotted to the merchant ships was none too good and collision and casualty due to dragging down in the November gales were not infrequent. In such a congestion of staggering ships there was need of vigilance and we temporary 'beachcombers' had at least that warrant for a post that was not otherwise exacting.

Chapter V

SAILING ORDERS

At Naval Headquarters in Glasgow one had to learn the rules. Security was served by curt contacts and a caller had to be amply documented when the base was established in Saint Enoch's Hotel. The elderly P.O. in charge of the gangway on the fourth floor was a grim custodian then and to be feared at first acquaintance, but missed later as the very figurehead of *Spartiate*—as the base was named—when he was retired or demobilised. My position in this early introduction to Naval Control was not that of an accredited and recognisable participant in hostilities but rather of a doubtless bothersome enquirer upon some trifling point of local interest. I had not then the warrant of a seagoing shipmaster to answer with the name of my ship when challenged concerning my business. I might even have to stand aside for a moment whilst a neighbour in the queue said, sharply and confidently, '*Empire Trout*, for my routeing orders!' and was immediately given his clearance Form A and directed towards the appropriate room number. No. For me the tide was not flowing at the moment. I had to wait while the very efficient old hand found a Boy Scout to escort me until I had been safely handed over at the cubicle where an answer to my enquiry might be available.

Early in December, 1939, I was in no such diffident position. My tide was making handsomely. It was in quickstep I came towards the gangway desk on the fourth floor saying '*Cameronia*, for outward routeing', and I could almost have sworn to a slight grimace of respectful approval on the old lad's face as he handed me Form A and waved me through to the corridor. For I had been appointed to a ship, to relieve the regular master on a voyage to New York and was due to sail on the following day.

Very few of the larger and faster passenger ships were left in their normal trades when Admiralty requirements for cruisers had been met. Of those remaining, it took short experience of sailing them in convoy with ships of lesser speed to prove such practice wasteful of capacity and indeed dangerous in action by reason of the liner's limitation in manoeuvre at such slow speeds. Independent sailing was then tried and, in the main, it was successful. No escort was provided. It was left to the ship to make the voyage under her own powers of speed, vigilant lookout, and steering zig-zag courses in clear weather. All these ships were armed and many were provided with naval ratings to instruct their crews in gunnery. The route upon which the independent ship was to proceed was plotted in advance of sailing. Throughout the voyage her approximate daily position would be known to Naval Control at the 'map room' in Whitehall. Should a menace be reported on her course, a coded wireless signal (which required no acknowledgment from the ship at sea) could be sent to shunt her to a less dangerous area. The *Cameronia* was of such a class. She was a quick eager ship of 17,000 tons and her speed was over sixteen knots. A passenger list of 1600 was no burden to her and she could carry a large cargo. I had seen to her construction in 1919 and had previously commanded her. I knew her well.

The Routeing Officer had doubts. His sailing orders for us were clear and understandable, but the date set for our departure seemed to disquiet him. Could we be sure of maintaining our best speed between Greenock and a position off Rathlin Island on the northern coast of Ireland? It was imperative, he said, that the ship should reach the latter point not later than 11 p.m. on the night of sailing. Otherwise, he would hold us up at the Clyde anchorage for twenty-four hours. Offhand, I could foresee no difficulty. Barring accident, I said, the ship could be there on time. As I mentioned 'accident' I thought Commander Wilson look even more thoughtful and disturbed. He studied a file of signals with close concentration, then confided that it was the possibility of accident he feared. It appeared that a considerable troop movement was in progress. A very large convoy of warships and fast troop transports, conveying the First Division of the Canadian Army, was due to pass through the North Channel at midnight of our day of sailing. There were uncertain factors. The convoy might be ahead of schedule—or astern of it—according to the weather they had experienced. He had given us one hour's 'backlash' to speed clear of the Channel before the military arrived in it. In thought of the weather forecast, which was not good, and the dimming or extinction of ship and coastwise lights, I shared his concern. Once more, I checked over the distances on the route he had laid down on the chart for us. Yes. Even at less than our best speed, we could be well clear of the North Channel before the incoming troop convoy was due. Reassured, he signed my orders and accepted my receipt for them.

In the elation of being again in command of a fine ship and throughout the stir and distractions of sailing day, the Routeing Officer's final injunction did not burden me seriously. It was only when we were held up at the Boom Defences off the Cloch in late afternoon that the consequences of delay occurred to me. For over half an hour we lay stopped awaiting the signal from the gateship to proceed: a straggling group of small coasters was coming in from sea and they had the right of way. With growing impatience and concern, I thought of the fleet of high-powered transports pressing on at speed towards the North Channel. Added to that disturbing thought, there was now the probability of further delay imposed by a new regulation of which I had just heard. The Clyde pilot, whom we had formerly disembarked off Gourock, was now to be carried on to a Landing Station off the Isle of Bute. More delay . . . and the troopships crowding on to their landfall!

I must have betrayed my state of mind when, under way again and having passed through the narrow gateway, I sought information.

'Pilot,' I said. 'What *is* this new idea . . . carrying you on to Rothesay Bay? It seems needless to me.'

Captain Duncan Cameron, the Company's special pilot for Clyde waters, looked curiously at me as he answered. (Pilot? Why that formal address? Was this the way to speak to a very old friend and former shipmate?)

'It may appear needless t' you, Skipper,' he said. 'but everybody isn't a local man with a license. Lot o' strangers coming inward t' th' Clyde now. We even have t' go down below th' Cumbraes t' bring them in.' He stepped a pace or two for it was cold and bleak on the bridge, then continued. 'And it's something special at the moment. It will be all hands standing-by in the cutter. A big troop convoy . . . coming in tomorrow, daybreak. . . . That what's worrying you?'

So . . . he knew too. I had thought the word of it most highly secret. But, of course . . . of course . . . the pilots would have to be informed. I admitted that the matters were not unconnected, and together we studied the weather. It was not promising. Daylight had gone; there was a fresh southerly wind and with promise of more to come in continuous heavy rain. We could just see the dim outline of the Cowal shore as we passed close by it. Then slow and stop to land the pilot at the station, and Duncan stepped off the side ladder. We switched off all lights and turned into the swept channel.

With this severance of the last link with the land, I recovered a measure of buoyant spirit. There was no longer the complication of outboard interference in the execution of the sailing orders that I had unsealed and laid open in the chart room for the guidance of the navigation officers. It was now for *Cameronia* to press on and keep her date and for us to maintain a sharp lookout. We were making good speed. As I stood out on the wing of the bridge to consider the prospects, my confidence in the ship was amply confirmed by a glance down at the divided water, whirling and spreading out in swift and cleanly pattern, under the forefoot. But a lifting of the eyes towards the outlook ahead brought me no assurance of our own ability to guide her as expertly as her speed demanded. There was no horizon, no division of sea and sky upon which the eye could focus in roving

The Clyde Pilot, Captain Duncan Cameron,
on the bridge of the *Cameronia*

intensity. It had grown dark and the unceasing rain slatting on the eyelids made lookout difficult. Nor was there a single point of light by which the range of visiblity could be measured and the radius of avoiding action be determined. In other and less emergent days this state of the weather would be met by a prudent reduction of speed to within the limits of prompt manoeuvre, but there could be no thought of that in this circumstance of a date to be established.

To stand still and do nothing but keep lookout is probably the hardest of all sailor tasks, for it is only by conscious effort one can capture wayward thought and return it to inattention, only by physical insistence maintain the eye at effectual alert and vigilance. Inevitably in the course of a watch it grows weary. There comes the twitching period, demanding momentary closure and a fingering caress of the eyelids, a stiffening of the shoulders and a brisk step or two. The critical period follows hard upon that when the chimera of imagined objects—shapes, lights, the spark of signals—comes to corrupt the balances of eyesight. As the hours passed, I was sensible of this. We had seen only two vessels on the long stretch down channel, close to, but both avoided without difficulty for they were stopped being probably naval trawlers, listening. I left the bridge to examine the chart of their position. The transit from the utter darkness of the bridge to the moderate glow of the desk lamp at the chart table was a sensible shock and it was some time before the detail on the outspread sheet became legible. Sailing orders lay open beside it and again I busied with pencil and dividers to figure out the prospects. We would be late twenty minutes but that was within the 'backlash' the orders conceded. We were approaching a turning point on which the course would be widely altered to head through the North Channel.

In wartime navigation, with coastal beacons dimmed or extinguished, routeing was designed for passage in the deeper waters. Thus, the many turns required to 'hug the land' were eliminated in favour of war channels that could be swept effectively by mine-sweepers. There was however a weakness in this due to the length of the safe waters. When, at the end of one 'leg' in it—and the course had to be set anew—the alteration was very large and had its dangers not only in the convergency of traffic but also in the habit of ships to over or under-run their distance in thick weather and thus enter unswept waters on one side or the other of the war channel. It was in thought of such an alteration, an angle of over 90°, I studied the chart and the orders. Within ten minutes, if our estimation was sound, we would be on the turning point. There was no margin for error. Nothing else could be done in the circumstance and I decided to turn 'by the clock' and trust the engine counter. It was one of the risks to be taken.

I had hoped that the visibility would improve in the more open waters between Scotland and Ireland but the outlook seemed even more dismal when we had turned northward. Only, we were running now, with the blustering wind and the driving rain coming at us from astern. In that, there was a 'fiddler's chance' of profit. Whilst our vision was improved, our hearing was discounted by the direction of the wind when we listened intently for the fog siren on the Mull or the gun at Altacarry. It was between these points in the North Channel our course lay, but we heard no sound from either nor did we see any gleam in the darkness from their dispowered coast lights. Whilst the Channel is wide, the swept ribbon in it was no more than a broad mile. Had we turned on the quadrant too soon or too late?

Position was surprisingly established by a sudden alarming incident. When we were by estimation five miles from Rathlin, the steaming lights of a small vessel flashed on for an instant, ahead and close-to. A quick turn of the helm averted collision and, as the stranger sped by on our port side, we put a blessing on the sharp eyes of her lookout who had seen our greater bulk in time. She appeared to be a destroyer. Almost at the moment we were turning again to our channel course, and with our own navigation lights momentarily exhibited, a second stranger lit up. She was apparently a large ship and steering to southward on a parallel course, but sufficiently clear to be observed without alarm. 'Ships that pass in the night' during wartime do not often speak to one another in passing, but a message can be read into the mere appearance of a neighbour on the seas. It could be considered bad seamanship to rely upon another and a distant sailor's navigations, but there was the reflection that we could not be very far out in 'dead reckoning' to meet him thus in the war channel. This was confirmed when, a little later, we heard the double-crack of Altacarry fog gun on the Isle of Rathlin. But it came down wind to us and from astern just as we were again turning under helm to head out into the open Atlantic. We were twelve minutes late, but the Canadians could go in now without apprehension and Commander Wilson could sleep well.

*　　*　　*

The writ of wartime sailing orders did not become invalid upon departure from the coastal danger zone. While the Battle of the Atlantic had not yet taken on its sinister pattern of pack attacks by squadrons of U-boats far out at sea, German surface raiders of large size and power were abroad. Only a few days before we sailed H.M.S. *Rawalpindi*, an armed merchant cruiser, had been sunk in gallant action with the pocket battleship *Deutschland* and her disguised merchant consort in northern waters, and the whereabouts of the enemy in the Atlantic was a constant dread on the voyage. We were fortunate in the weather which was not windy but marked by much rain and fog and mist. These conditions, that were our menace in coastal waters, were friendly on the ocean passage. Not zig-zagging, we made good progress. Twice on the voyage 'remote control' was exercised from the war room at Whitehall. From what dangers the ship was thus diverted we could not know, but there was moral encouragement in the signalled order to fly off at a tangent and to know that a keen visual lookout was not all we had for protection on the voyage.

Listening in without any special expectation of good news to the broadcast from London on the 14th December, we were startled and amazingly exalted by a short disclosure that the

Admiral Graf Spee had been brought to action in the South Atlantic and hopes were high that her raiding career was ended. British naval *forces* were said to be still engaged and the plural description of our arms aroused confident expectation of a victory at sea even if the German was known to mount power-ful armament. On the following days there were brief references to the action but it was not until we arrived off Sandy Hook on the morning of the 18th we heard the full story of the Battle of the River Plate. The pilot, whom we took on board there, almost stumbled on the side ladder under the weight of Sunday editions that he, so thoughtfully, had collected and brought out to us.

When relieving Captain Kelly in the *Cameronia* at Glasgow, we had talked of incident abroad. Naturally, the feeling in New York (that was almost a home port to both him and me) in respect of our war efforts had been discussed at some length. It appeared that we were not now as greatly esteemed there as once we had been. Even our friends had to fence with words to make their disapproval sound not too bitter. It was thought that we were not resolute enough, that we were not putting our backs into it. It was a 'phoney' war, they said, in which the Allies seemed to be shooting craps in the Maginot Line instead of meeting their enemy in the field. In his own way, the Captain put it that our name was 'Mud' over there!

But the bye-name had changed when we arrived. There was no precedent for the manner in which the news of the sea battle was conveyed to the American people, so amazingly to their taste was the round by round commentary that a fortuitous broadcaster was in a position to hurry over his system. The story, as related to me by the enthusiastic pilot in the intervals of conning the ship in the Ambrose Channel, was that a lone broadcaster of the Columbia Corporation was taking a morning stroll at Punta del Este, which is a seaside suburb of Monte Video. He saw ships coming swiftly from the north and the flashes of heavy gunfire. How he got his gear together and managed to link up was not known. But what was known to millions of excited listeners was that he described the fight from its early stages on through the salvoes and the hits, the smoke and the sounds of naval action—right through to the final frantic flight of the German battleship towards refuge in the harbour of neutral Uruguay. . . . Sunday's broadcast was no such unheralded occasion. Every network in the United States was 'on th' step', the pilot said, to cover the news as the worried Germans worked feverishly to patch up the ship's wounds and return to the fight . . . or the flight. The amazing story ended with the sailing and the self-destruction of the German ship. The pilot, visibly excited as he came to it, swore that he had heard the thunder of the explosion when the ship blew up . . . and he sitting at his ease in the messroom of the cutter at Sandy Hook! It is a curious and very unusual experience to see a 'Branch Pilot' emotional and excited. He was, when he told me the story. As it ended, we were turning to stem the flood tide off Quarantine before anchoring. So much was the British Navy now in good standing that, when he had shouted out 'let go!' he came from the wheelhouse holding out his hand to everyone. He said he was proud to shake.

★ ★ ★

On return to the Clyde (with a great cargo of uncrated fighter planes on deck) I learned that Commander Wilson had not slept at all well on the night of our passage outward bound through the North Channel. In the early morning hours he had been called up to identify a ship that was reported to be concerned in a serious casualty. She was thought to be the *Cameronia* and the Commander had unhappy hours until the matters were resolved.

When, in the morning, the great troop convoy arrived it was reported that one of the ships on the starboard wing had been in collision with an outward bound stranger in the darkness. The impact was miraculously confined to a swift 'side slice' in which the out-swung lifeboats of both ships were torn away and serious deck damages were sustained. The name of the outward bound vessel was not immediately known, but from description corresponded with the size and outline of the *Cameronia*. Later in the day, the damaged ship arrived in the Clyde, having put back to port to replace the lifeboats and their equipment. The outward bounder had originally sailed from the Mersey. By a curious trick of fate, the two ships involved in the collision belonged to the same great shipping company!

Chapter VI

THE MAGNETIC CAUL

In the duty room at the Clyde Pilot Station on Gourock Pier one could always count upon acquiring news of some detail in war operations affecting the Ocean Front. It was not that the pilots were unmindful of their obligations of secrecy in respect of shipping matters, nor that they were ever voluble or communicative in any assembly that was not convened on the bridge of a ship, but the duty room in wartime was a very private and special precinct reserved to the business of pilotage in the River and Firth and few strangers were admitted there. But an old familiar could be accepted, particularly on a winter's day of storm and rain when, having disembarked from his ship at the anchorage he had missed a train connection for Glasgow and was wet through. For him there would always be a seat at the blazing fire and the never-absent cup of steaming tea proffered.

On such a day early in January, 1940—having been relieved in the *Cameronia*—I sat there in modest comfort whilst the daily traffic of the port came under discussion and the pages of the big book of engagements were scanned by entering and departing pilots. There were not many, for it was the slack period—the tide being at half-ebb and the river channel deserted. Through the rain-lashed windows a pilot who was the 'next on turn' was gazing out pondering his assignment without enthusiasm. From my seat at the fire I could see the white and red bars of the pilot flag at the masthead of the cutter whipping and slatting in the wind and rain at the breast of the pier and, beyond that, the rough white-capped waters of the Firth. Suddenly, the watcher reached for a pair of binoculars and studied something in the estuary with close attention. It was a naval tug-boat towing a barge of some sort, a not unusual feature of the seascape in war-time.

'That Admiralty tug again,' he exclaimed, turning to the Pilot Master at the desk and holding out the binoculars towards him. 'I wouldn't have thought they would play around with th' "apple cart" on a day like this. I wonder why they use this state of th' tide to tow down. Always about half-ebb. . . . Steer better on th' flood, I sh'd say.'

The senior focussed the glasses on the tow and examined it with careful scrutiny. He agreed that it was an odd proceeding and invited me to take a look. I could see nothing strange about a tug towing a flat square-ended barge, on the deck of which there appeared to be a great coil of heavy mooring wire such as might be used with boom defences. But the unwieldy barge was sheering violently in the wind and tide and I thought it curious that the tow-rope should be of such long scope for river work. I said as much, and was told that the towing operation had some-thing to do with experiments in devising a sweep for magnetic mines—a counter to Hitler's secret weapon to which the Fuehrer had dramatically announced that there was no defence. There was said to be a magnetic 'loop' laid down on the sea-bed at the Tail of the Bank in an area in which the pilots were forbid-den to anchor, and it was in that water the tug and her charge passed up stream and down. Probably the Navy had chosen the quiet periods in absence of traffic for the experiments, or it may have been that the height of the tide was considered favourable for them. It was all very *hush-hush* and further comment was discouraged.

The Port Medical Officer came in for a warm up before heading for home. He had been off to a Clan Line ship at the anchorage inspecting the vessel's lascar crew amongst whom there were symptoms that might mean an outbreak of smallpox. He was in a mood of relief that his examinations had been negative. As talk of that went round, the doctor mentioned an odd circumstance brought out during his medical examination of the Mahommedan sailors. Nearly all, he said, had a charm or talisman of some sort suspended around the neck. It was thought that a phrase or verse of the Koran might be the inscription stamped on the little tablets, but he had seen at least one that was different. It was a little cloth bag containing a dried-up 'caul'— the membraneous film that sometimes covers the head and face of a newly born infant. Most of us had known of the superstition that such a charm was sovereign against the perils of the sea and particularly death by drowning, but that *credo* was thought to be confined to Europeans: the point that the belief had apparently extended to Asiatic seamen was novel and productive of much discussion and I had nearly lost my second rail connection in the enlivenment of interested talk on sea customs and traditions. Still moist from the warmth of the hospitable fire I hurried to catch my train. I recall that the 'next on turn' remarked on parting that I would need a 'caul' when again I went to sea.

It was a tiresome journey for we seemed scheduled to stop and idle at many stations and points on the line. I had ample opportunity for reflection on the conversation in the duty room and the terrifying problem of the magnetic mine, the new danger on the home doorstep of which I had heard dread opinion expressed on my return from the United States.

That a destructive force of such character could be lifted from the sea bottom to make contact with the hull of a passing ship in the way a child's toy magnet could pick up its piece of metal seemed hard of belief. But I had seen magnetic cranes in action at the dockside unloading cargoes of scrap steel and had noted how the magnet was neutralised when lowered into the hold of a vessel; then, energised by the application of current, how quickly and with ease it would attract an adherent mass of such awkward cargo to be hoisted and lowered again to swell the dump on the quays. But that would mean immediate control at some point and would not fit in with the rumours of ships being shattered unaccountably in the watched sea-channels that had been swept systematically for the well-known contact and moored mines. . . . We had not been told of casualties due to this unknown weapon, but it was common knowledge that many seaports, including London and Hull, had been at a standstill for a time pending the discovery of counter measures. Counter measures? What protection could now be devised with the poles of magnetism—the true compass we had trusted for so long—turned against us? The compass! . . . I had been indifferently schooled in the Physical Sciences and could not fathom their depths, but I had of necessity learned something about the mariner's compass and its compensations for permanent and transient magnetism. . . . (What was that stock jest that was always fired off by the lecturer at the classes on Beall's Deviascope? . . . Oh, yes. . . . About the expert who toiled for so long to shield the needle from the ship's disturbing influences upon it, only to find that he had also eliminated its terrestial directive force! . . . A good one, that!) But anything could happen now. It was not unlikely that the 'apple cart' I had just seen, probably energised in some way, represented the magnetic body of a ship. Maybe a measurement of its field was being made, else why the long scope of the towrope to remove it from the tug's disturbing influence? Beyond that I could find no other thought to ponder. With much snorting and a succession of irregular jerks, the train hauled to a stop at the platform and traverse of the wartime gloom of the Central Station put an end to my reflections on this sudden new sea peril.

About a month later I was sent on relieving duty to a ship in dock. She was in a stage of refitment after a long voyage to the East. The customary dismantlement for survey was being undertaken and the trim appearance of a ship just in from sea was not hers. Her decks were cumbered with engine parts, and gear and equipment, removed from working places for check or examination, lay untidily about. D.E.M.S. was fitting guns in her and shipyard workmen setting up armoured protection around the bridge and wheel-house. Among the naval specialists interested in the fitting out of the ship I noted newcomers, mostly R.N.V.R. and wearing the then unusual strip of green cloth between the gold sleeve-bands that indicated their rank. I was told that they were electrical experts of the new special branch of the Navy—the Degauss Department—formed to deal with protection against the magnetic mine. It seemed that we would have our 'caul' when again we put to sea. But we would not wear it. The ships would.

Hitler's 'Secret Weapon' had yielded its design and powers and manner of operation and the antidote lay in a belt of energised electrical cable which they were planning to instal in the ship. As I understood it, the object was to neutralise the ship's magnetic field by a counter-current passing through the cable and in this way render the magnetic needle in the German mine ineffective to detonate its explosive charge. Reduced to such simple terms, the counter-plot for defence against the terror that had caused so many great losses in shipping was understandable even although the mysterious co-efficients used in the scientific calculations employed in each individual ship was beyond my wit. The question of interference with the ship's compasses was naturally the subject of my immediate enquiry when the Degauss officers spoke of the plan. That too, they said, would be taped off by a dual adjustment, one with the protective current switched off and the other with the energy 'full on'. Upon completion of the installation, tests would be made on a range off Helensburgh Pier and thereafter the ship would be 'swung' for the adjustment of compasses. For operation of the belt, no special schooling would be needed. The ship's engineer or electrical officers could attend to it. The only adjustment the navigator would need to make was in respect of the compass course that was being steered and, for that, a fairly simple instrument would be fitted on the bridge. We were warned to 'keep the juice running' at all times when in port or in shallow waters. An instance of over-confidence was quoted: that of a ship only recently equipped. Upon arrival at her next port, the master thought he might safely switch off the protective energy when moored at his familiar wharf—with the result that the ship's stern was shattered by the explosion of a magnetic mine that had been dropped from the air, probably on the night before. It is not often that one has the key of extinction so readily at hand. We would need to guard that switch.

During my term of relief duty in the ship I watched the ship-yard workers harness the insulated belt around the hull on the level of the main-deckline: there seemed to be miles of it for she was a sizeable vessel. When the fitting was completed and the wiring tested by ammeter, she was said to be immunised and it only remained for the formulae to be approved by the results of the ranging off Helensburgh Pier before sailing. Certification was important before a programme could be prepared for the sequence of that test and I was required to call at Naval Head-quarters to obtain the document. I found the newly established division in the throes of settling in to what must speedily have become a major department of the Admiralty. Despite its new-ness and understandable congestion and apparent disorder, the experts so recently gazetted had found a slogan or motto for their 'trade'. That they had enrolled a classical scholar in their ranks was evident from a typewritten slip pinned up above the desk at which certificates were issued. It was a paraphrase from Pope's translation of the Odyssey—

> This potent girdle round thy bosom bind
> And sail: throw all thy terrors to the wind.

Chapter VII

CONTINENTAL EXPORT

IT was the matter of the Polish gold consignment that had brought me on deck in the early hours of the 22nd March, 1940. The *Cameronia* was in port at Glasgow, lying at the dock alongside and all ready to embark passengers in the forenoon and sail for New York on the tide. The loading of general cargo had been completed overnight but a shipment of bullion and coin (said to be over two millions of Poland's treasure) had been delayed on the rail journey from the south. Arrangements had been made to receive it during the darkness of the morning hours and embark it quickly without attracting notice. Special dockers had been told off to unload the boxes from the railway vans and carry them singly to the ship's strong-room. As staff captain of the ship it fell to me to supervise the transfer of such valuable property.

But for the working party and a group of officials and ship's officers, the quay was deserted. Two railway cars containing the treasure had been shunted to a stand-still at the gangway. As the boxes—of convenient size—were shouldered by the stevedores and carried, one by one, to the ship they were closely examined by the company's dock staff. I remarked that the consignment was not in the fresh and ship-shape condition customary in the transport of bullion. However shining may have been the inner content, the outer surfaces of the wooden boxes were scored and travel-stained—in some cases, mud-encrusted as though they had been immersed in river water. Many had their edges splintered and chafed by some form of rigid rope-lashings. But, in the main the containers appeared to be strong enough and without sign of breakage: only a few were put aside under guard for further examination. A bank official who had travelled with the consignment from London said the boxes had been 'on the road' for nearly six months. With him were two Polish military officers and one civilian, also Polish, who were to accompany the consignment to America. The soldiers were tall and lean, with deeply furrowed features and an alert observant air. They did not offer to speak English (which, later, we learned they understood) but held themselves aloof until all matters had been concluded. Standing apart on the windy quayside and heavily cloaked in swinging military garments, they might have been dramatis personae for first and second conspirators. But the Polish civilian was more companionable . . . and voluble. He spoke good English and seemed not to be at all worried by the occasional sharp remarks of his compatriots. He used his hands to large purpose in relating the Odyssey of the Polish Gold that he had accompanied in its journey from Warsaw. He mentioned that this consignment was only a small part of it. The sweep of his hands as he spoke conveyed the impression that the substantial dock sheds at Kelvinhaugh would be about the area in which the whole could be contained. But he was obviously truthful in description of the long journey. Although his English was good, it was not always easy to follow the flood of his words. His pronunciation of place-names could not be fully understood, although it seemed clear that railways—being in the hands of the German and Russian enemy—were not used. Somehow, he gave the impression of pack-horse or mule convoys over heights in the Gallician Alps, and the shivering contraction of his shoulders indicated the wintry weather of December in 1939. It was when he went on to describe a passage down the Danube River towards Constanza we found ourselves in better understanding. From that Rumanian port to Beirut in Syria the treasure was taken by sea in a small Turkish coasting ship. Nothing, we thought, could match the 'mime' of his sensitive acting as he showed us the Reis of the Turkish steamer grumbling and protesting the dangers of the voyage— or would it not be the matters of reward? The sea voyage was of long duration, for the vessel crept close inshore to take advantage of neutral waters. After some time at Beirut, the treasure seemed to have been shipped in a Messageries liner to Marseilles and then by rail to Paris and across the Channel to London.

The unchallenged boxes of the consignment had been carried to the strong-room, doubly-checked and agreed, by the time our pleasant friend had concluded his story. There remained only the investigation into the condition of the doubtful containers. Of these, there were five—but three, although discoloured and travel-stained, could be accepted. The boxes were of substantial construction, inch-wood, with the corners neatly chamfered. Strong bands of metal were bound around them and these led up to a recessed roundel where the jointure was nailed down and covered by an imposing waxen seal. The boxes were numbered and many had curious inscriptions stencilled on them. Although there was no sign that the boxes had been broken open, the seals on Numbers 40003 and 40077 had been defaced or broken and the metal bands slightly displaced.

The decision had to be made whether the damaged boxes were to be accepted and signed for or be returned to the custody of the Bank of England. The checkers' scales on the dock— more commonly used for the weighing of Scots' whisky in export—were brought into use and comparison made with other boxes of similar size in the consignment. There were discrepancies, but the London bank official did not consider them of serious importance. 'There were,' he said, 'many gold coins of differing sizes in the shipment and their packing would not always be alike.' He thought, too, that the suspect boxes might contain ancient well-rubbed pieces as the dates, stencilled on the wood and almost undecipherable under the crust of time, went far back into the last century. His instructions were that the consignment must go through to consignees at New York 'as a whole'. He was prepared to re-seal the boxes and accept a conditional receipt for them, endorsed in some such phrase as —'seals damaged: boxes said to contain bullion.'

The re-sealing of the damaged treasure-chests was attended with difficulty. At four of the morning on a wind-swept quayside at Glasgow, there are not the conveniences of a Bank Shipping Department in Threadneedle Street. Certainly, the damaged wax of the seals was there and could be heated again, and the ship's carpenter was at hand to align and nail down the metal bands, but who was to duplicate the fractured impress of the Polish Eagle and the curiously lettered inscription that sursurrounded it? The London bank official had a personal signet-ring on his finger that he was prepared to use in the emergency but, as he said, there ought to be another imprinting to establish the identity of the person 'of the second part'. Sailors are often known to wear earrings, (a talisman in favour of acute hearing, some say), but signet-rings are not commonly a part of seafaring equipment.

The difficulty was solved by the Chief Officer. With a penknife, he cut off the lowermost left-hand button from his uniform greatcoat and handed it to me. When the wax was sufficiently heated we put our respective signs on it. I had to spit on the button before a neat impression of the 'House Flag' of the Company appeared in countersense—a grounded anchor superimposed on a waving burgee. It was an old uniform button, belonging to the days when the Anchor Line had a splendid motto to go with a fanciful rope border on its insignia. 'SECURE AMIDST PERILS' looked well there, taking its place amongst the fractured hierograms of a martyred nation. But it read oddly foreign as—ƧƎϽUᴚƎ AMI⅁ƧT PƎᴚILƧ.

On this voyage I was not in command of the ship. A new routine had been established by the Owners in which the *Cameronia* was to be alternately in charge of one of two captains, the other taking duty in the alternations as staff captain. It had become increasingly evident that only by fairly constant seagoing could the senior officers keep apace with the new developments and regulations that came almost daily into operation. New weapons and training in their employment required constant study and direction: signalling and the use of secret codes had been enlarged and complicated by frequent amendment: there was a constant flood of circular advice from the Trade Division of the Admiralty, Naval Control, the Ministry of Sea Transport, and the Board of Trade: even the Post Office (Security Branch)—forwarding new schemes for the hushing of

Unloading at Yorkhill, Glasgow: March, 1940

garrulous merchant seamen—had a hand in our affairs. All these added responsibilities called for a serial understanding that could easily be disrupted by shore service and the distractions of 'standing-by'. But it was perhaps in consideration of life-saving equipment in the ships and the efficient observance of sea drills for their employment, the Company was the more emphatically decided. The tragedy of the 'open boat' had become commonplace, and efforts to meet and overcome its preventable hazards were many and ingenious—but few were simple in application and fewer still did not conflict with some other necessity or convenience. A ship's lifeboat, being designed for the normal perils of a sea voyage, is of restricted size. She is surveyed and measured by a nautical official of the Ministry of War Transport: upon these measurements she is certified to accommodate a certain number of persons. Under war conditions at sea many additional fitments and accessories had to be carried in lifeboats. These included extra sailing gear, signal apparatus and colourful canvas display for attracting aerial attention, weather cloths and stanchions for sea protection, extra blankets and weatherproof clothing. Food and fresh-water supply were increased in weight and quantity; the medicine chest—already a substantial burden—assumed almost the proportions of an ambulance aid station. With all this weight and bulk of necessary war gear, there was not—in the early years of hostilities—a remeasurement for body space: the number of persons to be carried remained engraved on the stem of the boat, unaltered from its peacetime advertisement. In a large ship transporting great numbers of civilian passengers, there was certainly the need for an additional senior officer to attend to little else but safety measures in the distribution of personnel.

But the new arrangement was not popular; not only with the masters who could say, with Abu Ben Adhem, 'How can two kings rule in Babylon?' but also with the ship's officers who saw in it some hitch in the scheme of promotion. But the latter had no need to be concerned for advancement. The outlook upon that was good. Our serious losses of merchant shipping demanded any practical manner of replacement and ships could be acquired from foreign registry—at a price. Many were thus purchased from the United States and, in their allocation to British management by the Ministry of War Transport, the Anchor Line had obtained a number of ships to man and operate in the North Atlantic. The American Neutrality Act of 1939 forbade what would otherwise have been the loading of a cargo in the purchased ships for a voyage to the United Kingdom under the American flag. Upon arrival, they would officially be transferred to British registry and the American crew repatriated under contract. But the new U.S. law (and the proclamations and regulations issued thereunder) withheld all American seamen from the war zones. So, officers and men had been recruited in British ports and, in *Cameronia,* we had embarked three such crews—they being sent to the United States to take delivery of precious reinforcements. Promotion had thus been rapid and substantial for many of the Company's officers: as for the diffidence of the established seniors, surely that could be met by tactful assistance and timely reliefs.

It was not unexpected that the exercise of 'boat drill' would have its difficulties, but I thought it curious to be enmeshed in the intricacies of the enemy's language right at the start of the voyage. I had long forgotten the little German that once I knew, and when endeavouring to stage a preparatory exercise before sailing from the Tail of the Bank was dismayed to learn that most of our large body of transatlantic passengers were refugees from Central Europe, all using that language and unable to read our Notice to Passengers posted up in all cabins and quarters. After struggling vainly in an attempt at translation, I was relieved to find amongst the travellers an efficient helper. The Purser had discovered Mrs. Bernstein in the lounge, surrounded by a group of migrants to whom she was explaining the measures to be taken. She had a copy of our notice in her hand. She was immediately invited to translate it for general publication on board which, willingly, she did. When set up and printed, the new notice had a formidable Germanic appearance, quite unlike its idle counterpart in English. The long German words came snarling out on the page of the leaflet like wolves'

teeth. 'Self-control is necessary' had become alarmingly passionate as 'GROSSTE SELBSTBEHERRSCHUNG IST DRINGENDST ERFORDER-
LICH'! and, having space to expand, a fearsome row of exclamation marks was carried to the margin of the page.

Mrs. Bernstein was very thorough. She knew something
about ships and shipping too. It was not long before we learned
that she had been an office worker with a large shipping company in Hamburg and the zest with which she applied herself to
expert manipulation of the purser's typewriter had something in
it of happy reunion with an almost forgotten instrument. She
was a small person of middle years and spare proportions, but of
amazing vitality and quick intelligence. She was untiring in her
assistance and seemed indeed to find some relief in being thus
busily employed. Like the Polish gold, the refugees had travelled
long and far. They were not quite the distressed and pitiful survivors from the full fury of the Germans that, later, were to become familiar amongst our west-bound passengers, but most
were obviously people of substance who had friends abroad.
Practically all were Jewish and were being expatriated to the
United States through an American agency. A feature of their
'way bills' was that all had some home to go to on arrival. They
would be disembarked to Ellis Island, there to remain until
claimed by their sponsors.

After a reasonable time interval, in which it was hoped that
the formidable *Achtung* would be studied, a second 'Alarm' was
sounded . . . and with astonishingly quick and novel result. Our
foreign passengers came struggling on deck towards their boat-
stations quietly enough but practically every one staggering
under a load of some sort of personal belongings. Whilst the
womenfolk carried bulky packages of clothing or household
gear, the men appeared to be less embarrassed by small handbags
—but the manner of their carriage of these suggested unusually
heavy and valuable content. A halt was called and the indefatigable Mrs. Bernstein was again brought forward. There was
much talk. One of the passengers pointed to a few words in the
German notice posted up nearby. '*Ist das eine kleine packchen?*'
yelled the little Jewish lady, pointing to a substantial bundle that

may have been bedding. My memory jogged by her word and action, and recalling callow days in a Bierhalle at Bremerhaven —I had half-expected the shout of assent in the manner of the Stitchenbank Song. But the bewildered people hung their heads. No. We would have to try again. As the passengers went below with their bundles, Mrs. Bernstein scored out a word or two in her translation. What had been German for 'Dress warmly whilst in the Danger Zone. Have ready a small package of very necessary items' was amended to read 'WARM ANZIEHEN ... 'Dress warmly'.

On the third attempt, which was conducted just before sunset and the ship at sea on her voyage, matters were improved—but there still remained the problems of weight and space in the crowded lifeboats. This time there was no quick rush on deck towards boat-stations. The refugees took up their allotted positions slowly and without excitement or interest. Having noted how quickly and with what animation they had come on deck on the former occasion, I was at a loss to account for this tardy and deliberate assembly, but it was soon evident that they had been guided by the amendment in the notices. They had indeed dressed warmly. They had not brought bedding, and household property could not be seen, but the multiplicity of heavy outer garments was unbelievably bunched up on their persons below the encirclement of bulky life-jackets—and the men were still top heavy under the weight of their handbags. There is no sumptuary clause in the Merchant Shipping Act and March in the North Atlantic can be a bitterly cold season. I could only agree with the resigned elevation of little Mrs. Bernstein's shoulder and the hopeless upturn of her outstretched palm. She said nothing until I invited her opinion on the transport of the money-bags. She thought the men would not go in the lifeboats if they were parted from their 'kleine packchen'.

Chapter VIII

BINOCULARS

THE fortune of war did not favour us in May of 1940 when, again in command of the *Cameronia,* I sailed out to New York. The campaign in Norway had ended in withdrawal. All western Europe was over-run, save for neutral Spain and Portugal: our Allies were on point of capitulation, and a new enemy had come against us in the Mediterranean. At sea, we were not as heavily pressed, but the Battle of the Atlantic was developing with intensity. U-boats, now hunting in packs, had extended their activities to 40° west and with successes because of the scarcity of destroyers and armed escorts, now in part withdrawn to protect our coasts against the threat of invasion. Matters did not look well.

But our luck as an independently routed ship still held and there was good prospect of safe arrival after a fast passage. There was the day when, south of Iceland and at dawn, we raised the smoke of a west-bound convoy ahead and steered wide to avoid it. The same night we picked up signals of distress indicating that three ships had been torpedoed. From the positions given it seemed likely that they belonged to the convoy we had sighted and from the time of origin of the signals it must have been in night attack. In Sailing Orders there was the warning that U-boats, in the absence of an adequate convoy escort, would operate in darkness on the surface. They were said now to have a surface speed of eighteen knots or more. It was a sober thought that *Cameronia* could no longer outstrip a submarine. The gun and the smoke floats would be our sole defence in that event. But our defence had been strengthened by the strange circumstance of a housing shortage—the dearth of naval barrack-accommodation in the Clydeside area.

Recruitment to the Navy, for 'Hostilities only', had exceeded all expectations and the joint problems of berthing, messing, and training that large body of men were perplexing the naval authorities at Glasgow. On hearing word of that, I made the chance remark to the senior D.E.M.S. officer, Captain Forsyth, that 'we could do with a few extra hands in the ship these days' ... and with a surprising result. A group of these 'H.O's' ranging from ten to as many as thirty young men was assigned to the ship on each voyage and probably to other ships as well. The arrangement served both camps and many good purposes. Under the expert instruction of our Col.-Sergt. of Marines the landsmen were drilled intensively in gunnery and rifle-fire. They gained too their needed sea-legs on the voyage and many attained a modest competence in ship-work that included steersmanship, flag signals, and a turn of lookout.

Entering the harbour of New York seemed to be like coming home again from another world. It was an afternoon of brisk wind and sunny weather and the high masonry of Manhattan, its chines and towers and monuments, stood out above the Hudson in brilliant light and shadow. Being a Sunday, there was not the stress of work-a-day traffic in the river but, at the Battery, the day's excursion steamers with all their bravery of festive flags and emblems turned in and out on their schedules, the broad and terraced decks peopled with gaily-dressed holiday-makers and the strains of dancing music sounding out. I tried not to contrast the gay fanfarade with the sober encompassment I had left in the east as we canted into our berth at Pier 45. But there, when we had tied up, I too could make holiday, for friends had learned in some way that I was coming to port and were there to welcome me.

★　　★　　★

BINOCULARS

I think the 'Binoculars Scheme', which was a private form of
Lend-Lease that antedated the generous and legal act of March,
1941, was brought about by the appearance in my cabin of the
ship's Second Officer as I sat there with my friends on that Sunday afternoon. Mr. Colquhoun had the duty of safeguarding the
instruments on the bridge and, when in port, keeping them
locked up. Amongst them were the optical instruments that included binoculars and telescopes. These had now become very
scarce and valuable. Many had been stolen from the ships, others
subjected to rough usage that reduced them to the character of
empty beer bottles. When the war broke out, it became impossible to replace them by purchase, all such equipment being
requisitioned and all output from the makers being reserved for
the Navy and Army. There was no possibility of replacement in
the United Kingdom and even repairs had become makeshift
and inadequate. In order to conserve the few passable instruments in our inventory, I had passed an order that they be
checked upon arrival in port and brought to my cabin for safe-
keeping. I glanced at them as the officer put them a-row on a
side-table before he withdrew. They looked shabby and work-
worn.

But we were talking together. One had to put up a bold front
even with our reverses in the war already known. I had no need
to act that part for my American friends were thoughtfully considerate. The war situation was but briefly mentioned and that
with concern and encouragement, then turned to what I could
relate of the incidents of the voyage. Later, the safe arrival of the
Queen Elizabeth at New York was happily discussed. The advent
of a new great liner on her maiden voyage is always a triumphant
occasion in the port and few events have a greater interest for the
travel-minded people of the United States. But none had ever
aroused such enthusiastic and widespread notice as the sudden
and unheralded arrival of the greatest ship in the world. There
was no advance publicity, no excursion steamers to meet her, no
convoying airplanes overhead, no flurry of newsmen and
photographers, no civic preparations, when the huge grey ghost
emerged from the Atlantic mists off Sandy Hook on the morn-

ing of the 7th March, 1940, and berthed quietly and efficiently at her up-town pier.

The friends who had come to meet me were all confirmed sea-travellers who had sailed with me on many voyages. It was natural that they should wish to see the great new Cunarder at her dock and with that in view we went on deck. As we passed out of my quarters Grover Higgins picked up a pair of binoculars from the side-table. The *Queen* could not be seen from our bridge for there is a bend of the river at the Chelsea Piers that shut her out from view; we had to saunter aft towards the stern until she ranged in sight—a new and huge marine skyscraper outstanding on the northern fringe of the Hudson. Unlike the many towers and turrets of the lofty neighbouring structures she bore no streaming flags at her mastheads: even the well-known House Flag was not hoist at her mainmast truck. Grim and grey, she wore only the Red Ensign of the British Merchant Navy on the staff above her massive stern.

When we returned to my quarters Grover did not immediately replace the binoculars that he had tried to use on such a magnificent and distant target. He sat there turning them over in his hands in reflective scrutiny. The use of rubber adhesive tape to bind a broken eyeshade seemed to be a point of interest. He remarked upon it and asked if they were all we had. I replied that we had a few others, and better ones—pointing to my own old but tried Zeiss glasses hanging at the doorway. I said too that some of the senior officers had their own personal binoculars of differing merit. The ones he saw there on the side-table were the ship's property, used by the juniors and the lookouts. We could not now get what we needed in Britain, the Navy and Army took them all and with the Treasury restriction on dollars we could not easily purchase good glasses in America. . . . Yes. I surmised that most British merchant ships were as badly off as we were. But we could manage. Grover pondered this. He was of the Law and sought all the evidence. He said we ought to be better equipped and thought that something should be done about it.

In my many years of trans-Atlantic ferrying I had made friends on both sides of the ocean, for shipboard is the right atmosphere for such ingathering. Out at sea there are not the entangling threads of social position, financial standing, international rivalry, industrial competition: the field is fair if not always level for the cultivation of long-enduring friendship and intimacy. I think it was Christopher Morley who fathered the word 'kin-sprit' in this connection, for I am certain it is he who knows that people of kindred taste and spirit are largely to be discovered on the decks of a ship. It was Mrs. Patrick MacDermot who spoke of that as we sat together considering Grover's suggestion that something might be done in the way of an intimate appeal to personal American friends for the loan of binoculars to aid our hard-pressed ships. At the Wakefield Bookshop where she presided, Ilah MacDermot had an almost complete register of mutual American friends who were also her customers. By their tastes in the books they sought she knew the yachtsmen from the bird watchers, the sportsman from the stay at home, the horsemen from the hill-climbers, and the depths in soundings between readers of Robert Nathan and Dale Carnegie. A public appeal could not be made, for the United States was neutral, but it was thought that a modest and private canvass might serve. The wording of that appeal was left to me to be composed, the collection of the instruments to the Wakefield Bookshop in the first instance, and the administration of the scheme to Grover Higgins and Roger Disbro of Cleveland.

Although privately administered, the Binoculars Scheme had official approval, so necessary for documentation and the issue to the right hands of the many magnificent high-powered instruments loaned or donated by generous well-wishers in the United States. The British Consul-General in New York, through the Shipping Department of his Consulate, undertook the issue and accepted receipt from the grateful masters for registration against recovery in better times. It was a feature of the plan that the recipients thus endowed should be given the name and address of the lender with a view to correspondence reporting what could be told of the fortune of their ships. But, for security reasons, this was later discontinued.

Perhaps some measure of the great success of the scheme may be found in the following letter. It is out of its serial date in the book, but belongs here.

H.M.T. *Circassia*

At Singapore,

13th September, 1945

Dear Senator P——,

I hope this letter will reach you. It is written from Singapore and you will perhaps note that it is dated shortly after our entry here on the occasion of the surrender of the Japanese. Doubtless you will wonder why I am writing to you. Let me explain myself as the Master of the British Transport *Circassia*. All I know of you is that you are the generous owner of a pair of Zeiss binoculars, 10 × 50, No. 1180906.

You may recall that, in 1940, a private appeal was made by me and my friend Grover Higgins of Cleveland, Ohio, for the loan of binoculars for use in the British Merchant Navy. I framed the appeal for we were desperately short of them at the time. I remember a phrase that I included in the request. The instruments were asked for 'in the pious hope but doubtful expectation that they would ever be returned'.

The British Consul-General in New York undertook the distribution and has a record of the donors, and I am now informed that steps are being taken by a Government Department in the United Kingdom towards recovering and returning the binoculars. I have heard that over 800 pairs of splendid instruments, many of high-power like yours, were received, but I fear that many have gone down with the ships and now lie beside their wearers. I have been fortunate, and the wars are over now. So, I would like to take your invaluable gift from around my neck, where it has been throughout much of the war. I have the thought of having them reconditioned before sending them back to you. The lenses have been well looked after, only the rounds are scratched a little by the rub-rub of uniform buttons. But perhaps you would prefer to have the sentimental (and even historic) interest in the binoculars preserved, for they have seen much since 1940. Would you let me know?

My dear man, I cannot thank you enough, nor convey my gratitude to all the generous American friends who helped us to see our way clearly when we were against a very powerful enemy,

Yours gratefully,

David W. Bone

Chapter IX

SEAVACUEES, AND BLOOD
FOR BRITAIN

Upon later consideration, I thought it likely that the Commodore of the large slow convoy we had sighted ahead had formed a dim view of *Cameronia's* conduct when at our best speed we parted company and set off on our own route across the Atlantic, for excessively quick and doubtless angry signals were flashed at us from the guide-ship, but were so quickly angry that we could not read them. Sailing independently from Glasgow on 14th August, 1940, we had come upon the north-bound convoy in the war-channel that is little more than a mile wide off Rathlin, and prudence had dictated a slowing down until more open waters were reached. But Rathlin was now astern and there was the whole Atlantic for sea-room, so speed was increased and the course altered to avoid the rearmost ships. Having no intelligible answer to his signals it was apparent that they were repeated to the destroyer on the port wing of the convoy's screen: a huge bow-wave formed quickly under her forefoot as she turned to investigate us and she poured black smoke as she came up from astern.

It was now nine of the forenoon and the children had been groomed and fed and were on deck, all primed for the day's engagements—the pain of yesterday's parting from parents and friends being doubtless no longer remembered. How quickly they recognised a special source of entertainment in the proceedings, how excited in the shrill calls one to another to join in furthering the occasion as the destroyer creamed up on us within hailing distance.

The Commander on the bridge of the escort had probably had a busy morning, rounding up the fractious merchantmen of three separate sections from the Bristol Channel, the Mersey and the Clyde, now forming up in one great convoy off Oronsay to make the Atlantic crossing. He was coldly polite. Precise, his words were chosen—like a pronouncement from the Bench. I felt like a defendant in the witness-box.

'Is the Master on deck,' was the first exchange. I identified myself by waving my arm.

'Why are you falling out of convoy? . . . What are your pennants? . . . Why do you not hoist your pennants?'

'I am not in convoy and I have no pennants assigned!'

No pennants. This called for a moment's consideration. I could see his gaze directed to the flare of our bows on which the name of a merchant ship is usually displayed. Ours was painted over and obliterated in accord with some new order.

'*Cameronia* from Glasgow,' I prompted. He acknowledged by a wave of the hand, then called—'Where are you bound?'

'New York.'

'What are your orders? . . . and where issued?'

'Independent orders. Issued by Clyde Naval Control. . . . We sailed early this morning.'

This also required a little reflection and it was with now fatherly interest the Commander and his party on the bridge of the destroyer surveyed the closely-packed lines of the cheering children on the decks above them. Independent sailing . . . and with all these kids on board! It seemed hard to believe. In the naval ship the news of the encounter seemed to have spread. Along the whole length of her exposed decks were the upturned smiling faces of the destroyer's men. It was perhaps difficult for the children to understand why the bluejackets did not return cheer for cheer, but at any rate the youngsters could be happy in the signs and signals that were made to them.

The Commander raised the 'mike' of his loud-hailer again. 'Sorry, Captain,' he said. 'Commodore thought you were one of his party. We'll wish you a safe voyage—a very safe voyage with all that crowd on board. I'll inform the Commodore . . . Goodbye!' He retired from the crow step, gave an order to the cox'n, and the smart little ship swung out to rejoin the convoy.

As she did so her crew broke silence unrebuked and returned the excited calls, hails and cheers of the little argonauts.

The transport of over four hundred young children in a ship would have been matter for grave consideration at any time, but most seamen would agree that such an embarkation in time of war was an almost unbearable charge upon all those responsible for their safety. Total war had imposed this strain upon us. Murder from the skies, in the cities and country towns, on the beaches and in the fields, had become the common crime of the exultant enemy after the fall of France. But at least the children could be snatched from the path of the Teutonic Herod and adventured abroad. There were kindly arms awaiting them in Australia, the United States and Canada. In the emergency, the merchantman was set to do his best to deliver this new and precious cargo despite the restraints of the King's enemies. But the task was never lightly undertaken. I would confess this voyage the most wearing and anxious of all my days at sea.

We had embarked passengers at Glasgow on the day before sailing. For me, it had been a trying day, marked by the visits on board of many friends and acquaintances whose children, sailing out with us, were committed to my care. It seemed heartless to assume a bearing of confidence, that I was far from feeling, in the circumstance of such pitiful leave-taking. The ship was not specially engaged in any scheme of evacuation but, for many of our younger charges, wardens had been engaged to take the children abroad and the attendants were to return with us on the homeward voyage. In addition to the children, we had embarked many adult passengers and the ship was crowded.

When the Company's clerical staff had concluded berthing arrangements, it was time for an attempt to bring the children under control. To stage a boat-drill with the ship lying at the quayside is rarely satisfactory for the distractions there and the coming and going of the longshoremen are all against the measures of routine. But the Ministry's regulations enforced it and their Surveyor was there to see it carried out. We had no success. About the most we could do was to change the children's toys, exchanging a ship's lifebelt for the civilian gas masks they had brought aboard. Captain Moir, the Surveyor, did not look as gravely concerned as we had expected. He had seen the same initial effort made in other ships and to no better effect: but he had interviewed the masters on return to gather information. All had agreed that ship life had imposed its own restraints and 'to make a game of it' was the thing to do. He said that one master had found it helpful to employ the elder children as look-outs, their reward being a post on the bridge and a ship-made armband. I was grateful to him for his advice when I accompanied him to the gangway to say good-bye. But my fears returned as I noticed the number of children's lifebelts thrown aside and discarded on the upper decks as I made my way to my quarters.

How right he was. When the destroyer had turned away a second attempt was made to regiment our capricious emigrants. It proved a long and tiresome business punctuated by tears and outcry and fits of temper. Inevitably, lifebelts were lost or mis-laid and had to be replaced, children mis-appeared or dis-appeared, straggled, fidgeted on the chalked deck spaces beside the ship's outswung lifeboats: the adult passengers who were not directly connected with the seavacuees objected to long standing at stations but, as moral support, could not singly be dismissed: there was, throughout, the shouted call and counter call from one group to another, the sudden dart from place and the shrill demand for the same standing-room on return: there was argument, near quarrel—indeed, a scrap or two developed over some points of preferment. But at length there had come some shade of attention that held promise of improvement with each succeeding drill. Even the almost despairing but indefatigable Mr. Squires, the Chief Officer, had the look of one who had achieved something when at last he came to report progress. Throughout all the excitements and clamours of the business there was one picture of contentment on the deck below my post. The babies in their cots and prams were sleeping peacefully for it was summer and the day was warm.

It seemed almost that Providence had set the day apart for the exodus of the innocents. There was no wind and the glassy but slightly undulating sea extended to a clear-cut horizon above which a few little clouds stood motionless. Only astern of us lay troubled waters where, in the tangents of her zig-zag, the ship had disturbed the calm. It was an unbelievably fine and sunny day and the ship a playground of ever-new discovery. Even the working seamen about the decks seemed happy in its character and endured the proffered aid, that was all too frequently obstruction, as they set about their duties. It was with a catch in the throat I noticed the interest our young charges took in the work of checking the provisions in the lifeboats, doubtless speculating upon the uses of the packages. (The 'First-Aid' boxes contained morphia.) . . . It was not easy constantly to remember that the fair day and tranquil sea were both suspect of treachery and that, at any moment, a blow might fall. Enemy submarines were known to be in the area and ships had been torpedoed not far from our line of advance only two days before. Although attack from the air was not at the time apprehended, there was always the possibility that the *Luftwaffe* might spare a distance Condor or Focke Wulf for a turn to sea. With some apprehension I focussed my glasses upon a growing speck in the sky astern and, with relief made her out to be a patrolling Sunderland of Coastal Command. The seaplane flew low over the sea and, at a distance remote enough to deaden the roar of the engines, had the appearance of a solan goose on the wing above the herring shoals. For many hours she remained within sight, circling, banking, turning again and again on inspection of the sea in advance of our route. It was evening when she signalled that she was returning to base. As a parting gesture she roared alongside and circled the ship. The airmen themselves, being enclosed, could not be recognised from our decks, but we would clearly be seen by them—a waving group of voyagers in a crowded ship sending thanks and farewell.

In August and in northern waters the periods of official darkness are, at the most, a few hours of troubled twilight. Any object seen on the northern horizon stands out sharply against the lingering glow of late sunset and early sunrise, whilst a ship on the southern sea-line would still be enshrouded under the darkling sky. By that accident of position it is possible we sighted the enemy before, if indeed we were seen by him. The high lookout on the foremast had sharp eyes and was the first to glimpse a tiny upstanding tooth on the clean-cut sealine to starboard. It could not be seen from the deck but rough bearings were taken and it was assumed to be a small vessel, possibly a trawler on passage to Iceland. As the morning light grew it was seen that we were converging for the stranger became visible from the bridge and I blessed the name of the kind American who had lent me his powerful binoculars. By their aid, I made out a submarine proceeding to the westward and it was time for us to bear away to the southward and lay on that little kick of extra speed that was reserved for a high occasion. Whether or not we were sighted by him could not be known, but he made no sign of it and at sunrise was no longer to be seen. We reported him to the police and continued on our way. But there was at least one thankful mariner in the *Cameronia* who gave praise for the fortunate turn of the zig-zag course that had brought us to the southern gloom and revealed him against the northern light.

On the forenoon of the third day out, it was thought there was opportunity for a gunnery exercise, now overdue. Sergeant Smith, the instructor, had many new D.E.M.S. recruits for training and was anxious to 'rustle them up' in actual gun-fire as against the dummy drills he had completed. A target had been prepared and of course, with its black flag, it held the eyes of the children when they came on deck in the morning. We had had long discussion of plans for the control of such an excitable 'gallery'. I was inclined to keep all the children below for a time, but realised that such a course would inevitably arouse apprehensions. The ship's surgeon said it would be unwise to expose the younger ones to the possibilities of shock, although he thought the elder children could be allowed on deck with some provision for cotton-wool ear-plugs. He thought some of them were well hardened and cited the case of two small brothers amongst them who could talk quite calmly of guns and bombs—fire too— when their home in Hampstead was bombed and fell in on top

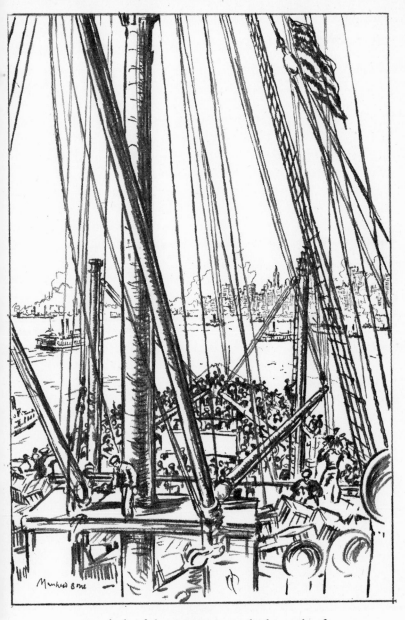

Foredeck of the *Cameronia* on the last mile of
an 'independent' voyage

of them! It was agreed to let the elder children stay, but all passengers would be confined to the fore-deck that was sufficiently far removed from the gun platform on the stern. The exercise was satisfactory and the target was hit by the fourth round at about 7000 yards. My interest in the shooting was marred by the need for frequent glances at the fore-deck where the longest necks I ever saw were craned overside to mark the fall of shot. We had no accidents and there was surprisingly little reaction to the concussion as the six-inch gun was fired. But I was glad when it was over and the children could return to less-exciting pastimes.

Fog extended all along the American coast when we made the land, and the deep-throated bellow of the Ambrose lightship was, for the children, the first sign of welcome to a new and friendly continent. It was a day of heat and summer haze and they were dressed for it in party best. I thought I had never seen the decks of a ship more splendidly adorned. But it was the old pilot, coming on board off Sandy Hook, who remarked on it. He was somewhat breathless when he mounted the bridge, for the long climb up the ship's side had winded him. But perhaps it was the unexpected greeting, the cheers from the joyous youngsters, that affected him for I thought his eyes dim as he said— 'What's this? . . . What's this? . . . Have ye brought the whole Royal Family across with ye this trip, Captain?' . . . I said I had.

★　　★　　★

Amongst the many special duties imposed on a shipmaster in wartime there is the important one of maintaining silence regarding the movements of shipping. Were this only a matter of self-restraint in conversation or correspondence it could be undertaken without second thought. But, in this duty, much more was required of him. He was expected to curb the natural loquacities of his crew and passengers and dam all rumour at its source. In what way this was to be done was never clearly laid down by regulation nor was he ever empowered to enforce an effective censorship upon personal disclosures.

But there could be no cavil at the exercise of mild persuasion and *Cameronia's* ON ARRIVAL poster—her 'Blue Peter' in reverse —was, for this purpose, prominently displayed in crew and passenger quarters as she entered port. Whether or not it had any effect in withholding information from the enemy we had no way of knowing, but there it was—the last six words of it reading like a chapter of adoption that may have influenced some one or two towards habits of reticence when safely disembarked from a ship in a port at home or abroad. It read:

ON ARRIVAL

Do not talk about the ship or whence she sailed or when. Do not say what ships were seen on the voyage.

Only tell your friends of incidents within the ship in your letters and do not mention the name of the ship.

Never give away the names or descriptions of other ships in company or of friendly aircraft that may have been seen.

Tittle tattle, idle gossip, and giving credence to rumours may endanger the vessel in which you have now so many friends.

For the same reasons of security it was not possible for us to send wireless messages from the ship at sea to announce the time and date of arrival. The hazy weather conditions that had attended our entry into the New York harbour channels robbed the signalman at Sandy Hook of his flag sight and we were not reported as having passed inward until anchored at the Quarantine Station off Staten Island. But Argus, in the persons of waterfront news reporters and press photographers, has his own sources of information and is rarely put off stride by an unheralded arrival of visiting celebrities within the port. When we had anchored and the Port Health Officer was satisfied that we were 'all well' the Customs cutter brought off the members of the Fourth Estate. Not very much escaped their initial survey and our temperate DON'T notice was immediately scanned and interpreted in a manner that had not occurred to its composer. 'Do not say what ships or aircraft were seen!' *Mm-mmm?* 'May endanger the vessel!' *Mm-mmm? Mm-mmm?*

It is unlikely that the children had paid any more than passing attention to the notice but, put on their mettle by a skilful newsman, it is astonishing what wealth of romantic imagination can be expended. When, later, the reporters—many of them friends of long acquaintance—confronted me with the evidence they had procured from our fertile moppets, I had my difficulties obtaining credence for the one fact that a distant submarine had been seen. Woven out of that indubitable incident there were many colourful figments to be dispelled. The gun-drill too, that we had conducted with so much care for their sensibilities, had been woven into the tale of an epic sea-battle in which we had of course been victorious! But the press photographers had a less nebulous report to make to their editors. For them the children put up many perfect pictures and, for the benefit of the newsreel cameramen, massed on the foredeck and sang 'There will always be an England' in shrill fortissimo. As a reward for that they were given the discarded flash-light bulbs with which many were able to stage a very realistic air bombardment until —in fear of the shattered glass—we had to call a halt.

Our stay at anchor off Quarantine had given time for the news of our arrival to circulate and the upper storey of the pier was crowded by the expectant friends and relatives of the incoming passengers when we docked. A strong ebb-tide was running in the North River as we drew in towards our berth and the operation of 'docking without incident' was perhaps long drawn out in consequence. In that slowly deliberate business opportunity was afforded for mutual recognition between the landsfolk on the dock and the voyagers within the ship, for *Cameronia's* outer rails were only a few feet distant from the upper stageways of the pier. It was a scene long familiar to me, but strangely, I did not quite accept it. Certainly, there was the same commotion in the welcoming crowd that thronged the upper storey, the same eager shifting of position to ensure a better view; shouts too, and words of friendly greeting. But only here and there did faces suddenly brighten, awake and aglow, in recognition. Framed in mass by the open windows and doorways, most showed expressions of puzzlement, perhaps anxiety, as we glided slowly in to our mooring.

To many of these kindly people on the dockside the children whom they had come to meet were complete strangers. Even if related, one cannot trace family resemblances without quietude, recollection, and reflection. They were so many in the pilgrimage, so many who looked alike, so many who could answer to an image preconceived.

This circumstance had been foreseen. Within the huge upper storey of the dock, on the tie-plates, letters of alphabetical sequence had been displayed and, as the children disembarked, they and their baggage were placed under the initial letters of their surnames until claimed by their sponsors.

The great floor of the upper pier resembled the concourse of Grand Central Terminal in holiday mood when I crossed the gangway from the ship. Around the agency and information-booths and fronting the bulletin boards, large questioning crowds had thronged and the loud-speakers erected above the doorways blared out the names of individuals requested to attend at the telephone or to identify themselves in some way as present. A few of the more ingenious had placarded themselves to establish rendezvous. 'UNCLE JAMES Campbell' of Newark, N.J., moved rapidly and expectantly from group to group in the crowds and a pleasant lady appeared to have her own shy difficulty in exhibiting a card 'Miss Jane Austin' that had also an oversize question-mark inscribed on it. After the comparative quiet and uniformity of the ship, the scene appeared sharply in contrast as one of confusion and derangement. But it had its own lines of planned direction and already the lifts and the staircase leading to the west-side driveway were thronged by a steady stream of departing voyagers and their tutelary benefactors.

My mission on the upper pier was personal. Many of my American friends had previously signed formidable legal documents in respect of the admittance of selected children into the United States and had accepted responsibility for their maintenance, clothing, education, and well-being for an unknown period of years. A small group of the children concerned in such Bonds had sailed out with us and, naturally, it was my duty to see these items in our export manifest safely delivered to the consignees, and, as well, to gratify my own pleasure in a reunion with cherished friends. My search led me to letter 'G' for George, but had I been blind I could have recognised the gathering by its character of high-strung and exultant allegro. It was abundantly clear that the children were already completely at home in a far country.

★   ★   ★

To link arms with a friend after long separation is no uncommon mark of affection, but to have him show discomfort at the gesture is odd. When the ladies of the party had thought the rigours of the day too much for their little charges and had carried them off to the less disturbing atmosphere of happy home-life on Long Island and Old Greenwich, I led my friend on board to spend a quiet hour in my quarters.

It appeared that he had just managed down to Pier 45 from an hospital in time to meet the children and my congenial action had maybe disarranged a bandage on his arm. At the hospital he had decanted (he used the word) a pint or so of his blood that was to be sent over to Britain to fortify our wounded in the battle there. There was a widespread scheme for it—Blood for Britain—and a formula had been devised for the oversea shipment of the living corpuscles. He thought it likely that *Cameronia* would include 'plasma' as special cargo on our return voyage. He said the tapping of the 'maple tree' was not attended by any serious discomfort: he was prepared to cultivate his very healthy allotment and submit to further transfusions when called upon. It was 'broadcast' time—a relay from London, and as we sat there in my dayroom, I could almost see the vital sap welling up in him as we listened to the calm even voice of the announcer—over three thousand miles away—stating the toll of the Battle over London. Out of the blue, we learned that during the previous week 570 German aircraft had been destroyed over Britain, that Mr. Churchill had said, 'Never in human conflict has so much been owed by so many to so few,' but there was no detail of the inevitable death-roll and destruction in the great city. My friend said only, 'Ah, London,' when the radio was silent again. I knew that his kind heart was there in shattered London, for he had spent much of his youth in England and knew the metropolis probably better than I did. Whilst my reaction to the news was perhaps a fierce interest in the turn of the great battle then raging, his reflections would doubtless be concerned with the area of the fighting and his thought with the fate of his many friends there.

Ah, London! The hackneyed and sadly overworked expression that 'blood is thicker than water' seemed to have acquired a real meaning as I sat there with my friend. American-born, and a stalwart upholder of his country's institutions and ideals, he is of old Suffolk ancestry and there must still be many of his ancient kin in that lovely part of England. Was it not curious to reflect that a loan was in process of redemption in this passing back to them the elements, perhaps purified to a degree by alien re-agency, from a common stream; to flow again in the veins of an undaunted citizen of London?

Among the items of an imperfect education, I read some-where that it was law in England in mediaeval days that yews should be planted and maintained in churchyards throughout the realm. It was thought seemly that the bows of the yeoman archers should grow out of the loins of their dead. Surely, there is here some analogy to the scheme of 'Blood for Britain' . . . if only I could express it rightly.

Chapter X

TROOP CONVOY

'You speak remarkably good English, Captain,' said the Naval Control Officer, looking up from his note-book in which he had jotted down my answers. Somewhat taken aback, I accepted the curious statement as complimentary, then suddenly realised that—the time being after sunset—our national flag would be hauled down. The officers of the Naval Base would not then see the Red Ensign worn by His Majesty's hired transport the *Nea Hellas* as they boarded her in the port of Freetown, Sierra Leone, in quest of the customary information. The ship and I were thought to be Greek! Their mistake was understandable, for Hitler's berserk rage in Europe had enlisted many nations' flags against him and amongst the vessels of the large troop-convoy that had just arrived at Freetown from the Clyde were Polish, Dutch, Norwegian and Belgian ships. What more natural than that a ship named *Nea Hellas* should be deemed to be of Hellenic registry? A brief explanation followed, and the business of the visit was continued. . . . 'Yes.' We would be re-fuelled in sufficiency for the next stage of our long voyage to the Middle East. 'No.' We could not be watered to full capacity. Fresh water was in short supply. In any case, there were only two tanker boats for the thirty ships of the troop-convoy: but they would do their best for us. We would sail again in three days' time. Convoy conference would be held aboard the *Cape-town Castle* at the anchorage and I would be advised of time and date. The matters concluded, the naval party disembarked, leaving me to pace the deck for a while and reflect upon the urgencies of the war that had brought me from the North Atlantic to equatorial waters.

Early in 1941, the tide of battle had risen to greater heights in the East and the old familiar pattern of troop-transport had been brought from the files of the last war and re-imposed. Italy's entry into the war against us had rendered the Mediterranean a *Mare Clausum* to Allied merchant-shipping for a term. The comparatively short sea-route by way of the Suez Canal had been temporarily abandoned for the much longer passage around the Cape of Good Hope. A voyage of ten or twelve sea-days had become one of nearly six weeks. In this emergency, the Department of Sea Transport was hardly put to it in providing troopship tonnage for the vital reinforcements demanded in Cyrenaica and Abyssinia. The requirements of troop transport call for ships of large size and reasonably high speed. They must have lengthy endurance in their economies of provision, of fresh water and evaporation plant, of bunkerage and fuel for power. They are of little use without space for the carriage of very large numbers of military personnel, their gear and equipment, their stores and munition. At this date not many such ships were available, but one fortunate circumstance went far towards solving the difficulty of procurement. After a wholesale and diligent self-scuttling programme had been carried out, there were no longer any German merchant ships engaged on commercial occasions at sea and, in consequence, the services of large oversea patrols could safely be terminated. These liners, requisitioned by Admiralty on the outbreak of the war and equipped as armed merchant cruisers had thus become redundant and—reconditioned and again under the Red Ensign—were available for troop movements overseas. Added to this useful list were many of the larger passenger vessels of our Allies. The *Nea Hellas* had been formerly the *Tuscania* of the Anchor Line and was transferred to Greek registry by sale in

1936. She was of a pattern with the *Transylvania* and the *Cameronia*—of 17,000 tons and had a speed of over sixteen knots. When hired from the Government of the Hellenes, it seemed sound practice to return her to the management of her former owners and, as I had formerly commanded her, it fell within the scheme of affairs that I should again embark and take a seat—back where I was in 1923. Within ten days we had armed, fitted and stored her, embarked Australian troops, and reported ready for sea at a Clyde anchorage.

We sailed in bitter wintry weather and the convoy went far into the Atlantic on our southward journey. On the passage we had seen nothing of the enemy but on several occasions the escorting destroyers had smelt him out, flagged the ships away from the area by emergency diversions, then shivered his timbers by depth charge . . . with what result we did not learn, but took good augury from the explosive tremors that ran through the hull of our ship which was the rearmost vessel in Column Four. At the Convoy Conference before sailing I had asked for this position in the formation. My request was not altogether based on the reflection that in the *Nea Hellas* we were a scratch crew and had not had recent experience of convoy; my old shipmate, James Spencer, the Chief Engineer, and I had our private doubts of her sea-performance. Haste in preparation and an urgent sailing-date were factors, and there were some matters of her internal economy we had to accept as reported by her former crew who could not be expected to hold friendly feeling for a boarding-party in their ship—however amicable had been the Hellenic owners' assent to the urgent transfer. It was as well we had taken up this humble station in the convoy (a position that afforded sea-room for her cantrips) for it was not long before difficulties developed. *Timeo Danaos* is maybe a hard phrase in its application to a new and very gallant ally, but I had thought of it only as applied to the ship's late stoke-hold crew. The important routine work of clearing, and maintaining clear, the boiler tubes—complicated as they were in *Nea Hellas* by super-heat—had either been neglected or indifferently performed, and if she did not quite display a pillar of fire by night she could certainly emit dense and sightly columns of smoke by day—the major of all crimes in wartime convoy. The engine counters too, by which the revolution of the propellers was adjusted, were out of register and could not handily be corrected whilst under way. When sailing independently as the ship had been, this erratic pulse would arouse no grave concern for it would be on an open throttle such a voyage was made. But convoy demanded an exactitude in revs. that the faulty dials could not display; the engineer officers could only guess at their errors in compliance with the incessant orders from the bridge, the ship barged here and there and the Commodore made angry signals. Yes! It was as well we had asked for sea-room at the tail of the convoy.

And now, anchored off 'King Tom' in the harbour of Sierra Leone, we had come in from sea to replenish fuel and water for the passage around the Cape to the next stop at Durban. Darkness had fallen as I tramped to and fro on the boat deck and thought of present logistics to be solved in one way or another. I had no relish for the Convoy Conference that would be held in the Commodore's ship at the anchorage. There would be a lot of 'heavy tonnage' there and maybe the masters would look askance at the pseudo-Greek who had made such a poor showing on the voyage. I would have much to explain. . . . My old ship was not now quite the sea queen that I had known when I took her over from the builders' yard so many years before. In that twenty years she had been engaged in what is probably the hardest and most exacting sea-trade of all—the North Atlantic with its rigid time-schedules. What wonder that she had her infirmities after all that service? But voices I could hear (stout Clydeside echoes, rough, rude but stimulating,) as I passed and re-passed the stoke-hold ventilators gave me assurance that at least one of her ills was under treatment and my shoes *crunched* upon the mounting layers of boiler-tube sediment that was being blown upward through the tall funnel from her hardening arteries.

I was not unacquainted with the transport of troops for I had entered the service of my Company during the South African

war in 1899 when its ships were largely engaged in the movement of our Army: the earlier World War had employed me
fully at Suvla Bay and in the Mediterranean and, in the piping
days of peace, occasional long voyages to the east had made me
familiar with His Majesty's Sea Transport Regulations. But the
new activities of 1941 posed problems that differed vastly from
its scheme of management. No one could now seriously pretend
there was no hardship for the voyaging soldier in troop-
transport overseas: the denial of the shorter route through the
Mediterranean and the urgency of reinforcement had over-
crowded the ships to a degree that rendered the extremes of
cold and great heat to be endured on the Cape passage an ever-
present burden. Nor were we in the *Nea Hellas* favourably
embarked to meet complaint. Our troops were Australian and
'Diggers' are not the men to be complaisant under stress. . . . A
curious distaste for cured fish in the dietary seemed productive
of an abnormal appetite in beer and, if that could not be satisfied
by canteen rationing, there were always mobsmen able and
willing to augment supplies. But, as I stepped on the boat-deck
resolving thought on this, not all the troops embarked seemed
to be busy concerting plans again to break into the beer stowage
in No. 4 Hold, for a large group had massed on the foredeck and
was in song there. Cheerful enough; but it was in some trepida-
tion I harkened to the voices, seeking some clue to the state of
balance in the choir. No. It was all right. It was not 'Roll . . . *out*
the barrel' in Dionysian fervour—the chorus they had used when
last they had helped themselves. It was 'Waltzing Matilda', and
the roar of it made me quicken my steps.

Pleasantly tired after my exercise, I went below in happy
anticipation of an 'all night in', a period of rest that had long
been denied me. But there is no rest for the delinquent in convoy
procedure. Yawning, I took up an urgent 'Hand' signal that had
just been brought off from the beach. It was addressed to us and
was from F.O.I.C., the Flag Officer in Charge, no less! It contained a sharp reprimand that caused me, wide awake, at once to
reach for the telephone and ring up the cabin of the Officer
Commanding Troops. *'Your ship'*, it began, *'is reported to be*

showing lights on deck. It is imperative that no lights be shown by vessels in harbour as the Port is possibly under air observation by Vichy French from Dakar.'

Damn! Against all orders, the Diggers must have been striking matches on the foredeck at their sing-song!

★   ★   ★

For quite a long period the old ship had been deserving of respect for good behaviour in convoy. Advantage had been taken of the three days' stay in harbour at Freetown to effect some adjustment and repair that, although only of temporary utility, had sufficed to avert the wrath of Commodore Hill. It was with satisfaction I could now turn the pages of the Signal Log when I came on deck and note that two hoists, sadly memorised by frequent reading in the early stages of the voyage, had not again been run up against Pennants 45. They were '*You are ahead of station*' and '*Keep closed up*'. In the engine-room the ship's engineers had skilfully corrected the faulty counters. Nor was there more ado concerning the emission of flagitious volumes of black smoke. True, there was still an undue density at the funnel tip, (and much greater heat at the base), but the Commodore's attention had been attracted by a competitor on the starboard wing of the convoy who had contracted an infection and was daily and harshly adjured to take measures.

At Durban, where we had again put in to port to supplement fuel and water for the long stretch north to Suez, the Convoy Conference was made remarkable by its unusual display of concord. No longer were defects, faults, and malpractices the main issues for discussion. We had all learned lessons and our association had in it the same character as that of a well-knit ship's company. It is possible that our good humour in Conference was heightened by the news of the day. Kisumayu had been taken and the South Africans were storming on beyond Mogadiscio. There was good news from all the eastern fronts and it was thought that the naval situation might justify the dispersal of the convoy. But no. We were still to keep together, for a powerful German raider was at large in the Indian Ocean and

Italian submarines, driven from harbourage on the Somali coast, could still find Vichy assistance in Madagascar. The long passage up the coast and into the Red Sea provided little incident and no alarms and there was the prospect of safe arrival in the Bay of Suez with all ships present and correct as they had sailed from the Clyde.

I had long known that Mr. Spencer was uneasy about the reserves of fuel oil in the ship and when we approached the end of the long voyage his concern seemed to increase rather than to grow less. It is ship habit for 'the Chief' and the Master to consult together daily at about noon on the events and prospects of the voyage and as we approached its termination it became obvious that he had grave apprehensions.

A transatlantic liner, the *Nea Hellas* had been designed for the comparatively short sea-passages of 3000 miles between Glasgow and New York. The capacity of her fuel tanks was based on that, plus a reserve to meet contingencies. There is a vast difference between the Atlantic tracks, even with fog and heavy weather to augment it, and the 4500 miles that separate Durban and Suez. Such a difficulty could normally be met by a reduction of speed to within the limit of the ship's ability to make port or by putting in to a way-port to supplement. But such simple expedients obviously could not be adopted in convoy. It was not quite the scarcity of fuel that worried the Chief Engineer but the doubtful quality of the last remaining reserves in No. 3 Tank. It was thought to be contaminated by a leakage of salt water and that was sufficiently known for the Greek engineers to report it when the ship was taken over. Certainly the weight and quantity were there but what would be the combustability of it when piped to the furnace burners was the vexed question? In the early stage of the voyage he had endeavoured to test the content by actual use. We all knew what had happened then The greatest volume of thick black smoke ever seen to come from a ship and the Commodore—after asking, '*Are you on fire?*—making a signal that we would have to return to port if matters could not be controlled! We had to fall out of convoy then for two hours to clear the supply lines and recondition the burners. As though that were not enough, there were kindred problems to furrow the brow of my old friend as he sat with me in my cabin on what we hoped would be the last full sea-day of the passage. The 'blood stream' of a ship, polluted, and flowing sluggishly in her veins, has its full effect on all the many complex auxiliaries. Generators, refrigerating system, pumps were all showing ominous symptoms. There would be a substantial list of repairs on arrival.

On arrival? . . . As we talked of it, I could see outboard the long white shaft of the Daedalus Reef Lighthouse standing out on the horizon to port. Three hundred and sixty-five miles from the anchorage at Suez. The sea was calm and the weather fair. Surely we could stay the course and anchor with the convoy. Mr. Spencer considered again the figures of expenditure of the good fuel we had taken on at Durban. He said he thought not. At some time in the early morning he would have to draw from the contaminated tank.

It was as he had feared. At two in the morning and in the Straits of Jubal, I was on deck in time to prevent the officer of the watch from shouting angry questions at the mouthpiece of the engine-room telephone. In the light following breeze the dense black cloud that proclaimed our breakdown stood high and funereal above the funnel; we had already lost speed and had fallen behind the convoy, now disappearing in the gloom ahead. . . . Thirty hours later we crept slowly past Newport Rock and limped to an anchorage in Suez Bay. We had arrived, but the manner of our arrival was not one of which I was proud.

*   *   *

When, southbound, we sailed from the anchorage again, we bade fair to emulate the Flying Dutchman in quest of a port for solid repair and refitment. Conditions at Suez had not been favourable for such operations, as always we had to have steam raised and maintained in readiness for sudden excursions when enemy planes swept over. From their airfields in the Dodecanese Islands to the Canal area is no more than a flight of two hours and the concentration of shipping at both ends of the Suez Canal was a target that the Germans, now operating from Italian bases, did not neglect. The canal itself was of course an object of attack and on one occasion was closed for ten days, having been mined from the air by one said to be a former ship pilot employed by the Canal Company. When a 'red' warning was broadcast, the ships at anchor were ordered to weigh and scatter out to sea during the attacks. There was thus no opportunity for thorough examination and repair of the boiler tubes, now badly choked by the use of foul oil-fuel. The *Nea Hellas* still advertised her whereabouts by a thundersome volume of dense smoke: speed too was greatly reduced and it was in this condition we were independently routed to make the return voyage to the United Kingdom.

On that route there were many ports of call for we were under instruction to load whatever cargo was offering on the South African coast. We carried only a small number of passengers, they being for the most part troop details or convalescents. At Port Sudan, at Aden, Kilindini, Zanzibar and Durban, we had requested dockyard assistance in refitment and repair but always there were prior claims on the machines and the engineering facilities of the port. (At Durban, every shipwright and engine-fitter in the yards was employed in repair of the gallant H.M.S. *Illustrious,* to make her again seaworthy for the long voyage to a dockyard in the United States.)

Our controlling authority, the senior Sea Transport Officers in these areas, being usually R.N.R. and sympathetic to a merchantman's difficulties, might listen with understanding to our catalogue of imperfections, but all they could do was to promise to report our woes to Sea Transport in Berkeley Square at London, then urge us to continue to the next port in the hope that something might there be done. Meantime, as they said, there was cargo on the wharf alongside: we would have to load it on board at express speed and get out to sea again. In this manner we limped from port to port down south from Suez.

The 'Stop Press' of our instructions, revised and renewed to date at every port of call, held few entries concerning enemy action in the Indian Ocean and our invalid status on that part of the voyage did not arouse serious apprehension: but Naval Control at Durban supplied us with the picture of the Atlantic and it was vastly different. U-boat activity in that ocean had been intensified and the waters off Freetown would be decidedly unhealthy for what was now no better than a ten-knot ship—and of a size that no sober torpedoman could possibly miss. It was in fervent hope of a restoration to our former useful speed we smoked our way around the Cape of Good Hope and docked within the harbour at Capetown; and it was somewhat in the mood of the tragic Vanderdecken I hurried from the ship to the Naval Base to report arrival and seek assistance in repair of our defects.

The S.T.O. (Sea Transport Officer) had not been briefed from Durban that we were in difficulty. Indeed, he seemed unsure of our identity or at least somwhat confused by it. He had expected a small foreign ship to load a modest cargo. And now he had a large Greek ship under the Red Ensign, fitted for the carriage of a great body of troops, but detailed to carry merchandise on commercial account! And requesting a stay in port for necessary repairs! No wonder he ruffled his iron-grey hair. Certainly our case—loss of speed, state of the boilers, the extent of our dangerous smoke outpourings—was appreciated, but he had no authority to approve the expense and delay in the voyage that was contemplated. Rustling through a file of signals, he studied a message from Headquarters in London. He read it out to me. 'Nea Hellas to load to capacity on Ellerman berth for U.K. Urge utmost despatch.' He pointed out that we were already three days late in anticipated arrival. I agreed, but suggested that if our speed could be worked up by the measures suggested we could make that good on the passage to Freetown. I urged that the delay at Capetown in repair of the boiler tubes would not altogether be time lost; we could employ it profitably in loading a greater cargo. I recalled the text of London's signal. We were to load to *capacity*; we were to take whatever the ship could carry when loaded to her marks. I thought it needful to introduce a profitable suggestion and told him there was in the ship a 'deep' tank, at the moment containing ballast water. I said I would be forever ashamed to carry dirty ballast water back to the Clyde and that the reason for its being in the ship was that the tank could not be discharged when at sea and we had been given no time for that operation on our very short stays at the way-ports. I proposed to pump the tank out and to clean and prepare the space of it. When I mentioned that I had the ambition of stowing a thousand tons of suitable cargo in place of the ballast water, he agreed that there was matter for an urgent recommendation by cablegram to Headquarters in London. On the day following a guarded approval was received: it was contingent upon a survey being held to consider the defects. Again, 'Urge utmost despatch' concluded the message.

★   ★   ★

At sea again and headed northward towards Freetown as the next port of call, it was the funnel tip that vied with the round of the horizon in my eager lookout. I could not keep my eyes from it. I would admit that swirling volumes of steamer smoke may have their own artistic and impressive formations, not unpleasing to the eye and perhaps even significant of high speed under certain conditions; but we had dwelt with that picture for overlong and had fathomed its treachery. So it was with mounting confidence I noted the absence of our Indian smoke signal of disorder. There were no more than gaseous fumes ascending in the rarified air of the south-east trade winds: I remarked too the fanwise spreading wash of our smooth displacement at sixteen knots. The Globe Engineering Company had done well in the eight-day period allotted to them for removal of the choked superheat tubes: we were loaded down to our marks by a bumper cargo: all was well again and the *Nea Hellas* pressed northward on zig-zag courses with every indication of seemly behaviour. We saw nothing of the enemy on the passage to Freetown, but almost daily we had wireless reports of his activity in the waters through which we sailed. It became clear that long-endurance Atlantic type U-boats had now concentrated on the trade routes to the south of Gibraltar and extending as far down as to the Bight of Benin. Of the numbers and positions of enemy submarines we had no other information than that contained in the brief SSSS messages of stricken ships. The naval signals we received, broadcast from Simonstown, Lagos, or Freetown, rarely contained mention of enemy activity. This was understandable for the same procedure of Remote Control that we had known in the Atlantic was in force.

At Freetown, where we refuelled and watered, we gained information of the enemy's activities at first hand. For passage to the United Kingdom, we embarked a number of D.B.S. (Distressed British Subjects.) They were Merchant Navy officers and men and also civilian passengers who were survivors of ships torpedoed and sunk in nearby waters. For the most part they seemed soberly resigned to the fortunes of war that had, for a time, returned them to the beach. They had lost everything but the tropical clothing in which they stood. Freetown was not then adequately stored to refit distressed seamen and it was well that, having made the return voyage from the Middle East with only a small number of servicemen as passengers, our canteen stores and clothing supplies proved ample to meet these new requirements. These new passengers had not been long on board before I was gratified by many offers from them to take duty as boat and lookout men for the homeward passage. Some had had bitter experience of hardship in 'open boats' before making the land and they were detailed to examine our lifeboats and give us the benefit of their hardly acquired experience. Others were posted as extra lookouts. In *Nea Hellas* we were adequately manned, but could always find place for such interested and experienced volunteers.

There was some delay as we lay anchored (in 'the slavers' berth') off King Tom awaiting instructions to proceed to sea. I had been on shore reporting at Naval Headquarters and sensed some indecision there. I thought that, with cargo loaded to the marks and all in order, with a signed speed of sixteen knots, we would immediately be ordered on the voyage. But no. There was other thought of our employment. The instructions were to maintain steam ready for immediate departure: Routeing Orders would be sent off when forward.

It was nearing sunset when our Orders came. We were to proceed at once to Gibraltar: the booms would be held open for us beyond the hour of official sunset. The Naval Control Officer, knowing the value of fore-knowledge to a merchant-man, had added a pencilled note to the typewritten instructions. It read that we were intended to evacuate civilians from 'the Rock'. There was cause for wonderment in the text of Sailing Orders. We were routed to pass through the Straits of Gibraltar in darkness, then return on a westward course so as to arrive off the Rock—coming apparently from the eastward—at sunrise. That was curious. Was Spain gathering against us too?

Chapter XI

MOVEMENT EXODUS

As we rounded Europa Point and entered the Bay of Gibraltar on the 26th May, 1941, there was silence within the harbour and a curious impression of grave event in the absence of shipping movement. There were no warships in the port—other than the elderly aircraft-carrier the *Argus*, whose stony camouflage blended into the texture of the terraces and bastions above the Dockyard Basin. I had not ever known the Rock and its waters thus devoid of ships and craft. On the many former visits I had made, the early morning hours had always been brimful of incident and naval activity, for the gun at sunrise marks the moment when the water gate of the Citadel is unbarred and the occasions of the day commenced. The afternoon might be quiet and devoted to the rite of the *siesta,* but not the fresh of early morning. It was then that the fishermen put out from Irishtown and the Old Mole to cluster off the Point and seek red mullet there; naval picket boats and launches furrowed the smooth waters of the harbour and the Admiralty pilots with attendant paddler tugs took opportunity before the wind had risen to trim and cant the ships within the Naval Dockyard. But on that day there was little movement. *Nea Hellas* lay silent and quietly too, stopped off Rosias Bay awaiting the pilot to enter the port.

Unbusied and inanimate as the scene within the harbour appeared, the vista of the Bay was as fair as ever. The morning sun, that was hidden from us by the lofty ridge of the Rock, glinted on the distant landscape of the Spanish land and coloured the ranges of the far surrounding mountains. Even the squalid shacks and tenements of La Linea and the neutral ground acquired a gentility from the morning light that also touched the gracious distant spires of Ronda and San Roque. Upon a high hill to the northward the rays brightened the grey old martello tower that marked the site of the Queen of Spain's chair where Isabella waited in vain to see the banners of Spain again hoisted over Calpe. Perhaps by now there was a jack-booted Gauleiter seated there. Would he too wait in vain to *heil* the swastika?

With the coming of the harbour pilot we were quickly enlightened as to the unusual appearance of the port. Did we not know that the *Bismark* and the *Prinz Eugen* were at sea and that the Fleet had sailed? We had learned when on passage from Freetown that the great battle cruiser *Hood* had been sunk by enemy action at sea on the 24th but the circumstances of her loss had not been mentioned in the brief item included in a news broadcast. For a time, we affected to disbelieve it, for it was originally quoted as from German report and had not the *Ark Royal* been sunk on paper by Herr Goebbels so often before? But there had come no denial and sadly we accepted the news that the great ship had been lost. The pilot went about his duties with grave deliberation. I surmise that he would know the *Hood* well for, in her quarter century of supremacy, she had often been based on Gibraltar. When we had berthed at the detached Mole and his job was finished, he swung his arm in a sweeping gesture towards the empty quayside and the Dock-yard almost as though he were urging his paddlers to swing a ghostly ship into position. 'That was where she lay,' he said.

When I reported on shore to Naval Headquarters, there was an atmosphere of tense expectancy in the Duty Office. I felt somewhat an intruder there amongst the naval officers. Of course there would be sadness at the grievous loss of the *Hood* but expression of it was unspoken in this dire moment of suspense. I surmise that our dispositions in the North Atlantic would be well known to the senior officers. The Duty Com-mander at his desk looked grim but exultant as he scanned the signals that were brought to him from the War Room. It was long before he considered my report. Quite naturally, 'Move-ment Exodus' in which my ship was chiefly concerned could await the outcome of much more serious events, but the good man did reward me with an assurance before he settled down to deal with *Nea Hellas*. It appeared likely that the *Prinz Eugen* had escaped to harbour in Brest, but the *Bismark*—as he said—was doomed beyond possibility of error. She had been brought to action and great news was expected at any time.

We were to embark about a thousand passengers for transport to the United Kingdom. Most were Gibraltarians of the shopkeeper class. Further reference to the signal files brought out that a number of passengers had still to collect their embarkation orders. The Commander surmised that these were British residents withdrawn from Cadiz, Malaga and Tangier. He appeared to know more about them than about the tradesfolk of Main Street and the Water Gate, for there had been much correspondence regarding their accommodation in the ship. They would come under the heading of 'indulgence' passengers. It was with a half-smile, he quoted little excerpts from the letters on his file. The writers, he remarked, were mostly retired officers and civil servants long absent from Great Britain. Judging by their communications, the Commander thought some of them might be critical of wartime ship life and amenities, and might even prove skilful in composing 'Letters to the Editor'. How *were* we fixed in *Nea Hellas*, anyway—in respect of accommodation, food and service? I assured him that we were reasonably well found in most particulars. We would have to re-arrange the berthing plans to accommodate the numbers he had mentioned. We would be seriously crowded, but not overcrowded. I was afraid the indulgence passengers might have reason to complain upon their first introduction to austerity in the ship, but we would do our best for them. Food? We had stored to capacity at Capetown. For the rest, we were well manned and equipped. A sudden thought prompted me to think of perishable supplies, of fresh vegetables: we had been digging in tins for over a week. Could anything be done in Gibraltar? The Supply Officer was brought into the conference. He said he was afraid not. He added that, if fresh vegetables and other provisions were stacked abundantly in the market, there would be no need to evacuate so many civilians from the Rock. The neutral ground had been a closed area for some days. I

'The Rock' from the eastward

noticed the Commander and his junior exchange expression of some common thought, brought about by such a trivial topic in the conversation as our request for a head or two of lettuce. Was it not possible that the great news, hourly expected, might have the effect of toning down El Caudillo's belligerency and re-opening the frontier?

Embarkation was a lengthy proceeding occupying the best part of three full days. Whether or not some form of persuasion or indeed of compulsion was enforced in respect of the local emigrants was not known to us, but our passengers seemed loath to take shipping abroad. Many of them I had known in the flourishing days of tourist traffic when the Rock, being one of the first ports of call to Mediterranean 'cruisers', held the initial advantage in display of tricky but attractive bargains. How, in these days, they would stand astride their doorways in Main Street extolling the treasures within! How now, unfortunately redundant in a garrison of fighting men, they had come aboard to cluster at the ship's rails for a long look at the towering Citadel whence their roots had been torn and their communal ties disrupted. Not a one of them had eyes for the seaward vista; in that direction lay the empty sea. From where we were berthed at the detached Mole, the treasured view was shore-wards towards the terracing of the Alameda Gardens, then the length of the bastions and the upland villas of the town, and finally an upward glance towards the serrated ridges of the Lion's Mane. Once embarked, we became a 'sealed' ship for security reasons, under orders to allow no further traffic with the beach. (It was common knowledge that there might still be Spanish eyes and Spanish ears within the Rock itself.) But there seemed no serious restriction on prolonged farewells. Daily, almost hourly, the friends and relatives of the evacuees rowed out to us in small boats and lingered alongside to shout late remembered messages or only to wave in wordless salutation. With embarkation completed, there came the customary grouping of all crew and passengers at boat stations, each girdled by a lifebelt—strapped and adjusted. What the friendly occu-pants of the rowing boats thought of such sinister precaution could only be surmised. Perhaps, knowing now that the great and powerful *Bismark* had been destroyed, they could take comfort from this evidence of the ship being prepared and ready 'in all respects' to proceed to sea.

We had to await escort before sailing. A new regulation had come into force that ruled out independent routeing for merchant ships carrying more than one thousand persons. It had been long since such ships had joined convoy at Gibraltar and none was expected. Force 'H' with every available destroyer had not yet returned from operations that led to the destruction of the *Bismark* and, as I gathered, the fuelling of naval ships concerned in that action had been the cause of delay in return to base. After a day's hold up when embarkation was completed, it was decided that we should sail in company with H.M.S. *Argus* to the Clyde. Although listed as an aircraft carrier, this fine old ship rarely put her planes into the air herself. The transport of aircraft was more properly her designation and, in that duty, she plied between the Clyde and Gibraltar. At the Rock, her cargo of fighter planes was transferred to the *Ark Royal* and from her were manned and flown off at a position in the Mediterranean to the reinforcement of Malta's defences. The *Argus* had a useful speed of eighteen knots, but was not considered 'handy' for escort duties. At conference, the Captain warned me that we might have our difficulty in sighting his signals as his mast was no higher than a cottage flagpole. Together, we sailed on the evening of the 29th, and made good progress into the Atlantic before darkness fell. But at midnight both ships were ordered to return and at daybreak we re-entered the harbour and berthed as before at the detached Mole.

The Pay Commander who boarded the *Nea Hellas* on our re-arrival seemed unperturbed by the situation that had brought us back to port. For him, it was doubtless only an incident in the day's work, but my interest was in the prosecution of the voyage and it was in no complaisant mood I contemplated further delay in port. Already, there was alarm and disquiet amongst our passengers at the overnight proceedings. What expression it would take when, inevitably as the day progressed, the rowing boats came swarming around us at the Mole was a matter of concern. Could not some statement be made to allay apprehension? It seemed definite that an escort could not be provided for some days, But the Commander was reluctant to authorise the posting of such an admission. The ship was to remain at four hours notice for steam: no shore leave was to be granted. With these instructions I was left to the uncongenial task of pacifying the excitements and ill content of our protesting passengers.

Throughout the period that might someday be termed an historic week in Gibraltar we lay immobile at the Mole. On the 2nd June Force 'H' returned to base from battle in the Atlantic and the harbour once again assumed its normal spirited appearance. It was afternoon when the ships came in, the *Renown*, flagship of Admiral Sir James Somerville, leading the *Ark Royal* and the *Sheffield* and escorted by a flotilla of fleet destroyers. In our weary position at the detached Mole, the *Nea Hellas* suddenly assumed importance as grandstand in a naval occasion. Every point of vantage in the ship was quickly crowded. Langour, and inquietude were swiftly dispelled by excitement and enthusiasm as we cheered the fighting ships to their berths at the quayside. Nor was this our sole distraction in the days of waiting. There were the diplomatic exchanges. With the Fleet visibly in harbour again, the Governor, Lord Gort, had the courteous thought to call upon his opposite number across the Bay at Algeciras. Later, his visit was returned and we had opportunity to study through high-powered binoculars the demeanour of the Spanish grandees as they were received by a guard of honour at the Flagstaff landing steps. When, in the afternoon, they returned from what had doubtless been a Lucullan feast, we in *Nea Hellas* were interested specially in certain packages that were embarked in their barge with them at the last moment. We had the thought that the comity of nations could be well served by our ship's contribution to it. Certainly, the Spanish visitors could be in no doubt regarding the abundance and quality of rations in the garrison of Gibraltar —for our chief baker was especially proud of the batch of fine white bread that he had drawn from his ovens that very morning and that we knew to be wrapped up in the packages.

On the 6th of June we put out to sea again. The convoy in which we sailed was small but of unusual formation. Only three large ships comprised the convoy proper of vessels bound to the United Kingdom, but there was a considerable escort during passage through the Straits and at least two Catalinas were in the air ahead. It was in late afternoon we sailed and the westerly wind and sea had risen to the customary strong breeze that comes before sunset. A day of extreme visibility that was not without its dangers by reason of that. In 'line ahead' the *Nea Hellas* was sandwiched between two large aircraft carriers, H.M.S. *Furious* being the senior and leading ship and our former consort H.M.S *Argus* taking station astern of us. When south of Carnero Point, signal was made to zig-zag as course for the open Atlantic was set. Throughout the tangents of the zig-zag there were certain wide angles of progression in which there was the illusion that we were back in port again and moored calmly between two stone breakwaters. This was in part due to the massive camouflage of the naval ships, but greatly heightened by the absence of masts and superstructures above the long sheer of their landing decks. The single funnel of the *Nea Hellas* was tall and of substantial girth. I surmise that, viewed through the lenses of a periscope, the convoy might present an uncommon spectacle to an enemy commander— that of a solitary vessel suddenly resolving into three as the turns of the zig-zag opened and closed the bearings. Nor was this the only deviation from the normal formation of a merchant convoy. At frequent intervals we were sharply exercised by the Senior Officer in a form of evasive manoeuvre not often practised in merchant ships. It was a combination of zig-zag with changes in formation from 'line abreast' to 'line ahead'. It cannot be said that we became quickly expert in such evolutions, but we did acquire a modest competence as we joggled our way from Gibraltar to the Clyde.

Chapter XII

PAPER SALVAGE

It was always a custom in the sailing ships in which I served during my early years at sea to devote any odd time to the clearing of the decks. Let the ship be snugged down or hove-to in a gale and the peril of high seas on the open deck preclude all shipwork there, the energetic Mate could always find opportunity to outwit Satan by providing occupation for idle hands. Usually, these were light tasks undertaken in the comparative comfort of a sheltered 'tween deck and of course within hail of the officer's post on the weather side of the poop. They were not important; they could quickly be abandoned when there was call for some action aloft or for another hand to the wheel.

I was reminded of the old days when I returned from the lengthy voyage in the *Nea Hellas*. Whether the circumstance of that ship's surprising recovery from early functional disorders had been remarked in the board room is not known, but it seemed significant that both the Chief Engineer and I were relieved of our posts in her and instructed to proceed to the United States to take over another aged vessel, the U.S.S. *Catlin*, then being fitted as a troopship in the Navy Yard at Philadelphia. If advancement can be assessed on a tonnage basis,

the 'Chief' and I were doing well. The *Catlin* was a very large
ship . . . but rumour had it that she was, to say the least, somewhat difficult.

It was whilst awaiting passage to the United States and being
at home on leave I thought of clearing my decks. Desk and cup-
boards were littered by the accumulations of many years of
delayed action and recent transfers from one ship to another had
overloaded my domestic storage. A 'Paper Salvage Campaign'
was in full flurry in the city of Glasgow and neat little Boy
Scouts were constantly at my door to remind me of a patriotic
duty in the general war effort. I think it likely that their initial
harvest whetted an appetite for more, and I had occupation
enough in helping to load up the little hand cart that they
rustled so smartly to the door.

But I too found a harvest of my own in the dusty business of
turning out and sorting the budget of remembered years. There
was a fragrant dust aroused in the handling of old letters, news
cuttings, note books—brave scraps of unfinished verse, the
'diaries' I had started so valiantly in the Januarys of forgotten
years and whose pages remained unsullied as from March. Unfinished essays into long-forgotten and imperfect schemes went
'by the board', but it was with the photographs I dallied for
long in indecision: what to destroy and what to preserve? . . .
Was there ever a day when I stood like that at the head of the
Captain's Table in the *Transylvania* to approve a festival haggis
on a 'Burns Night'? And the ship's piper at my elbow waiting
for me to pour his dram before awaking the echoes in the
dining saloon with '*Gabhaidh sinn an rathad mor*', doubtless to
the amazement of our American guests. Yes. The print is old
and faded, but that would be Duncan my old quartermaster . . .
who was lost in her in 1940.

One souvenir I held long in my hand. I think I had kept it
because of its illustration and the legend printed below. It was
an old dining car menu of the L.M.S. Railway belonging to
the days of pre-war travel. The picture was a good line drawing
of a classical incident, of the maiden Nausicaa helping the sorely-
tried Odysseus to embark from the Isle of the Phaceaces. The

legend bore her parting words to him—'There is good hope that thou may'st see thy friends.'

Thus reminded of such a happy prospect in the United States, I could afford to consider the labours of my new assignment with less distaste. I had looked up the particulars of my ship in Lloyd's Register and, with some dismay, had recognised her as the old German liner, the *George Washington*, a veteran of transatlantic sea travel in byegone days. I had thought her long since condemned to the ship-breakers' yard. I noted the date, of her construction at Stettin. 1908 seemed like something stone-cut on the base of a museum piece! Without a doubt she had been a fine ship in her day, but that day was long past. Sabotaged by her German crew in New York harbour in early 1917, her cylinders and boilers had been patched and repaired by American engineers and she had served as an United States naval transport in the First World War. She had gained distinction by carrying President Wilson to attend the fateful Conference of Versailles in 1918. Certainly she was a colourful old ship, but somewhat out of picture for a war purpose after a third of a century afloat. Amongst the items detailed in the Register was the information that she was a coal burner and consumed 350 tons of fuel in a day's progress at nineteen knots.

It was with misgiving I pondered that problem. Where, if anywhere, could able stokers be found to lift, shift, and fire forty thousand shovelfuls of coal in a day at sea? The breed of rip-roaring but competent seafarers by whose strength and stamina and singular skill at feeding steamship fires great records had been made in the North Atlantic passage, like the square-rig sailormen they displaced, had died out. The use of oil fuel in modern liners had brought about an incredible reduction in the physical labour of stokehold crews. As a consequence less stalwart recruits had become acceptable and the traditional North Atlantic 'firesmin' followed the old-time sailor into the limbo of forgotten tradesmen.

But how well I remembered him. I recalled the twilight of his stormy career when, as a young officer in transatlantic steamships it was often my duty to attend the gangway on sailing days at New York. How the roaring lads, fortified by last-call potations in the Dutchman's saloon across the waterfront would mount the gangway and swagger past with fists clenched, the wrists turned insolently outwards, and each arm performing a rhythmic curve as expressive of scorn of a 'deck' officer in a frock coat and white gloves. How, prudently, I preserved a neutral and uninterested demeanour—and endeavoured to ignore their challenging remarks. But I could remember too how, when sobered to their hard task below in a reeling ship at sea, the insatiable furnace fires were fed. And passengers in the comfortable old-fashioned smoke room in the *Columbia*, hearing the rattle of shovels on the foot-plates of the stokehold below— the constant demand for more coal from the trimmers—would adventure a few additional dollars on the Auction Pool of the day's progress! I had contacted an old shipmate who was almost the last of the breed, a good old hand but past the years when I had known him *make* a man take up the duty he had signed for . . . and do it. He was glad to sail with me again as leading stoker in the *George Washington*, but he had no rosy vision of recruiting skilled assistants to feed the transatlantic fires in a ship. The best he could promise was bodies—hands and feet, in manning the stokehold and bunkers of the ancient vessel.

In this reverie of byegone years, I recalled that I had seen her in undress and retirement as she lay drowsing on the tides of the Patuxent River in Maryland, the date about 1930. There, at her lightest draft she looked singularly high-sided and impressive amongst the nondescript vessels that were moored with her to await some fiat of disposal. I saw, in her, the hull of a good ship. As I viewed her from the low roadway that runs by the tidal riverbank, I felt all of the sailor's instinctive reaction to fine design even although the rust of long detention and inaction was thick on her structure and proclaimed the lowly state to which she had been reduced. A discoloured commission pennant fluttered at her masthead and indicated that she was still a U.S. Government ship in reserve. My host (Bill Footner had an eye for ships too) said she had lain there for years. But there was common talk at Solomon's at that date that she

and the other hulks moored beside her would be towed away
to be broken up for scrap, Japan being then the foremost bidder
in that international market. The islanders of Solomon's had
hopes of benefit in that proceeding for, as they told me, the old
crocks were moored right above their most lucrative oyster
beds. But the rivermen thought the *Catlin* was not completely
derelict. They said that, unlike the other hulks, a naval maintenance party was berthed on board the big ship. They said too
that, on occasion, Government Maritime Inspectors from
Washington came down to hold survey in her, doubtless to
justify some vote in Congress on Naval Appropriations.

I remembered that view of her and there was some reassurance in the recollection. No Government department
could afford to postpone the interment of a corpse. That the
ship was, at the moment, in the Navy Dockyard at Philadelphia
undergoing refitment and repair held out some prospect of
rehabilitation. The way I considered it, someone expert in
ships had decided that the old German liner had good metal in
her and a competent survey must certainly have been held
before contracts were agreed. Even with generous and timely
Lend-Lease in operation, the great expense of re-conditioning
such a vessel would not be undertaken lightly. I looked again at
my instructions. Upon completion of refitment at the Navy
Yard the U.S.S. *Catlin* was again to become the *George Washington* and to sail under her third national flag—the Red Ensign.
A crew of over five hundred men would be required to man
her. Already a number of officers and leading hands had been
sent out to the ship at Philadelphia to gain experience of her
reconstruction and it was proposed to send the others to camps
in Nova Scotia until the ship was sufficiently advanced to
require their working service. I was heartily in agreement with
that arrangement for it would be impossible to provide occupation for them at 'stand-by' in an American Naval Dockyard.

On this assignment I sailed from Liverpool in the *Lochkatrine*
on the 25th May, 1941. But for a passage across the North Sea
to join my first ship at Antwerp in 1890, I had not sailed abroad
before without having my signature on the Articles of Agree-

ment in a ship. It was a strange experience to have no job on board and its novelty was emphasised by the many formalities attendant upon departure 'out of uniform'. For too long I had been accustomed to stepping on the bridge, pulling a brass-bound cap over my eyes, and saying 'Let go, aft! . . . Let go forr'ad!' to begin a voyage. There were not many passengers, for the ship was a cargo carrier and had few berths for such idlers as I. We sailed in late evening together with other ships in a 'slow' convoy of which the *Lochkatrine* was guide. The Commodore was Admiral Sir Bertram Thesiger who, with his expert signal staff, joined us in the river.

The voyage was long, for the convoy—augmented from the Bristol Channel, Belfast, the Clyde and the east coast—aggregated nearly fifty ships when at length we formed up off the Butt of Lewis and steered for high latitudes near Iceland. I found the passage tedious and its only exciting incident was a night attack by a U-boat pack, assisted by an enemy 'shadowing' plane that, at his distance, held the convoy under observation for a long period on the day before. In this engagement it was said that two of our ships were torpedoed and lost, but—so large was the formation—I had no knowledge of that until the morning came. With my room-mate, I was up and down all night and it seemed curious that the loss of ships should have occurred with so little evidence of casualty. . . . But the great convoy extended over many sea miles. My companion was Mr. Reid, a courier of the U.S. State Department, and seemingly in no way embarrassed by the weight of his impedimenta. A good room-mate, unperturbable, he had made many passages in war-time. I think he was not long doubtful of me, for he had agreed to let me assist in disposal of his heavier consignments if the need came. The light one, not inconsiderable in size, would have needed the services of a blacksmith to deprive him of it as it was constantly chained to his wrist. He had acquired the habit of eating with one hand.

The use of a new defensive apparatus was revealed to me during the attack. It had become the tactic of the U-boat packs to surface between the columns of a 'slow' convoy and rely upon their speed and the confusion into which the formations would be thrown to effect their swift and sudden purpose. 'Snowflakes' had been devised to counter this form of attack. They were rockets firing a high-powered illuminant, and these had a parachute attachment for long continued suspension in the night sky. The glare was steely and intense and by its light the escorting destroyers could bring the submarines to surface action with some prospect of success. (At a later date and when 'Radar' was perfected, 'snowflakes' at sea were largely discontinued.)

We were not again attacked and, in about 40° West longitude, the escort that had served us so well was detached and held away southward, doubtless to join up with a home-bound convoy. A day later, the Admiral dispersed the large convoy and came down from the bridge that he had not left since sailing from the Mersey.

Chapter XIII

MANNING A SEA GHOST

By some odd circumstance the taxi I had engaged to transport me to the Philadelphia Navy Yard traversed a flag-bedecked avenue. During stops and starts as the traffic was controlled, the friendly driver explained the occasion as the Great Mammoth Convention of the American Legion. The avenue was crowded by upstanding men who, if a little beyond the best years, were yet amazingly active and enthusiastic. Some wore uniform but the most were in civilian clothes though sporting the khaki fatigue cap of the war of 1917–18. Stands had been erected and in them were ladies seated to watch their men-folk parade in quickstep. There were many military bands, some standing at ease whilst others exercised in preparation for the event of the day. At the lower end of Broad, one ambitious bandmaster was testing out for key and the strains of Sousa's 'Stars and Stripes' rang out in full volume. It was in this manner the taxi was ushered almost to the main gate of the Navy Yard. The driver called it League Island. He said, pleasantly, he knew I was a 'limey' for no one in the Quaker City called it the Navy Yard. As I paid him off he wished me good luck and said I was in time for the music all right.

'In time for the music!' It was curious he should have reminded me of that . . . for it recalled an incident of the earlier World War, when, as in August, 1941, the United States was neutral. It was at New York in the autumn of 1916. Halted at the crossing of Broadway and Twenty-Third, I had been stirred by the same excitement and the same patriotic march as long columns of United States regular troops swung by on their way to embark at the North River in a demonstration against Mexico. Within six months of that date the United States had joined with us in the war against Germany. I thought it a good augury as I explained myself to the Marine sentry at the Admiral Commandant's office.

Rear Admiral Watson was helpful, but I had not been long in conversation with him before realising that the *Catlin* was not popular with the authorities in the Dockyard (she was known there as the 'Rip Van Winkle'). A date in October had been set as that of completion of repairs and conversion, but there was a doubtful cast in the Admiral's words as he mentioned it. He seemed the more particularly interested in the date on which the British crew would join to relieve the four U.S. officers and over sixty naval ratings who had at the moment the care and maintenance of the ship. I could not assure him of a definite date but reported that my crew was at sea and on its way out to join. The interview pleasantly concluded, he set me on my way to visit the ship.

I was not happily impressed by the first appraisal of my new command when I saw here lying lubberly and forlorn at Pier 5 in the Navy Yard, but one does **not** expect any ship undergoing extensive repair alongside to be pleasing to the eye and it was with due allowances I surveyed her from the dockside before going on board. I was again struck by the patent strength of her construction and the 'fineness' of her lines. She was 720 feet long but the proportion of beam to length made her seem narrow in any comparison with more modern steamships. Her four masts had been shortened for some reason and that gave her an unkempt appearance her two pipe-stem funnels did nothing to dispel. But these were minor imperfections to which one could become accustomed; my main encouragement lay in the state of the hull. She had lately been brought up from the backwater in Maryland and although her upper works seemed to have been cleared from rust and glowed in red oxide paint she had not yet been in dry-dock for survey of the hull underwater. The ship was not upright but lay at an inclination from the dockside and this list presented a good view of the lower plating. The encrustation of shell on these plates had almost the proportions of a breakwater. But a small section had been scaled for examination and there the bright Swedish steel was clean and uncorroded.

It was about noon when I climbed the long gangway to board her and the inactivity of the mid-day break heightened the appearance of disorder on her littered and deserted decks. I thought of all the hard labour involved in restoring her to shipshape condition and pondered the Admiral's enquiry concerning the employment of our British crew in her. What could be done at this stage of reconstruction with a mob of merchant seamen, doubtless softened and ill to organise after long shore-dwelling and an idle sea passage? It was no good prospect and I felt that a major problem would arise if the Admiral insisted on his small maintenance party being immediately relieved. I saw no sign of them, other than the P.O. at the gangway who looked suspiciously at my civilian clothes and seemed unsure of my identity. Nor did my meeting with the Company's merchant officers who had previously been sent out to join her allay my premonition of difficulty. Staff Captain Steuart had his working ills and frustrations to report and my happy reunion with James Spencer, the Chief Engineer, was clouded by his already poor opinion of the old ship's boilers and the measures the dockyard people proposed to take in their reconditioning. Both of the senior officers agreed that it seemed hopeless to adventure upon protest with the Naval Authority controlling the ship's conversion, but they thought matters might be advanced if the British mission at Washington could be approached. . . . Cautiously, but in good hope, I entered upon my duties. I had not had any part in the scheme of conversion. That had already been decided upon by the British Ministry of War Transport and the United States Maritime Commissioners under a Lend-Lease agreement. My task for a time was not unlike that of a Clerk of Works and, in the last resort, it was the Naval Constructors and Engineers of the dockyard who were the ultimate arbiters. I thought it a situation that called for tactful restraint in any submissions to be made.

To shipbuilder and engineer the repair and refitment of an old ship is a much more vexatious task than new construction from keel to truck. The problem involved being the adaption of existing structure to serviceable design cannot be other than of

a makeshift character. Nor is there the sense of good craftsmanship in the workman's hand for he is constantly affronted by the
dissimilarity of the material he has to join. In the *Catlin's*
reconversion these already great problems were aggravated by
the absence of many of the original plans, diagrams, blueprints,
of engines, boilers, and internal systems on the ship. Some of
these, I was informed, had been destroyed by the German
sabotage in 1917 whilst others had been mislaid; their replacement called for new measurement and investigation throughout. But it was in respect of her twelve great 'Scotch' boilers
that the old lady provided the father and mother of all headaches
to everyone concerned. They were the originals of 1908.
Certainly they were then well constructed but all metal grows
old, and boilers—subjected to frequent alternations of great
heat and cooler temperatures—perish more quickly than less
actively excited components in a ship. It was admitted that this
heart of the old vessel was diseased, but the ship doctors with
their improved panacea of electric welding held to the considered opinion that the boilers could be made serviceable.
Venturing to express my doubts, that submission was brushed
aside by the experts . . . who would not have to sail in the ship.

Philadelphia is a friendly city and at League Island in the fall
of 1941 its sympathy with the Allied cause was undisguised.
Consequent upon the generous provisions of Lend-Lease, there
were several British warships undergoing repair in the Navy
Yard. H.M.S. *Furious* lay across the basin from us in process of
refitment that could only have been vicariously effected under
the menace of air attack in home dockyards. Many of our
smaller naval auxiliary vessels, corvettes and sloops, were also
in course of repair and the White Ensign was a not uncommon
emblem in the area. The *Catlin* still wore the American ensign
and starry 'Jack' and the commission pennant of Lieut.-
Commander Zachary Taylor Jones, U.S.N. fluttered at her
main masthead. The actual transfer of the ship would not be
made until conversion had been completed, but amongst my
many preoccupations there was concern to meet Admiral
Watson's repeated enquiries for relief of his officers and men in

the care of the ship. In October, when I reported to him that a sufficient crew had arrived in Canada and was accommodated at camps there, he seemed courteously impatient. Why were the men not brought down?

I had learned that American ships used for the transport of troops and military munition were manned in much the same way as our own armed merchant cruisers under the White Ensign, the men being enlisted and subject to naval discipline. I thought there might be a misapprehension here, and replied that we were not a regular naval ship and that my men were merchant seamen. I had no need to explain that I feared difficulties of control throughout a lengthy stay in harbour and particularly in a naval dockyard area. In many conversations the Admiral had expressed his admiration for the British seaman in the Battle of the Atlantic, but there was finality in his decision that my merchantmen were to remain in Canada until the ship was ready for sea. I felt relieved if chastened by the instancy of his change of front.

The matter of relief in care and maintenance duty was curiously resolved when H.M.S. *Manchester* arrived in need of urgent repair. She had been badly damaged in action—in the Mediterranean as I understood—and had voyaged the Atlantic to the dockyard in that condition. It was said that her dead were still in the flooded compartments. Immediately upon her arrival I called on Captain Drew. It was known to me that the naval barracks attached to the dockyard were already over-crowded and that there was little accommodation for the crew of a damaged ship elsewhere in the busy harbour area. *Catlin* had ample troop-deck space and temporary messing arrangements could be made. My suggestion that his men be berthed in the old ship was welcomed by Captain Drew and was later approved by Admiral Watson. With the debarking of Lieut.-Commander Jones—to whom we 'limeys' owed much for helpful guidance in the ways of the dockyard—and his men, a situation that was almost prophetic in design arose; of British naval officers and men serving under the 'Stars and Stripes' and regulated to a certain degree by a British merchant shipmaster.

Refitting for war service on the Clyde: 1940

Surely that was an earnest of our Allied co-operation, later to come about.

October passed . . . and November. The ship was placed in dry-dock and the growth and shell that she had accumulated in the long years of immobility at Solomon's were scaled away. When that was completed and the hull glistening in new paint, the floor of the dry-dock was ankle-deep in scleroid Maryland territory brought away from Calvert or St. Mary's County in Maryland. When undocked and moored at her berth again one could almost sense a quickening in this third rejuvenation of the old ship. Work on the troop-decks and upper sections was largely completed and she had taken on much of the outward appearance that had once impressed the transatlantic traveller. On a late date in November the main engines were tested in dock trials. Although unforced to much more than walking speed the great shining cranks of what was probably the largest set of quadruple expansion engines in the world revolved steadily and well. Recalling my view of her in the mean days of her retirement, I had the feeling that confidence had at last been hammered into her at League Island. Only the constant throbbing of the mobile units of welding plant on the dock alongside the position of her boiler spaces imposed an uneasy note in my hopeful calculations.

7th December, 1941. A Sunday and the Quaker City in the quiet mood of relaxation from the labours of the week. From my window on a high storey of a mammoth hotel I was idling in enjoyment of the view. It was a bright day of clear blue sky and a high wind that ruffled the Sunday's flag display on the surrounding skyscrapers. Neatly tucked in at an angle between high buildings, the cupola of Independence Hall could be seen and near it the tall slender flagstaff on which a brave ensign streamed in the wind. It was late afternoon. The telephone rang out. I was sleepy and pondered whether or not to lift the receiver. But no sailor with the keys of a ship in his pocket can afford to do that. It was the British Consul to tell me that the Japanese had treacherously attacked Pearl Harbour. . . . Clotho, of the Fates, had spun a grim new pattern in the East!

America's entry into the war had the immediate effect of hastening the date of our departure from the Navy Yard. Serious naval losses had been sustained that would call for all the skill and industry in the great arsenal. With regret, but understanding, I learned that the programme of sea trials in the sheltered and protected waters of Delaware Bay—on which I had relied with good hope—could not now be carried out. We would be quickly stored and equipped and would proceed to New York for further orders. There would be opportunity for such trials and tests as the presence of the enemy would permit on that passage. We were to be ready for sea on the 7th January.

I took my Christmas holiday in Benjamin Franklin's own old hospital, recovering from an operation. It had required my acquiescent signature on a sombre document before the clever surgeon tucked up his sleeves—for I too required a spot of welding. But I was in very good hands there and recovered quickly. In convalescence, I felt more than ever my kinship with old 'Rip Van Winkle'—now renamed the *George Washington* and wearing the Red Ensign. Strangely, I found my recovery aided and not retarded by remote bedside control of events at Pier 5 in the dockyard. I had neither time nor inclination to dwell on my own infirmity—the many needs of the ship calling for immediate attention and quick decisions. As a consequence, I was in reasonably good trim again at the final stages of preparation for sea.

Towards the turn of the year the crew had been brought down from Montreal and Halifax and as far away as Sydney on Cape Breton Island. They were in funds. I learned that many had sought outside employment in Canada whilst awaiting the manning of the ship. They had found that employment profitable but the effect of such uncommon riches—a manna from strange gods, with the conveniency of a great city in which to consume it—taxed the patience of the ship's officers in the busiest days of reconversion. Although Admiral Watson's thought of disorder was not seriously confirmed by the dockyard guard, there were incidents and anxious moments. The patrol wagon was never absent from the gangway and I found it not too easy to explain to the dockyard marine guards the limitations of the Merchant Shipping Acts under which my men were engaged; it was thought ridiculous that I had no legal powers to restrain and punish the men when, not being employed on the ship's affairs, they went rip-roaring uptown.

There was, too, considerable and understandable dissatisfaction with the conditions of shipwork on board and, as is so often the case, the least amenable to discipline of the large crew had the misfortune to be the most hardly handicapped in the routine of daily duties. It was, of course, known to the stokehold ratings before engagement that the ship was a coal burner but few could have had experience of such a labyrinth of bunker spaces and such mammoth boilers as those in the *George Washington*. It had been possible to fit electrical 'Link' conveyors in the more distant bunkers but even such aids could not greatly reduce the manual work involved. Then the long period of idleness in the Canadian camps had put many of our men out of temper and condition for labour and it was with apprehension I thought of the commitments of our sailing date.

We sailed on the morning of the 10th January, 1942, a bright day but bitterly cold, and the Delaware River a grinding mass of shelving ice. It was well that the cold weather was salutary and bracing for we had taken many elements of potential disaster to sea with us from Pier 5 on League Island. Long experience of fractious incident at the outset of a voyage had hardened me—and doubtless all the ship's officers—to the business of settling down. But the abnormal ill-temper clearly evident in the stokehold made all former difficulties seem insignificant by comparison. For some days before sailing I had pondered a rumour that was current below decks—that the ship would not be 'fired' beyond the Delaware Capes. Most commanding sailors are accustomed to crossing unfamiliar bridges at the first approach and are allergic to hearsay, but this seemed a possibility. As so often before when in difficulty, I consulted my friend Captain Drew of the *Manchester* and, as always, found him helpful. He offered to provide me with a draft of naval stokers from his ship, not as an armed guard to compel duty but as a 'stand by' group upon which I could call for assistance if necessary to the progress of the passage. I was happy and grateful to welcome his men on board again.

As we were towed into mid-river from Pier 5, I turned my binoculars on the dockside from which we had been withdrawn. In the six months of my ship's husbandry every plank in it had known my tread and even the air of it became familiar with my private hopes and fears. It looked strangely deserted in the grey half-light of early morning. My gaze swept over the discarded items of shipyard plant that littered the dockside where our gangway had been, and wandered up the well-known pathway leading to the Drawing Office, the Pattern Shop, the Boatbuilding Yard, the Equipment Warehouses, the Gunnery Stores. In quest of information and guidance, I could not use that road again. I was no longer the 'Clerk of Works' in daily contact with superior direction: the telephone had been disconnected at last. I had crossed 'The Shadow Line' towards a much greater responsibility and the ship and her men were within my keeping.

We had with us on the voyage a group of dockyard men—overseers, foremen, and working squads—upon whose expert knowledge and advice I could depend in adjustment of technical difficulties. But not all the tools and gear for running repairs had been brought away with them. Looking back as we turned into the river fairway and headed downstream I saw the many welding units stranded and silent on the dockside with their power leads hastily coiled—just as they had been withdrawn from our boilers at the eleventh hour—and the Chief Engineer had already reported another 'double-ender' as showing signs of over-strain.

Chapter XIV

CONFIRMED INVALID

THE new war situation in the Atlantic had brought the U-boat packs to swarm on the eastern doorstep of the United States. In January of 1942 many of the enemy's long-range U-boats were operating on all the coastal routes from Florida to the State of Maine. For long they were successful and it appeared that they were even able to establish a choice of particular target in the oil tankers conveying fuel from the Gulf. Counter measures could not immediately be brought into practice and it took time for the Navy Department to organise efficient convoys. Independent sailings were still continued and the toll exacted by the enemy from this progression of single ships had reached an alarming figure. Possibly for some inter-state reason, the enforcement of total 'blackout' on the populous sea coast towns was not quickly carried out and the enemy submarine commander lost no opportunity in seizing advantage of a state of affairs that revealed his victims at night time against the glow of coastwise lights. For this his general practice was to remain submerged offshore in the daytime and out of sight of air patrols, then surface and close the land in expectation of easy victims when darkness came.

All this I learned from the British Consul at Philadelphia when I called on him for routeing orders. He had no special route plotted out for me. The distance from the Delaware Capes to New York was only 150 miles; it was thought the *George Washington* could accomplish that journey in daylight hours and it was left to me to proceed as I considered best. It was unlikely that the enemy had sown mines on the sea routes and the Consul had no knowledge of any American minefield on the coast. No surface escort could be provided for the passage but I was informed that air patrols were in operation from a base in New Jersey. To one accustomed to the precisions of our own Naval Control this preview of our sailing seemed casual. It promised an adventure for which the ship was not yet sufficiently prepared. Her guns were well-placed and fitted, and there were trained and efficient gunners in our manning, but the surface weapons were of British pattern for which the resources of League Island had been unable to provide ammunition.

Into this troubled area the old sea ghost headed on the morning after she had sailed from the Navy Yard. It was made abundantly clear to us on the long river passage down the Delaware that we would not have speed in the ship until many correlated alterations and adjustments had been made. Off Ship John shoal we had to anchor for attention to heated bearings and this delay caused the loss of tide and compelled us to remain at anchor until daylight. Even then we proceeded slowly lest the patient become unduly excited. Although the weather remained bitterly cold there was little wind when we passed Cape Henry and gained the open sea. The sky was clear and, despite a falling barometer, it seemed that we could count upon moderate conditions for at least some hours. After we had passed the Capes, I learned that the voice of authentic Clydeside in the stokeholds and bunkers, though still mutinous and threatening, was not yet definitely pitched to active revolt. We made the pitiful average speed of about nine knots during the forenoon: erratic and unskilful firing set the range of that as low as seven at the cleaning of the furnaces and, at times, as high as thirteen knots. It was a sad performance after all the labours of the dockyard but at least we were afloat and at sea.

Five Fathom Bank is marked by a sturdy lightship and is a common and prominent landfall on the coast. Ships pass close to it on passage up and down the inshore sea route. In normal times it is a busy rendezvous for coastal traffic but when we approached it we found an area devoid of shipping that I considered suitable for the ship tests denied to us in the sheltered and protected waters of the Delaware. My choice of a proving ground at a point of landfall was dictated by the state of the weather and the incidence of good visibility in which to adjust magnetic compasses, but it was patently a sea area that would favour the operations of an enemy submarine. All morning we had been keenly on lookout for a warship patrol or a scouting aircraft overhead, but we had not expected to be challenged by a substantial airship of the U.S. Coastguard that grew serenely into sight from the direction of the land at about noon. Without a doubt we would appear highly suspicious to her commander for we were then running amok, under way without helm, by reason of a breakdown in the steering gear. To the airship's challenge we reported our particulars—name, where from and whither bound—but there ensued a long pause in the exchanges by which I guessed that even such an honoured American name might not yet be found in her code books. I had the thought of making 'formerly the Rip van Winkle' but when 'ex-U.S.S. *Catlin*' was spelt out and acknowledged, the matters seemed to be made clear. I was asked if anything unusual had been sighted and on replying 'No' was given the welcome news that she would remain in the vicinity for a while and signal any suspicious indications.

It was as well we had this far-seeing eye aloft for protection as the old lady was protesting the adventure and exhibiting her infirmities and hidden sores in ominous progression. The hydraulic system for control of water-tight bulkhead doors had proved imperfect, the forward stokehold was awash in sea-water through a fractured valve, the transmission power in the telemotors was defective, and it had become evident that the water-test of the boilers—calmly and steadily applied in harbour—had not revealed the weaknesses now disclosed in a working ship at sea. But with all our difficulties, our irregular stops and starts, our berserk courses—in which we ourselves on the navigation bridge had no more than a casual sense of the ship's intentions—there was a certain reassurance dimly to be pondered. To the eye at a periscope that may have been focussed upon us it might well have been that the presence of the airship and our incredible gyrations below her were considered sufficiently puzzling to instil caution before attack lest a new type of 'Q Ship' be found in commission. Our tests and trials were unattended by outboard alarm and by late afternoon we had obtained a practical knowledge of the faults to be reported upon arrival at New York. Despite her manifest imperfections, the old lady had shown a sufficiency of 'good metal' to offset many of her senile blemishes. The dockyard technicians and their mechanics had brought many of them under temporary control and, in a modest confidence, we continued the interrupted voyage.

The face of the barometer had not lied as I tapped it when off the Capes. A north-east gale had arisen in its sudden manner and with it a considerable head sea that brought out at least one admirable feature in the ship. She exhibited good temper in the rising gale by the way she 'shouldered' the seas and, even at such a slow speed, displayed a surprising response to helm action. To a certain degree, I had anticipated that her great length and the curious old-fashioned sternward projection of her propellers might promote an ease of handling, but I had not guessed at her sea kindliness in adverse weather. For that alone I warmed towards her. As we thrust our lumbering way towards New York I had little opportunity for optimistic reflection, but the ship, if not quite seaworthy yet, was certainly worthy of the sea again. It was in this mood, chastened as it was by the need for alert in a blinding snowstorm, I saw her anchored safely off Staten Island at New York.

★　　★　　★

I had come to recognise only too well the signal of distress that was my ship's manner of protest, but my guests seemed alarmed by the rising clamour of it as we sat together after lunch in my quarters on board. It was a farewell occasion and we lay at anchor in the stream off Halifax in readiness to put to sea on the following day. The date was the 2nd February in 1942.

Much had occurred since, slowly and ingloriously, we had limped into harbour at New York three weeks before. At that port and away from the conservative practice of the naval dockyard we had been free to exercise a more intimate commercial control in rectifying the defects revealed by the testing passage from Philadelphia. The local director of the British Ministry of War Transport, Mr. Philip Rees, had now directed our affairs into the hands of a mercantile shipyard. Whilst my duty had been the professional one of carrying out higher orders in the reconversion of the ship, his had been the much more difficult task of steering a tactful course through the intricacies of Lend-Lease finance with all its political cross-bearings. He had expert knowledge of shipping and its requirements and had expended many months of anxious thought and planning upon the acquisition of the ship from American ownership and her alteration and equipment for service as a British troop transport. The entry of the United States into battle had the understandable effect of lessening the naval dockyard's interest in such a problem ship as the *George Washington* and it was doubtless with relief the technicians and their mechanics (who had certainly 'worked their passage' from League Island) disembarked on our arrival at New York. With them there went the draft of the *Manchesters*. It had not been considered vitally necessary or indeed politic to employ them in the stokehold on the passage from Philadelphia. At times there had been sore temptation to do so: but there was always the tempering thought that the crew we had signed on our Articles of Agreement were the men—good, bad, or indifferent—with whom we would have to live and work for months to come. It seemed certain that the moral support of the presence on board of naval stokers had imposed a curb on our 'hotheads' and for that I was grateful to Captain Harold Drew.

To the Bethlehem shipyards our repair was entrusted by the Director. They had already a long acquaintance with the ship and her needs, having served her when she wore the crack house-flag of the Hamburg-American Line and held prestige as a transatlantic liner; many of the shipyard workmen had wrought in her to repair the sabotage of the Germans in 1917; later, when under the ownership of the United States Lines, her many repairs and adjustments had again been carried out by the same shipyard. Our engines and power systems were familiar to their men and we counted ourselves in good hands. Even the foreman boiler-maker affirmed that he had known every rivet in her big 'Scotch' boilers—though he confessed (with a rueful half-smile) that he had difficulty in recognising them now after the League Island welders had so liberally patterned them with a maze of cicatrix.

Nor had the crew been maintained in idleness during our ten days detention in the port. There had been difficulties, for the waterfront saloons nearby the Chelsea Piers are singularly convenient for a quick 'warmer' in working hours, but in-discipline was no more than was to be expected in the early imposition of ship routine. Opportunity had been taken to re-allot many of the incompetents in the stokeholds to lesser duties and constant 'watch and watch' training at the fires had produced a modest improvement in maintaining steam—an improvement that had enabled us to make a steady speed of fourteen knots on the passage from New York to Halifax when our repair had been completed. On that passage we had exercised defensive equipment. We could now fight back, for ammunition had been taken at the powder anchorage before sail-ing. Paravanes, that are our protection against moored mines, had been streamed and approved. With the Degauss installation we had perforce to rely upon the scientific accuracy of its designer for there was then no testing range available to us in western waters. On deck and in troop quarters the ship had taken on a worthy appearance and, as we lay anchored off

Halifax, I was proud of her at the final inspection by Canadian naval and military authorities when we met after lunch. A total of 4110 troops (officers, men, and nursing sisters) had been embarked and the Inspecting Brigadier had certified them as suitably berthed for overseas passage. In T.64—the minutes of the occasion—where the question is posed 'Has the Master received his Sailing Orders?' there was answer that he had. We were to proceed in convoy to the Clyde and I had been appointed Commodore. Convoy Conference had been held and all matters seemed to be efficiently resolved. Up until that first *purring* at the funnel-tip, our comment and our expectations had been hopeful. The pattern of events had seemed woven at last into a good design. The old ship, vibrant and alive again, had become a dowager in good company.

There is nothing unusual in the *purring* of a feather of steam at the escape pipes when a ship is being brought to 'stand-by' for engine movements, but when the murmur mounts in crescendo to a tortured uproar and the sound takes the furious notes of the lash and crackling of multiple whips, then it is clear that the valves have been opened up and the high-pressure steam—so carefully raised and tended—is of purpose being thrown wide to the wind. With that din in my ears, I had no need to reach hastily for the engine-room telephone nor to await hopefully for the lessening of it that might denote a lifting of the safety-valves in trials. As I watched through the day-room window the uprush of blinding white steam, I knew that when it had subsided the Chief Engineer would be framed in my doorway. There, he would stand for a while, silent or not saying very much: but his hands would be outspread—the palms uppermost. There was no need for words. It had happened . . . so often . . . before. It would then be my business to make an urgent signal to the shipyard for the welders and their plant to return to the ship. We would try again.

But that was in the days of reconstruction and preparation with the dockyard telephone at my elbow, not as at anchor off the piers at Halifax with troops embarked and everything otherwise in readiness for departure overseas. There would now be a

Board of Enquiry and a further technical survey be made of the whole boiler situation.

*   *   *

Daylight is long of coming at Halifax in the winter time. From an early hour I had been pacing the sheltered deck, pre-occupied with thought of our frustrations. It was bitterly cold. Snow had fallen during the night and the silent ship was blanched on the open deck, the upperworks, masts and funnels —almost as though the old lady was taken in terror of her age and invalidity. There were many problems. Two of her main boilers that had not hitherto been gravely suspect had developed cracks and there were signs that at least one other would not stand up to pressure. At a late conference overnight, many disturbing issues of the situation had been discussed. How long would it take to effect substantial working repairs—now agreed as the fitting of strengthening plates in addition to extensive welding? The Halifax dockyard was overburdened by repair and salvage work—being at the roadside on the route for crippled ships. Near us in the darkness many vessels that had been lamed in the Battle of the Atlantic lay anchored to await their turn. No date could be set for our place in the queue— even with first priority. A curious and complex point was raised. The only berth in the docks at which, by reason of her great draft of water, the ship could be brought alongside, was remote from the power station. Even if operations could immediately be undertaken, the power transmitted was likely to be en-feebled by long distance leakage. The disposal of the troops in the event of the Board deciding that the voyage be abandoned had been considered. The men could not be accommodated in the troopships sailing in the convoy, now almost due to proceed to sea. All the ships were embarked to capacity and no other was available to take our place. There was not then in Halifax a barracks or transit camp in which troops could be billeted for a time. The Brigadier (of Movement Control) was of the opinion that they would have to remain in the ship and be withdrawn in drafts as alternative shipping became available. For that we were well stored and victualled . . . but would we be able to maintain heat and lighting in the great spaces of the troop decks with so many boilers under repair and the temperature at zero? . . . There was too the regimentation of troops and crew at the harbour piers. Would not the Dock Board, the Health and Sanitary Authorities of the city, the Police, even, be interested in such a sudden increase of the waterfront population? . . . Over four thousand personnel and a crew of five hundred! . . . The commitments seemed endless. No wonder we had our difficulty in composing that last night's urgent signal to headquarters in Ottawa.

As I tramped the long length of the sheltered deck, the thought occurred that the Board might condemn the existing boilers and recommend the installation of water-tube boilers in their place. The notion was not new. Far back in the early days of reconstruction at the Navy Yard at Philadelphia and at the time of the first hydrostatic test of the welders' efforts, the frustrated charge-hand had damned the ancient metal in no uncertain terms. A good craftsman, he was doubtless unhappy in his task—knowing its importance to safety at sea. From him I learned that a complete set of water-tube boilers, originally intended for the ship, were stored away in the Boiler Shed in the dockyard. As I understood it, there had at a time been the intention to refit the ship for service as a transport under her own flag, but that the scheme had been abandoned in consequence of the great cost involved. The water-tube boilers of which the foreman spoke were not quite new but reconditioned to a serviceable standard. I think my seniors knew of this for, when I mentioned it, I was somewhat sharply informed that if provision of other boilers had come under consideration the ship would not have been transferred to British Registry. . . . But one could indulge in dreams . . . of confidence in a fine ship, had they been fitted.

Dawn had come and ship life was stirring again. A bugle sounded off the morning's reveille and khaki-clad figures appeared on the upper decks, adding a note of colour to the drab and fugitive iron-grey of our war complexion. The snowfall had abated but the clouds were still lowering in threat of more to come. As I watched the harbour scene, I saw the convoy that would not now come under my direction weigh anchor and proceed 'being, in all respects ready for sea'. The captain of the *Largs Bay* had taken my place. She passed close alongside on a brief traverse to gain the deepwater channel, leading the other ships of the convoy abroad. Our decks were by now fully peopled and hers were crowded by the muster of troops strangely patterned by the bands of their life-jackets. In the tumultuous exchanges between the ships that followed— the shouts and cheers, call and counter-call, ironic jest and its rejoinder, brief messages . . . and good-bye—there was stir and encouragement. I saw the captain on the bridge of his fine ship and waved to him God-speed. But when the shouting and the cheers had died away and I saw the line of outbound ships growing grey in the distances of the sea channel, I confessed to envy in my heart and prayed for the day when we too could proceed to sea in such spirit and in the same high confidence.

★   ★   ★

Some time later, in October of 1943, I anchored my ship— the *Circassia*—in Bombay Harbour to await instructions for the disembarkation of troops we had brought from Kilindini. In the interval of waiting there was opportunity for a survey of the other ships in harbour and, among them, I recognised the *George Washington* berthed at Ballard Pier. Except for one funnel having been removed, she was little altered and was wearing the American Ensign and the starry 'Jack' again.

At Naval Headquarters on shore I met the Captain—was it Captain Batchelder, U.S.N.R.? He was very proud of his ship. Water-tube boilers had been fitted in her and she now burned oil fuel instead of coal to raise and maintain power. The elimination of coal bunker spaces had made possible the enlargement of troop decks and she could now transport 5000 men in reasonable comfort. A speed of over eighteen knots could be made without special effort and she had an endurance of 12,000 miles at that speed. She was, as I had known she would be, a grand 'sea boat' and was quick and handy in manoeuvres. Her only awkward feature, the Captain said, was a tendency to 'list' when, towards the end of a long sea passage, the oil fuel tanks in the double bottom had become exhausted. He was enthusiastic. He invited me to visit his ship and take lunch with him but I found some convenient opportunity of excuse.

It was not that I was unfriendly. I would have liked to survey the old lady from within again but there was too much of my own 'old iron' worked into her and I felt that the experience would revive too many memories, hopeful and despairing, sanguine and fearful, confident and perplexing, of my long and unproductive work in her. There would come again the thought of two months' immobility at Halifax whilst the boilers were being patched and strengthened; of the long process in gradual dispersal of the troops we had embarked: of the arrival on board of specially expert welders—from Baltimore, of all places— together with their mobile 'boosters' to enliven the flow of current from the distant power station in the fitting of the end plates; of insubordination and loss of morale amongst the crew; of seemingly endless plan and abortive argument. And when at length the work was completed and the tests applied and approved—when I had reported to my superiors that the ship was ready for sea, it was only to learn that the voyage would be short . . . to New York where she was to be handed back to the U.S. Maritime Commissioners.

No. I was not unfriendly. Sensitive perhaps, and inclined to brood upon the sources of defeat, I felt that I would not relish a ship visit to my old command . . . but I wished for her many safe and swift voyages for nothing is completely lost that goes into the custody of a friend and ally.

Chapter XV

'CIRCASSIA'

MY experience in the old German liner had been that of long preparation for sea service and an unsatisfactory and abrupt conclusion when I was instructed to hand her back to her former American registry. It was under a very differing circumstance I came to command the *Circassia* that was to be my home afloat for upwards of four stirring years. She was fully charged and equipped for sea on the day I joined her, the Master whom I relieved having suddenly been taken ill. Troops had been embarked at Glasgow and she lay at the Tail of the Bank off Greenock in complete readiness to sail. There was just time for me to take over from the ailing Captain, nip ashore to the Customs House to have my name entered on the Register, then attend a Convoy Conference at Marymount. We were to sail at daybreak of the morning in a large convoy of troopships conveying reinforcements for the Middle East, proceeding by way of the Cape of Good Hope—the long way round. Reinforcement was never more urgently needed, for Tobruk had fallen and the enemy was storming on towards Egypt and the Suez Canal—only 200 miles away. To meet the threatening situation and provide troop transport for so great a movement, almost all our remaining armed merchant cruisers had been hurriedly converted to become troopships and it was as one of these the *Circassia* came again under the Red Ensign. Built at Fairfield on the Clyde in 1938, she was a modern motor vessel of good speed. Naturally, the fact that she had no main boilers commended her to me from the start. On the outbreak of war she had been requisitioned and fitted as an armed merchant cruiser, largely employed on ocean patrol service. Much of her armament had been retained on board. Her naval captain, whom I met, had a very high opinion of her—an opinion that

I was quickly to endorse—and I was happy to be afloat again in a fine and seaworthy ship.

In the early hours of my first night on board I had the curious experience of hearing myself speak to a radio audience whose number in millions I could only guess. Having been long absent from home waters I was unacquainted with many of the new aids and devices that had been installed in the ships for war purposes. In *Circassia* we had fallen heirs to a new naval type of public address system that could be connected to the ship's broadcast radio reception. I was unfamiliar with this adjustment and when, in anticipation of an early start in the morning, I had turned in, I neglected to snap off the switch. At about two o'clock—which would be 9 p.m. of the day before in New York—the Overseas transmission of the B.B.C. aroused me by blaring out the words of the 'Sailor's Day' broadcast that I had made at the microphone a few days before. My voice sounded alien, and I did not quickly recognise the recorded version. But there it was:

'. . . *Certainly, we know of casualties and are in no doubt of what is happening at sea.*' Widely awake now, I heard my voice say that. But did we know of all the casualties, and were not the totals of the sinkings and our dead at sea mercifully withheld from us? . . . Again, '*I have good grounds for thinking that we sailors are doing none too badly in delivering the goods.*' . . . Was I ever as confident as all that or was I but whistling in the dark? . . . When the voice was at length silent, I rose to switch the gadget off, then lay long awake pondering this strange overture to a sea voyage.

We made a swift and uneventful voyage. The convoy was heavily screened by a naval force that included the battleship, H.M.S. *Malaya*, and an unusually large escort group of destroyers. For a time and until the latitude of Gibraltar was reached, an aircraft carrier sailed with us and provided a scouting patrol during the hours of daylight. We called at ports en route and did not linger there but made a fast voyage to Suez. I surmise that there could not have been less than 50,000 troops in this vital overseas movement, for the *Circassia*, although only 11,136 tons and one of the smallest of the twenty-two transports, carried within her no less than 2500 officers and men. In addition to troops, many of the ships in convoy had loaded munitions, aeroplanes, heavy tanks and armoured vehicles, all specially constructed for desert warfare. We were a self-contained and substantial relief force whose timely arrival in Egypt went far to retrieve the critical position at El Alamein.

As the ships were disembarked and unloaded, re-fuelled and watered, they were put quickly to sea again on 'Independent Sailings' to return to the United Kingdom. We sailed under orders to embark Italian prisoners of war at Durban for passage to a British port. Upon arrival in Natal the ship was surveyed by officers of the Royal Engineers with a view to the disciplinary control of the Italian prisoners who were to be under guard of a Polish detachment. In this way we became an Ark of Babel that was later emphasised by the many tribal dialects of Nigeria and the Gold Coast. Colour-sergeants all, a group of West African soldiers was embarked. The wars in Abyssinia having proved their worth, they were being returned home to their bases to train more warriors in the methods of civilised warfare. To herd the prisoners we did not employ barbed wire and other encagements recommended by the officers of the R.E. A visit to the internment camp nearby revealed them as mild unfortunates, only too willing to be quieted and fed. The ship's Officer Commanding Troops accompanied me to the camp and it was upon his review of the prisoners the embarkation was arranged. He thought the ship's normal troop routine would suffice, but there were to be spoons only for mess utensils, not forks or knives, and all food was to be drawn from the kitchens in hashed condition. No Italian officers other than medical were to be embarked. As I watched the dejected bearing of the prisoners at the camp, I thought of another and a very different scene when I had last viewed Italian soldiers in such a mass formation. That was in 1936 when Abyssinia had been invaded by them and overthrown. In the *Cameronia* we were northbound in the Suez Canal and had the right of way. A large Italian troopship, the *Conte Biancomano* I think, being south-

A page from the artist's sketch book; Minelayers and other naval units at sea in heavy weather

bound, was moored at the bank to let us pass. Her decks, life-boats, rigging and derricks were brown with the swarm of troops she carried. As, at slow speed, we neared to pass her, an outcry arose. Jeers, calls, whistles, slogans sounded out from her decks. We had known we were to pass her and the troops we were transporting home after long service—the splendidly-disciplined First Battalion of the Cameron High-landers—had been warned to maintain silence. That they did, standing tolerantly amused as the cries 'Evviva Italia! ... Evviva Mussolini! ... Evviva Facismo! ... Evviva Umberto!' rang out from the Conte's crowded decks. But our merchant crew was not quite as well disciplined as the Camerons. Choosing his moment, a galley porter on the deck below (whom we later discovered to be the son of an ice-cream vendor in Camlachie) shouted something in a shrill piercing note that mounted the vituperation to a howling crescendo. When brought to book, all he had cried was 'Evviva Caporetto!'

Colonel George S. Lockwood (of the Lancashire Fusiliers) was our O.C. Troops and a sterling shipmate in the Circassia for a period of years. The duties of his office—as I understood them—call for comment. Not too many of the ships employed as troop transports were as well circumstanced as we were, or their Masters as happily befriended. I had heard complaint and argument at convoy meetings about high-handed doings by the military in the transports and there were frictions reported.

In the earlier World War the military (or naval) officer responsible for the daily routine and discipline of troops or ratings on passage was chosen from amongst the forces em-barked. A Ship's Adjutant, Senior Medical Officer, and an adequate orderly-room staff were also recruited in this way. The O.C. Troops who was then generally the commanding officer of the largest battalion on board, was rarely seriously interested in the lesser detachments nor, towards the close of the voyage, in the documentation whereby the ship's military accounts were rendered. It was understandable that, with the battlefront almost within sight at one end, or the prospects of leave or demobilisation at the other, it would be the good ordering of his own regiment that would occupy his closer attention. Doubtless it was in consideration of all these points that, in 1939, the War Office appointed permanent Military Ship Staffs to troop transports and these units remained established in the vessel for long periods. I can testify to the smooth and better working of the new arrangements, but its good currency on such extended service together required considerable tact and tolerance on the part of Master and O.C. Troops alike, both being in a commanding position without any established cachet of seniority on board a merchant ship. It could be all very well for the Master to consider all troops as passengers committed to his care. He was in command of the ship and all her people. He held the keys of the larder in his keeping. All very well. But, being sensible, he should admit the duty of the O.C. Troops to be interested in the quality and the quantity of its provision and in preparation of the meals for issue to the troops. Nor would he be wise to protest publicly against the military officer's manner of routine in maintaining troop-decks in cleanliness and good order. On 'Master's Rounds' it would be well to reserve comment for a more private discussion. On his part, the soldier could be well advised to forget many of the sharp habits of the Guard Room in barracks and adapt himself to the more liberal atmosphere of shipboard. With agreement on these lines, it was not difficult to dispose of minor argument in the smooth running of His Majesty's Sea Transport Service. In this close association of two seniors in a ship there are maybe the elements for a mutually destructive rupture but there are also the constituents of a lasting friendship. To a degree both are lonely men, isolated on board ship from the communal intimacies of their juniors. I like to think that it was under these conditions George Lockwood and I worked so happily together in the *Circassia* for so long.

The Polish detachment was not quite representative of the gallant army I was later to know when on transport service in the Mediterranean. Not all were trained combatants, for the group had been assembled in India from refugee camps there, had been clothed and equipped in British battle-dress and shipped to South Africa as an intermediate halt on the way to Britain. How they had wandered so far after the bloody conquest and partition of Poland was never explained to us. We took them at face value, but always in our broken converse we had to remember not to mention the exploits of the Russian Army—now our Allies—then so bravely defending Stalingrad. Many had themselves been prisoners of war but strangely—or perhaps because of it—were inclined to be unnecessarily harsh with the Italians when on sentry duty. That, we had to temper and control, but we got on reasonably well together. The prisoners gave no trouble. Indeed, as the days of the voyage progressed, they seemed to attain to some measure of content and happiness. True to type, there was much song amongst them and with their many odd scraps of baggage brought from the wars in Ethiopia were musical instruments that they played skilfully and well—even under the disapproving eyes of their stern northern custodians.

We sailed on the voyage in company with the troopship *Rangatiki* and the *Carthage*, an armed merchant cruiser. An enemy surface raider was reported to be at large on the Cape coast and the ship was held at anchor in Saldanha Bay for some days until the hue and cry had died down. It was said to have been this raider that had laid down a minefield off Cape Agulhas, but southerly gales and the swift currents in the area had set the mines adrift and disclosed its dangers. On passage through these waters, we had sighed floating mines and had taken a crack at them without visible result. Our D.E.M.S. gunners were excellent marksmen. Hits were scored on at least two black spheres, but not then or at any later date did we have the satisfaction of 'putting up' a floating mine. The 'Ross' rifle was used for this practice as it is said to have a greater penetration, and there was the hope of 'holing' the mine and leaving the seawater to sink it.

Enemy submarines of a large ocean-going type had been active in the waters off Freetown and many ships had been gunned or torpedoed when making passage to the port. Two days before our arrival there we were met by an escorting destroyer who accompanied us to harbour. On the night before arrival an incident occurred that gave rise to considerable speculation. In the black darkness the destroyer, manoeuvring ahead of the three ships, suddenly switched on her searchlight and pinpointed a strange vessel that appeared to be crossing our line of advance. We had only a momentary sight of her, then it was dark again except for a faint dim signalling between the destroyer and her discovery. The ship was friendly. . . . But how did the destroyer come to know that a ship was there in the darkness? There had been no ranging of the searchlight in quest of a target. Its operator must have known exactly on what bearing he would find an object when he lit up so suddenly and accurately, then blacked out as quickly. We knew there was Asdic but Asdic was said to be only effective in underwater detections. We were puzzled by the exhibition. . . . But we learned later that we had seen Radar, the new secret electronic device, in operation.

From Saldanha Bay we made a good passage to Freetown to disembark the contingent of West African colour-sergeants. Well-uniformed and equipped and with their brilliant crimson sashes making a brave note of colour—and all of upstanding physique—we had thought them a splendid body of disciplined troops likely to attract attention and a host of recruits. But when the tender lay alongside the gangway and the order was given to march on board, it was in great pain and obvious distress they broke ranks and stumbled in untidy procession. Their British officer had been too ambitious to display his men in all their furbished equipment to the Inspection Officers. The good sergeants were wearing ammunition boots that, as far as I could learn, they had never put on their feet before. An order was quickly given and as quickly obeyed. The men reformed, three long lines on the deck of the tender, upright again and smiling—every man among them with a pair of shined and blackened brand-new 'Number Twelves' slung around his neck —but now bare-footed as was his wont! In high good humour on all sides they were cheered away as the tender cast off and we put to sea again. Twelve days later we arrived safely in the Clyde.

Chapter XVI

ONE SHILLING A MONTH

EVERYONE engaged or carried in a ship at sea must have some warrant to be on board for there are Shipping Laws, and the Regulations of Ports and Harbours demand compliance. Even the captain's wife or children, that he may take on the voyage with him for company, are signed on in the ship's books in the same way as the seamen. As it is law that a contract must be cemented by a payment, a 'luck penny', there is allowed the pleasing fiction of her and their emolument being stated as 'One shilling a month'. The 'books' of a merchant ship are the Articles of Agreement that binds her crew to duty at the wages set forth. Contrary to common belief, the Agreement is not one between the Owners of a ship and the men engaged in her, but between the master and the mariners. At one time, God himself was invoked to fortify this senior position of the leading sailor. The preamble then read—'for a voyage towards the sea in the good ship or vessel called the *Nonsuch* of which, under God, John Christian is the master.' ... But the Deity is not now officially implored to extend his benefice, although the shoulders of the master must still bear the strain of furthering the voyage— to the 'books' of which he makes the initial signature.

'Signing-on Day,' as I remember it from long ago, had the

atmosphere of holiday at the Shipping Office, for there were colourful people there to encourage the hands to step up and touch the pen: white-stockinged wives and rosy children these, but others were the crimps and boarding-house keepers intent upon procuring the advance note for a seaman's first month's pay. It is work-a-day now and its colour has gone. But, if less noteworthy, the business is still conducted on shore at the Shipping Office, for the vast majority of ships carry crews that can there be accommodated at the office-desks. It is not so with the larger vessels with crews in the hundreds and it has long been the practice for them to sign on board the ship as she lies at her quay berth. It was thus when the *Circassia's* books lay opened on a long mess-table in the troops' recreation hall. In groups and parties, the men were brought in from their working tasks in the ship to sign for another term of sea service—the character of which, as yet, they could only guess. There was no particular order in the crowded assembly and no sense of importance in the confused jangle of casual talk. Perhaps, here and there, a man might dust off his working overalls, twist his tweed cap, or wipe grimy hands on his thighs, out of respect for the virgin page that lay before him, but there seemed no serious attention paid to the words of the Deputy Superintendent as he read out the text of the Agreement. When he had done that, his assistant —scanning the Purser's list—called for someone by name to step up and sign as 'Deck Hand' at twelve pounds per month—plus war allowances in current effect,—and so the engagement proceeded.

In contrast with the miscellaneous garments of the working seamen and the informality of their muster in crowded quarters, the D.E.M.S. gunners who were detailed to sail with us were dressed in uniform of the day and stood lined up together at one side of the hall. They too were to be linked up as shipmates for the voyage and all, including their officer—a lieutenant of the R.N.V.R.—signed on the ship's Articles as 'Deck Hands', but at the rate of One Shilling—twelve pence, not pounds—a Month.

This transaction that places enlisted members of the armed

forces under the control of the civilian masters of the merchant ships is, of course, largely dictated by International Law, for the gunners sail in the ships to neutral ports and otherwise might legally be interned there. But it is a convenience in many ways, welcomed by the men themselves, for the ship can be considered a branch office of their distant depots where matters of service pay and allowances can be made and adjusted. Then, too, the monthly 'arles' of a silver coin confers one dubious benefit. The majority of the men assigned to duty in merchant ships are elderly and generally of settled disposition. They are notable for good conduct but on occasion there are venial faults that come under consideration of the ship's master. In that event, a D.E.M.S. rating can elect to have his case taken up under the Merchant Shipping Act and no entry is then made in his Service Record. There are two types of D.E.M.S. ratings in the larger ships, naval and military. The *Circassia,* having augmented armament, was allotted a group of twenty-eight of whom twelve were grizzled gunners of the Maritime Regiment, R.A. They made a compact little force standing at ease in the recreation hall at signing on.

The D.E.M.S. Department of Naval Service, that had come so quickly into operation on the outbreak of war, had expanded enormously in the defence of merchant ships at sea. What, in 1939, had been thought adequate in the supply of weapons and the training of merchant gunners to serve them was soon proved insufficient when the enemy quickly developed air attack on the ships and set his improved submarines against the convoys in 'pack' formations. New arms and devices were introduced; all requiring expert handling. Their upkeep alone demanded constant and unremitting attention that could not adequately be given in the average merchant ships. This had been foreseen. As early in the war as the spring of 1940 recruitment to augment the D.E.M.S. forces was rapidly encouraged. To the substantial cadre of trained gunners (ex-naval and Marines) was added a great number of new men drawn from 'Hostilities Only' entrants. It can be surmised that this enlargement required some form of selection, for these gunners would serve abroad from their units, in small groups, and of necessity under non-service direction. (It took time too, to correct the not unnatural propensity of shipmasters and officers to utilise the D.E.M.S. ratings for duty that was not theirs in a hard-worked ship.) It was later in the course of the conflict when the military were brought in to assist in the actual defence of merchant shipping. This may have stemmed from the practice in troop transports of using the soldiers with their Bren guns to augment the ship's ack-ack weapons—a 'fatigue duty' that, compared with the cleaning up of troop-decks, was eagerly volunteered. It is not known if the Maritime Regiment of Royal Artillery was a new development or some revival of an old, but the gunners quickly grew sea legs and seemed to find the role of shipman no deterrent to good shooting. The D.E.M.S. Department became enormously expanded. In 1940, their whole establishment numbered about 2000 officers and men: in 1945, it had grown to 35,000!

From such a significant comparison it could be assumed that the merchant seaman had been unable to battle through without the aid of a specially trained corps. That is true. But there is bright evidence that the purely merchant gunner, hastily trained by D.E.M.S. in the early stages of the war, was not lacking in spirit or intention even though the task was found too great for him in later days. Curiously, it was not often the larger, faster, and better-manned merchant ships that set the examples of resolution and good shooting in action against the enemy; the case of the little *Highlander* may be cited.

Air attack on voyaging merchant ships in 1940 was at its worst on the east coast and in the North Sea. Weapons for air-defence were pitifully few and rarely of greater calibre than the Lewis or an occasional Bren, both so hard to come by after Dunkirk that the local administration deprived the coasters of them upon arrival in port in order that they could be issued to a vessel upon point of sailing on the same tide. It may have been in such a circumstance the *Highlander* undocked from her berth at Aberdeen on the night of the 1st August, 1940, and headed out to sea on her customary passage towards Leith. She was a coastwise vessel of small tonnage and about twelve knots speed, carrying passengers and cargo on the regular schedule she had maintained for many years. She was lightly armed with one Lewis gun and a Holman Projector—the latter, an early form of rocket entanglement—and her weapons were served by her own seamen. It is possible that her routine of weekly sailings up and down the coast had not passed unnoticed by enemy airmen who, after the collapse of continental allied defences, had been particularly active in the area. She would not appear at all formidable to the pilots of two German aircraft when they sighted her off the coast at Stonehaven in the lingering twilight of an August night. To them she would doubtless seem a suitable target for a practice session. They could not know the heart that was in this little merchant coaster. It is unlikely that the *Highlander* mustered more than four hands in the watch on deck and, with one at the wheel and one on lookout, only two would be available for quick first action until the alarm had brought all hands on deck. She carried no special naval ratings for gunnery duties, but her men had been trained and exercised at D.E.M.S. establishments on shore at her way-ports.

The ship's Official Log is the factual record of all events upon the voyage. Entries are brief for every shipmaster is fearful of over-statement and the perils of attestation and remembers how, in case of casualty, any lawyer may stab him with a misplaced comma and bar all explanation by the visible evidence of a full stop. Captain William Gifford would have that in mind when he penned the first of his five entries in the *Highlander's* blue-backed log.

This to report that at 11.45 p.m. (1st August, 1940) vessel was attacked by enemy aircraft with machine gun fire and one aerial torpedo which missed vessel passing close under stern. Fire was opened by ship's machine gun and Holman projector.

Quite properly he would not be inclined to elaborate the circumstances of the attack or to detail the state of the weather and the visibility—then darkling with the long twilight almost gone —in which the Second Mate, who was on watch, did not sight the enemy until the torpedo was slipped. (But he was sufficiently alert to avoid it.) . . . The aircraft then flew down the port side of the ship from forward to aft and raked the decks with machine-gun and cannon. All hands would be on deck by this time and the crack shot had reached his post at the Lewis which was mounted on a little platform at the stern. The second item reads:

This to report that at 00.10 a.m. (2nd August) Enemy aircraft which was still attacking and low over vessel, was struck by gunfire from ship and crashed, partly on deck and partly in water in flames.

Considerable damage was done to ship's superstructure rails etc. Lifeboats No 4 and 5 were smashed, Wireless Aerial put out of action, Holman Projector also put out of action and William Birnie A.B. and Bert Whyman, Fireman, who were operating same received facial injuries. The said injured men received first aid treatment on board.

The Captain thought it unnecessary to record a seaman's plain duty to examine his ship and establish her seaworthiness to continue the voyage towards Leith which was seventy miles away. There is no mention of that in the Official Log, and it can be taken that the thought of turning back to Aberdeen (only eighteen miles distant) for repairs and the replacement of the shattered lifeboats did not occur to him. . . . There was the voyage to be made and already there was the drone of another aircraft, plainly audible but unseen in the growing darkness. Attack again developed, this time from a torpedo-bomber whose pilot may have witnessed the fate of his compatriot.

This to report that at 00.30 a.m. this day, vessel was again attacked by enemy aircraft, and two aerial torpedoes were seen in close vicinity which again passed close astern, ship's course being altered to avoid same. Aircraft also opened fire at close range and gunfire was returned from ship's machine gun and kept up until 00.50 a.m. when Aircraft was hit and crashed into sea about 100 yards astern of ship. On both occasions Geo Anderson, A.B. and Lawrence Halcrow, 2nd Steward, were operating machine gun.

The fourth entry in the Official Log records briefly that rockets were fired from the *Highlander* when the first attack was in progress and a wireless warning was broadcast before the crash of the first aircraft put the ship's installation out of working order. That the message was received by Cullercoats Station is made clear by the final and fifth paragraph in the book, the ship being then safely at anchor in Leith Roads:

This to report that at 10 a.m. this day, Navy Launch with Doctor and nurse fetched injured men W. Birnie, A.B. and Bert Whyman, Fireman, to Hospital. These two men suffering from facial and other injuries owing to enemy action.

(sgd.) William Gifford, Master
T. P. Ogston, Mate

No. It was not quite the merchantman's inability to serve his weapons that led to the huge enlistment of D.E.M.S. gunners at 'One Shilling a Month'. The job had at length become too great for us.

Chapter XVII

SEALED ORDERS

At the port of Glasgow throughout the war King George the Fifth Dock, known as K.G.5, was the Military Embarkation Dock at which troops were marched on board ship up a long sloping gangway (or brow) whose other end might ultimately rest on Norway, Africa, India, Burma or Australia, wherever the fortune of the day required them. It is sufficiently remote from the city and public observation of troop movements. A network of railway lines flows into it on the western side and it was generally in darkness the long troop trains drew into or hauled out from the dockside halt on rail connection with all parts of the Kingdom. At all times the main gate and minor entrances were well guarded by security patrols and always one required dock permits and identity documents to gain admittance to the dockside.

In October of 1942 an even stricter control was enforced. One had almost to claim kinship with Saint Peter himself to gain entry at the main gate: all others were barred. A known face was no recommendation and it was of little use to become impatient when a constable of the Marine Division, who had known one for many years, held the dock permit up to the light to scan the water-mark. It was 'in Orders' for him to do this and, at the Embarkation Sheds where the 'red caps' of the Military Police held court, it could be consolation to note the thoroughness of their scrutiny of uniformed Commodores and Brigadiers. Nor were the merchant watchmen less liberal. Even on the topmost step of the gangway the master of a ship was due to be challenged by his own quartermaster. All the signs forecast a major operation and the secret of its location was well guarded. Up until that date there had been clues by which, noting skis and northern equipment stacked in the sheds, we could punch the troops' tickets for Norway: or, observing sun helmets and the lighter battle-dress of the men embarked, sense a reinforcement of the front in India, Burma, or the Middle East. But Movement Control had seen to it that there were no signs of 'whither bound' at the dockside on this occasion as we set about our preparations for another voyage. It could be noted that the advance baggage and equipment of the troops intended was singularly light in tonnage and there was a certain signifi-cance in the order to transfer rifle-racks from the armoury to be placed nearer to hand in the troop-decks, but there was no hint of destination in these proceedings. The Department of Sea Transport was as cautious to avoid disclosure. The clue that had often before given us a hint of how the ship's head would lie when again we put to sea was denied to us. Formerly, upon arrival in a home port, it had been our business to correct the ship's charts in the light of informations of wrecks and obstruc-tions, new mine-fields, and dangerous areas. Often, our far-away port could shrewdly be identified as, in small hand, the navigator pencilled in the amendments. But not upon this occa-sion. By Order upon arrival inward, all our chart folios and sailing directions had been packed up and sent to the Admiralty Chart Depot at Saltcoats. We had no charts to amend and no sailing directions to study although, by every post, the relative Notices to Mariners fell upon us like the leaves of Vallambrosa. It was clear that this was to be a very *hush* adventure. It was to be a 'dry' naval occasion too, for by imperative command, we were no longer to roll out the barrel for refreshment of troops on overseas voyage.

But of the formidable character of the operation there could be no doubt. We were intended for a landing on some hostile sea-coast. The signs were plain that it would not be a high-spirited raid on a strip of coastline like those of the Lofotens, Vaagso, St. Nazaire and Dieppe, but a long-planned full-scale massed assault upon the enemy's sea approaches. There was visible evidence. When we had come in from sea in mid-October and taken our pilot at the booms, it was with care and at prudent speed we made passage through the press of anchored shipping massed in the Clyde defended area. Throughout the war the Clyde anchorages had never been other than busily occupied, but this spectacular assemblage had the proportions of a not infrequent sailor's nightmare in its variety of obstructing vessels and the apparent hopelessness of clearing them. We found the Rule of the Road difficult of application and I remarked upon it. The pilot, in an interval of steadied progress, said the ships had been thus crowded at anchor for some days. 'All intended for the same big job,' he said, pointing towards a group of large liners berthed off Kempock Point. River steamers—the favourites of the Firth, now drab and dingy in their battle-grey —were tied up alongside the great ships transferring troops on board. I remarked the novel 'Martian' headgear of the khaki-clad soldiers on the broad decks of the transports. They had resemblance to an apian swarm by reason of their rounded headpieces, and I was not surprised to see the huge outstanding hive, whence the American troops had come, anchored off Greenock. The great *Queen Mary* had arrived in from an Atlantic voyage on the day before and it was from her the 'Yanks were coming'.

We embarked troops on the 29th October—2700 officers and men—and steamed down river to join the anchored ships off Gourock. Although the troopships of the first assault convoy had sailed on the day before and we, with others of the second, were in the berths where they had lain, the press of shipping in the Firth and at the Tail of the Bank seemed in no way diminished. In *Circassia* we were classed as a 'sealed' ship and traffic with the shore, unless upon urgently necessary business, was forbidden. But what need had we for the distractions of the beach when such a pageant of maritime strength and beauty lay close around us, displayed in a setting that no other harbour in the world could surpass? Late October in 1942 was a gracious period of fine weather. There was light rain at times, but the passing showers only added to the clarity of the view, leaving the colour on the distant hills more brilliant and the outlines of the anchored ships more sharply revealed.

It is not often there are 'days of grace' in a troopship fully em-

Casualty; the gallant little *Highlander* survives a bombing attack in the North Sea and makes port at Leith

barked for the voyage while yet the ship is retained in a safe anchorage, and advantage was taken of that unusual circumstance to set all in order for the passage. There was much to be done, for we had been hastily embarked. Troops were units of the British First Army wearing the new shoulder badge of the Crusades. The largest detachment belonged to the Corps of Motor Cyclists—the modern light cavalry. With them, we took on board their 'iron horses' and we found them intractable in the matter of stowage on deck and below. It seemed that every rider must know his own mount, where it was placed, and in what order it would subsequently be landed ashore, for there was a scheme of serial releases from the side of the ship in the programme of assault. Fortunately we had also embarked a sizeable squad of the Dock Labour Battalion, Royal Engineers, and with their help were able to restow the awkward vehicles to some agreement. But it was the task of finding a safe compartment in which to stack their cans of petrol that taxed our ingenuity the most. Strictly, and under an Order in Council no less, it is forbidden to carry more than a very small quantity in a troopship, but the case was 'needs must' and we found a lair for the jerricans in the swimming-pool on the sun-deck. There, the cans were placed at the bottom and water was run in to a depth of about three feet. It was not thought likely that this would be at all protective under air attack, and leakage would possibly occur and mount to the surface where a match-stick or cigarette-end could start a blaze to spread alarmingly. With troops meandering on the upper decks, that was an ever-present menace. When it was noticed that we had embarked officer details of the Sea Transport Service, it was not without satisfaction a memorandum was made out to the senior amongst them. As it was their department that had loaded the inflammable consignment on board, what could be more appropriate than that the officers should take care of it on 'passage duty' under Article 18 of the regulations? Being merchant sailors in a peacetime avatar, they were competent as fire guards.

It was whilst scanning the nominal roll of personnel embarked, in search of suitable recruits for passage duty, I recognised *Cir-*

cassia's place in the pattern of the expedition. Excluding the cycle corps, not more than a third of our people were of front-line combatant status. We were intended—in the second fast convoy—to 'hold jackets' for the fighting men until foothold had been assured and as well to transfer their heavier tools and equipment. Even their pocket-books would be in our hands for I noted a cadre of the Army Accountants Branch included amongst our passengers. Many naval officers were included but, in the reserved habit of the Navy, their special appointments were not appended. There were, too, civilians listed in the roll. Salvage experts, a dockyard divers' squad, surveyors of hulls and engines, a few merchant shipmasters and officers were amongst the entries. There were several Esquires and I learned later that at least two were owner experts attached to the Ministry of War Transport and detailed for control of transport in the area to which we were bound. Within her own bulwarks, *Circassia* seemed to hold the nucleus for the founding of a distant colony. Turning from the pages of the roll to gaze out again through my windows at the great fleet of ships anchored in readiness around us, I thought of the skill with which the vessels had been stored, stowed and furnished and of the fore-thought that had been expended in the distribution of the 'bodies'—the crusaders embarked for the task. I had noted the variety of their special occupations in the lists, but the numbers seemed few for so great an undertaking. Doubtless, amongst the anchored ships, our lists would be many times duplicated to en-sure that if one or more were struck down from amongst us in the convoys the operation would not be too seriously impeded.

In the Clyde area it had been customary for Convoy Confer-ence before sailing to be held at Naval Control Headquarters at Marymount, a modest villa residence set on an eminence above Gourock Pier: but on this occasion masters with their next senior and wireless officers were instructed to attend on board the *Narkunda* in which the Commodore of the convoy was em-barked. This unusual departure from established practice pro-voked comment and conjecture as we foregathered on board the P. and O. liner in the early afternoon of the 1st November.

There were those amongst us who thought it portended a full disclosure of the secret rendezvous, but the most part were doubtful. After all, what vital purpose would be served by the knowledge? We could as efficiently act upon immediate orders or 'proceed as previously instructed'. But it could not be denied that we were curious and it may even be that there was mild resentment at what some thought a denial of confidence. Almost as conspirators, we whispered together our guesses at the outcome. One had the opinion that Dakar in Senegal would be our objective. 'Was it not well known', he said, 'that Vichy planes from there shadowed our convoys and directed U-boat attacks? Losses off Freetown were mounting alarmingly. We'd have to put a stop t' that.' . . . Fortress Europe, somewhere in the Bay of Biscay, had the greater following. With thought of November weather in the Atlantic, I ruled that out in my speculations. Dakar, I thought sensible but the apparent weight of the offensive seemed out of all proportion to such a minor task.

Conference followed the customary lines. We were to weigh and proceed at 2200 hours, passing the boom gateships in the order detailed in sailing orders. Clyde pilots would be disembarked off Rothesay Bay. Thereafter, the ships of the convoy would continue in single line ahead until instructed by the Commodore to take up 'Formation B' which would be maintained until daybreak—or as otherwise ordered. Ocean formation was laid down in diagrams 'A' and 'A.1'. Would the masters please check up on their convoy pennants and agree that the matters are fully understood? A pause whilst spectacles were adjusted; papers rustled and eyes lifted from the mimeographed sheets to a blackboard facing the company and silence was accepted. The Naval Control Officer went on to detail the initial movements in the oversea voyage. In the event that we might separate through stress of weather or other cause, points of rendezvous for the first two days of the passage were emphasised: beyond that, there was no mention of further advance in the direction of the enemy. 'Any questions?' said Captain Crooke? One stalwart, somewhat diffidently, rose to mention that he had no charts for the voyage. What about that? 'That', said the Navy, not to be drawn, 'will be attended to in due course,' and again he drew our attention to a bulky sealed envelope in our files. It was marked *Top Secret,* heavily underlined, and bore the inscription 'Not to be opened until instructed by the Commodore'.

The slow convoys of munitions ships had sailed from the anchorages in the Clyde in the last days of October and the ranges of the Firth seemed vast and open again after apparent contraction in the pressure of the greater gathering of shipping, but already the ships were coming in from sea to be woven into the scheme of events. And from the berths up-river, early units of a third troop-convoy, fully embarked, had been brought down on the tide to take up positions on the starting line. As I watched the newcomers dropping their anchors in our near vicinity, I thought it prudent to plot out the whereabouts of the vessels included in our own convoy schedule. In the dark hours of our sailing it might be useful to know their place and movements at departure and how we could best bear up for the gate-ships when our turn was due. Whilst engaged in this memorandum, the charts were brought to the bridge-house—a substantial bundle of folios. Only one of these, that for immediate use in British waters, was unsealed. All the others, like our top-secret envelope, were marked 'not to be unsealed until instructed by the Commodore'.

Chapter XVIII

OPERATION TORCH

WE were not quickly enlightened about the destination of our particular convoy in support of the projected landing. It took five wondering days of an Atlantic survey for the news to come through. All had gone well and easily with us since we had sailed from the Clyde. Commodore Sir Richard Lane-Poole (Vice-Admiral, retd.) had been indulgent and only mild rebuke had, on occasion, been addressed to the ships under his guidance. We thought this leniency curious for it is in the early stages of the passage that the whip is commonly applied and the convoy sharpened up in readiness for whatever may happen. It seemed that we were due somewhere in mid-Atlantic without loss of time. In about the latitude of Gibraltar—and still far from the Rock—we were flagged to make the rare manoeuvre of turning sixteen points of the compass to retrace our course to the north-west. It was then that the Commodore was at pains to drill his charges in a long-continued period of exercise and manoeuvre far beyond the normal. Gun practice with anti-aircraft weapons was understandable and the clouding up of the convoy under smoke screen a wise provision, but the turns and twists so often signalled could only be designed to mark time on the sea-route in expectation of further orders. It was in the sunset hour of that day, when the convoy was firmed up and heading to the east again, that the long-awaited signal was made to open Sealed Orders and be guided accordingly. We were the Second Fast Convoy of Operation 'Torch.' Planned to set the fires of freedom alight again where, for so long, they had smouldered or gone out, the operation was well named. The great seaport of Algiers was our objective.

Naval orders, while admirably lucid and precise regarding what is to be accomplished, are rarely communicative in detail of the larger purpose of the operations of which they are a part. The sealed envelope that had lain for so long in my safe was no exception. We were to land our contingent of the First Army at Algiers. How it was to be landed and how received at that port was not detailed. Certainly, there was reassurance in that omission. But it was from another source we were informed regarding the great objective. A copy of the 'First Army Information Bulletin' that I was privileged to read when the seals were broken gave us the scheme of the assault in detail. When we sailed from the Clyde we had not the slightest inkling that we were still in touch with the distant Eighth Army on the borders of Libya. Of course we knew, and took unction, that the troops we had landed safely at Suez on the previous voyage had done their part in halting Rommel's advance towards Egypt and the Canal. But we did not know that—as we turned and circled in the Atlantic—we were awaiting a decision in the same field now two thousand miles away. The bulletin made that plain:

Our object is to clear the Axis forces out of North Africa, acting in conjunction with our comrades of the Eighth Army in Egypt. Unluckily, to reach the enemy we have no choice but to use French ports and territory as our base, though neither we nor the United States wish to fight the French, nor do we covet their possessions. In an endeavour to make this absolutely clear to the French the initial assaults of the Allied Force will be almost entirely American. First Army will follow through and move eastwards as fast as we possibly can to meet the Germans and Italians.

On that reading, it was understandable that the large American forces we had seen to be embarked in the ships of the First Assault Convoy in the Clyde would be fully employed. We had not the information that, just over the horizon to the south of us, a great U.S. task force of warships and troop transports was pressing on—direct from the United States—to attack the port of Casablanca and the beaches at Safi and El Mehdia in Morocco, or that our sister ships of the advance convoy were at the moment in the Mediterranean and about to land troops at Oran and Algiers. The 'Torch' was to be widely applied.

All that we learned later. The breaking of the news on board opened up a surprising chapter of revelations. It came out that Commander Sharp, R.N.R. (who had joined with zest in comment and conjecture throughout all the five days of our innocence) was the Naval Control Officer appointed to duty in Algiers. His bond discharged, he was at liberty to tell me of the formidable character of the operation and the great naval forces employed in its prosecution. From him I learned the Royal Navy was in strength to the northward and in the Mediterranean and the United States Navy to south of our position. He said, with a glance at the clock, that 'the balloon might go up' at any minute, but the succession of events was not quite as swift as that. Thus early, it was not expected that the official broadcasts of the B.B.C. from London would refer to naval doings abroad but we listened anxiously. On the 7th November a brief report of heavy and continued air raids by the R.A.F. on the port of Genoa aroused interest. This item of news was not considered important by the many listeners at the loud-speakers in the troop-decks for the amazing victory at El Alamein was still burning up the current in frequent despatches and all ears were tuned to them. Only a wing-commander of the Air Force listened professionally to the lesser news item. He wondered if the air attacks on Genoa were timed to mislead the enemy who must now be aware of an impending sea-assault in the Mediterranean? (It would not be for the 'flip', he said, that an unidentified—probably German—plane had shadowed us for the best part of a day when we were off the Azores: the weather had been very clear then and it seemed unlikely that the greater advance convoys had not been similarly observed.) Genoa seemed the right place to be stirred up and alerted.

Commander Sharp was not the only safe-keeper of the news in our ship's company. It was not long before I learned that, all unwittingly, I had been taking my infrequent spells of rest prone over unimagined wealth of sterling. When embarkation was in progress at Glasgow, I had thought it odd for the senior officer of the Army Accountants Branch to ask for special stowage of his 'stationery'. Offhand, I agreed to the placing of the packages in my quarters, for sentries were posted nearby. It was a surprise to be informed that the packages contained half a million—a special print of military money in bank notes of pounds, shillings and sixpences for the use of the Army in occupation!

We passed through the Straits of Gibraltar in the darkness of early morning, the 11th November. It was a novel experience to see the coastal lights on Cape Spartel, Malabata, Tangier, and Tarifa in the north, shining out at full brilliancy as though there was no longer menace in the quiet waters of the Strait. Brightly illuminated neutral steamers passed us and alongshore the glow of town and village lights stood reflected in the stream: only the high dark face of the Rock showed no sign of habitation. At that time the convoy was formed in two long lines and steering close to the southern shore. When we passed the Spanish fortress at Ceuta the quick-stabbing beam of the lighthouse on Almina Point caught each ship in an instant's flash as though counting us off in procession. That our progress would be observed by German watchers there was to be expected but the information could not now be of first importance, for we knew that Algiers was in our hands, Oran was on point of surrender, and the news from Casablanca, though critical, was good. All the world could know that the torch had been applied.

For good reasons, the London broadcasts of the B.B.C. did not uncover all the serial incidents of the operations. It seemed enough to announce (on the 9th) that—'Allied forces, landed early yesterday morning, captured initial objectives in two vital areas of French North Africa.' We were not, however, left completely in the dark regarding the progress of the adventure. Through the goodwill of an officer who had formerly sailed with me, we were given scraps of information. My friend was in command of a frigate, one of the nearby ocean escorts. Naturally he had to veil the substance of his news, but the Navy is singularly apt in paraphrase. We had the first news that the assault had begun from him. He made—'It's reported that Vichy blood transfusion has good result but patient still on dangerous list.' At a later date we learned that one of the destroyers, having crashed the harbour boom at Algiers, had subsequently sank off-shore, and it seemed clear that there was little prospect of a welcome in the port. The First Army Bulletin had anticipated that situation:

> . . . it is quite likely that some at least of the French armed forces will oppose our inruption into their country, though few will have their heart in a fight waged not of real conviction, but only as a genuine, though mistaken, gesture in defence of their honour. But whatever the motive we can brook no delay.

Our anxiety was not of long duration. In late afternoon of the 11th, the Commodore made a general signal that an armistice had been signed. Now, we thought, the assaulting troops would be in need of their jackets and heavier equipment and it was high time the First Army was landed and away to the eastward before the real enemy had taken second wind. But there was no call for acceleration in the speed of the convoy. Indeed, as night fell, we were again reduced to 'playing for time' and carving wide and intricate patterns on the calm of the Mediterranean. The beach-masters and the docks pioneers were not yet ready for our supporting entry.

The night out had its excursions and alarms. In darkness, we became involved with the slow convoy of munitions ships that had sailed from the Clyde two days before us, and found the pre-arranged conjunction somewhat too accurate for our peace of mind. But we drew apart without known casualty and turned to the northward for more sea-room. Submarines were reported in the vicinity. Although we were not attacked it was not long before we had word of their activity. During the night our wireless picked up an SSSS. It was from the *Viceroy of India,* torpedoed and sinking not far from Cape de Gata. Before morning we had news of other losses. The ships were those of the assault convoy that had sailed before us. Commander Sharp, who had the logistics of the operation at his finger-tips, thought that they would be returning from the beach-heads unescorted after landing troops and making for Gibraltar, there to form up in convoy for passage to the United Kingdom. He was gravely perturbed at the news and impatient to be disembarked at Algiers where his first duty would be the organisation of routes and escorts for the returning transports.

★   ★   ★

Hostilities in the Bay and at Algiers had mercifully been of short duration and had concluded without any notable sign of serious conflict. When, on the morning of the 12th (D day plus 4) we entered the harbour we were in expectation of finding the city and the port brooding sullenly under the menace of the guns of a powerful fleet. But the great warships—if ever they had steamed into the bay with guns unhoused—had been withdrawn, and in the city and on its surrounding hilltops the flags of France still waved happily, perhaps even in a greater profusion than would be shown in normal days. There were other ensigns here and there, fluttering as handsomely. Atop the administration buildings and on the forts that dominated the bay, the Union Jack and the Stars and Stripes ruffled in the breeze—hoisted no higher than the Tricolour that waved beside them. Entente had been established: at the port offices and on many flagstaffs along the waterfront, the White Ensign was prominently displayed, indicating that the great harbour with all its machinery and appliances intact was in our hands.

Awaiting further instruction we anchored in the bay where 'dan' buoys had marked off an area swept clear of mines. Naval minesweepers were still engaged in exploring the eastern waters and the incoming 'slow' convoy had its difficulty in finding room to bring up and let go in the restriction of the roads. All ships lay with protective balloons hoisted at operational height, for an air alert had been signalled in early morning and the warning flag had not yet been hauled down on the Breakwater Station. The spectacle of so many tethered blimps floating and swaying in the light breeze above such a vast and closely-packed assembly of shipping was disquieting, for there could be no safety in numbers in such a gathering and the mass of silvered fabrics, glinting in the sunlight, was certainly a beacon in the sky for any hostile aircraft. It was not long before this was appreciated and the signal made to haul down to masthead height. With that advertisement removed, the ships themselves came under attention. All were familiar to us for we had ridden together in the Clyde anchorage before setting out. Only the backdrop was changed. Instead of the purpled hills of Argyll and Dunbartonshire, there was the low sandy coast-line of the eastern littoral of Algeria, pointed to seaward where the forts on Cape Matifu were wreathed with smoke—still smouldering, as we learned later, from a naval bombardment on D day.

Strangely, of all our personnel embarked, the 'dockers' were in greatest demand. We had not long been anchored before a signal was received that Docks Operations, R.E., were to be disembarked and in haste we had them mustered and counted off by the time a barge was brought alongside to receive them. It could be seen that the need for them was urgent. From where we lay anchored, the congestion of shipping within the break-waters could be plainly observed. Every available berth was occupied—in some cases, double-banked by overlapping hulls. From time to time there would be movement—a 'light' ship, discharged of her load, would disengage and turn out to anchor amongst us, whilst another waiting ship would be signalled in to take her place. With the 'dockers' we landed our naval and transport units, but there was no signal to call us into a dockside berth and disembark our impatient 'Light Cavalry' of the First Army.

We remained at anchor throughout an uneasy night for we were bedded down under a great smoke screen of almost lethal concentration which began on the approach of sunset. An air attack was apprehended and all ships were signalled to 'make smoke'. We obeyed quickly and conjured up a stagnant cloud whose like no one amongst us had ever experienced. The city was as quickly alerted and to our great volume added the nauseous fumes of hastily-improvised crude petroleum flares. Possibly the full effluvium that so many alarmed agencies could set up, and that in a confined and windless area was not immediately foreseen. The order to diminish or to cease—by some form of siren—would be taken as 'All Clear' and it was in the height of our distress we heard the drone of bombers overhead. In vain we had closed down all apertures and ducts: in every part of the ship the fumes persisted. It can be admitted that we had effectively disarmed ourselves. Although the hoses were run out and the decks' water service running at full blast, the men to man them were out for the count and could do no more than gasp and cough and spit.

Strangely, we were not called upon to do more than that. It was apparent that the enemy was disconcerted to some degree by the foul blanket we had spread. For an anxious period we heard the planes circling overhead and at least three explosions in the city, then again the roar of engines followed by distant bomb-bursts on the eastern side of the bay. At midnight there was quiet again and we waited anxiously for the 'All Clear'. It was long of coming, but there were signs that many of the anchored ships, like ours, had put the dampers on the smoke floats: some were seen to be afloat on the surface of the bay and still emitting spiteful plumes. It was three in the morning when the wail of the siren encouraged us and almost blessed daylight again before the morning breeze had lifted the pall. We entered between the breakwaters in the early hours—but it was a red-eyed and begrimed detachment of the great army we disembarked.

When we entered the docks a capable French pilot came out to *Circassia* and conned us in to a berth at the Grande Mole. Certainly, we could have made shift without him, but the inevitable difficulty of protracted docking in circumstances of confusion and congestion and without tugs or boatmen, was not one to be cheerfully engaged by any deep-water shipmaster. Much time would have been lost and possibly damage incurred. I would admit that it was with relief I made out the pilot's flag on the little motor-boat that boarded us off the breakwaters and noted the powerful tugs waiting to cant us into the crowded berth. When the pilot came to the bridge, he addressed me by name and his handshake was firm and friendly. He had apparently recognised me at once as one who had accepted his services in the almost forgotten days of peaceful trading, for often I had brought a cruising liner to the port. To him, I was probably a friendly ghost of bygone years: to me, he was a symbol of the regular sea commerce to which I longed to return.

As I watched the immediate disembarkation of the Motor-Cyclist Corps and noted the ease of it I was reminded of a retort much quoted by sailors. To the protestations of a foreman stevedore who complained of difficulty in unloading an awkward cargo from a ship, the comment of an energetic mate was— 'What *you* want is a cargo of canaries. You could open up th' hatches and let th' little beggars fly ashore!' . . . While that acceleration was hardly within our powers, there was a modest similitude to it on the busy mole alongside. There was ample space for the troops to be mustered and counted off, but that was not the procedure of the new light cavalry that streamed on shore as soon as the gangways were lashed on board. All had previously been briefed on their objectives and there seemed no need for a nominal roll-call. From every point on the inshore side of the ship on which a running tackle could be slung we landed their machines and petrol for the journey. There was a constant roar and whirr and thrash of motor engines as the swarming troops tested out their mounts. Then, in ones or twos or flights of twenty or more, they spurred away up the long Rampe des Docks to the highway. There, they turned left on the Route Nationale towards Constantine or Jidjelli over two hundred miles away to the eastward. We were quickly cleared of our 'canaries'. As the rearguard flight wheeled the corner and was lost to our sight, I thought of contrast with the last occasion on which I had helped to land soldiers and their mounts in time of war. That was in the open 'roads' off East London in South Africa in 1899, when the mounts were the magnificent horses of The Royal Scots Greys. I remembered these noble animals, slung by a midship belly-band and dangling overside above the open landing-barges as the *Australia* rolled violently in the high ocean swell. How they whinnied in fear and alarm at that necessary but brutal expedient! . . . Across the mole away from the ship's side, a squad of the R.E.M.E. (Royal Electrical and Mechanical Engineers) had set up a workshop for repair and adjustment of defective motor-cycles. These mounts too made complaint in sudden stop and whirr at starting, but this protest was mechanical and in keeping with the new warfare.

Not all the ships of the first troop movement were signalled in to land their men at Algiers. Whether or not the sudden change in the weather to heavy rains had clogged the routes to the east-ward against truck transport or that the railways for want of fuel were inoperative we did not learn. But the sea had proved a useful highway on the flank of an advancing army before. Some of the first and second group of transports were ordered on to Bougie and sailed on the night of our arrival. Three of the ships that had sailed with us from the Clyde were included in that sailing—the *Narkunda, Cathay* and *Awatea.* When dis-charged of our military equipment we were ordered out into the bay to await their return and then sail in convoy to the United Kingdom. They did not return. All three were destroyed in aerial attacks when disembarking troops in the roads off Bougie. When the news came through, it was in sober reflection we hove up anchor and proceeded on the return voyage to the Clyde. Now, with the First Army on the march, it was not going to be easy to support it in carrying the Torch eastward, for every sea-mile of that passage was within close operating range of the enemy airgrounds in Sardinia.

Chapter XIX

STORM AND MOONLIGHT

THE winter of 1942 will long be remembered by sailors—and soldiers then afloat—for bitter weather in the North Atlantic, the like of which had not been experienced for many years. It was a season of continuous westerly gales and that long continuance set up the most terrific seas ever remarked by even the most aged of active mariners. In convoy, we sailed again in mid-December to North Africa and took our share in tempest.

The *Circassia* had been built for a special trade between the United Kingdom and India, her purpose being to carry no more than 300 passengers and a great lading of goods that varied in bulk, or weight, or character. To meet this trade, she was designed as a 'stiff' ship and, to secure ease in a seaway, was intended to carry her weights skilfully distributed somewhat higher in the cargo holds than is common practice. In war condition as a troopship, this placement could not be made. The requirements for nearly 3000 troop personnel and crew made it necessary to stow ballast or military cargo low down in the ship. As a result, she rolled violently, viciously, outrageously—when running to the south'ard before the great Atlantic gales. No seamanlike remedy could be put in practice for in convoy an individual ship cannot be eased and humoured in a heavy seaway as she would be in normal circumstance. She must keep the course and speed that is ordered by the Commodore and it is for him to slow down or perhaps, within the limits of the route, make an alteration of course to ease the hard-pressed ships. As the Commodore had his own choice of a ship to sail in he would naturally prefer a good sea boat, but no ship was good in these tremendous seas, or good enough for one to stand or sit or lie, to eat or sleep, and the most the Commodore could do to ease our situation was to order a straight course—not zig-zagging.

Any thought of comfort in the ships was over-ruled by urgency at the distant beach-head in North Africa, and he was determined that the E.T.A. (Estimated Time of Arrival) of his K.M.F. convoy would be honoured to the hour. (All allied convoys were identified by a number and a simple form of lettering, 'K' stood for United Kingdom, 'M' for Mediterranean and the final letter indicated 'fast' or 'slow'.)

How she rolled as we laboured on! With concern, I thought of the harsh conditions in the crowded troop-decks, for the hatches and companion-ways had been closed and battened down and no one but the ship's duty ratings was allowed on the open decks for with each succeeding lurch she ladled the tops from the running seas and set them to thunder within the bulwarks. Of visible damage to the outswung boats and deck-houses there was much to note and reports of illness and injury amongst the troops and breakage of troop fittings was almost hourly made known on the bridge. But always there is the graceless and unholy ray of comfort to be derived from comparison with others' trials and difficulties. I had only to look at the gallant little ships of our escort that still managed to keep up with us. Two had been detached and 'hove to' to await a lessening of the heavy weather. The three that still remained performed an incredible feat of endurance in maintaining even the semblance of a protective screen. One watched them in the height of the fearsome running sea and muttered a fervent thanksgiving when again and again their buoyant hulls were up-thrown to sight in the thrash and whirl of breaking water. How their men endured it passed my comprehension but, if example of resolution were needed in the convoy of larger transports, it lay there.

In eight days of incredible misery we made the Straits of Gibraltar and passed the Rock that had no summit but a hard high crown of broken storm-wrack. The weather had then faired to a degree and we had opened up the ship to the remedial draught of moist southerly winds. The sea was moderately smooth again and our sorely-tried people could escape from the noisome stench and squalor below to recover—as quickly they did—in the free and open air. The ship was for long unsteady in the new and better weather conditions. She, like a fretful child in convalescence, seemed unable to throw off the habit acquired in the long seas of the Atlantic and preferred to maintain her staggering gait in the comparative calm of the Mediterranean. Zig-zag was resumed in the finer weather and the convoy, that had been for so long ragged and in poor station throughout the days of storm, assumed a sensible neatness in formation. Off Gibraltar the escort had been strengthened by three destroyers of the 'Hunt' class and our numbers were augmented by four additional merchant ships. The coming of the 'joiners'—cargo vessels of modest speed—reduced our progress to twelve knots, but the eastward current set up by the long continuance of Atlantic gales was helpful. We had high hopes of making our date.

When passing close to the port of Oran on the following day a number of the ships in convoy were detached and sent into that harbour. In the re-arrangement after they had left, *Circassia* was given station immediately astern of the 24,000 tons *Strathallan* in which the Commodore was embarked. Speed was increased to fifteen knots when the freight ships had departed. When night fell there was an unclouded sky and brilliant moon, almost at the full; the sea was flat calm and the ships stood out in it in uncommon clarity—the visibility that often preceeds the fall of heavy rain. We were in good station and executing No. 30 zig-zag which is devised for use in specially dangerous waters when, at eleven, the *Strathallan* was torpedoed. To us, in her 'next astern', it was a curiously quiet, deliberate and unspectacular calamity. It took a moment of thought to realise that the great ship ahead—still upright and steering her course—had been hit and that the not alarmingly reverberant explosion carried its fateful message to the four thousand people on board. We saw no flash or flame of the exploding torpedo. The underwater shock was not severe nor the sound remarkable, but that deadening might have been effected by the positions of the ships. By her immediate whistle signal of casualty, it was broadcast that she had been hit on the port side. In that case and on the angle of the zig-zag she would interpose her great hull between us and the point of impact: thus, deflecting the full sound and shock of the blow that doomed her.

It seemed long ere we overhauled and passed her, although the interval, at fifteen knots, was only the matter of a few minutes. She had carried way for a distance, then had stopped and fallen out of line with the red signal of 'not under command' throwing a satanic glare on her funnel and masts and upperworks. There was no sign of alarm or disorder on her broad decks. I could see many Army nurses in their white coifs mustering on her promenade and troops lining up 'to the Birkenhead drill' on the decks below. If our approach seemed slow, our departure appeared surprisingly rapid as we left her to her fate. (We learned later that she was lost whilst endeavouring to return to Oran: it is in that story that good discipline and seamanlike measures averted a heavy loss of life in her.)

With the Commodore thus retired, the Vice-Commodore took charge of the convoy. He was Captain G. B. Kelly, Master of the *Cameronia,* in which fine ship he and I had alternated in command during the first year of the war. Wisely, he set off no fireworks to mark the change-over when it was seen that *Strathallan* had been hit and was unable to carry on. We had the course, the speed and zig-zag were as previously ordered: there was no need for signals and their absence augured well for steadied progress. Astern, in the bright moonlight, we could make out the stricken ship still afloat and upright. There was a considerable volume of smoke plumed above her and we feared that fire had broken out in her, but a destroyer of the escort was standing by to await developments. Another naval ship was questing in the area and there were tremors in our ship at intervals as depth charges were sent down. Although the Commodore would not himself arrive with the ships he had urged so resolutely, his E.T.A. seemed likely of fulfilment.

* * *

Upon arrival at Algiers most of the ships of the convoy were ordered in to disembark, but with *Cameronia* and the *Clan*

Lamont we were instructed to anchor in the bay and await further orders. This looked like a turn to the eastward, perhaps to Bougie or an offshore landing at Jidjelli. We had come in in late afternoon and when daylight was almost gone received our sailing orders from a naval launch. The coxswain was in haste to deliver the package, but he paused long enough to mention that evil birds were on the wing and the port would be blacked out very quickly and soon. As I examined the new instructions, the intermittent wail of the siren on the breakwater sounded out and soon the foul taint of crude oil fumes was in the air: two destroyers were circling to seaward to blanket the bay with black smoke. The weather had turned to heavy rain and frequent squalls of nor'west wind.

We were to continue towards the small port of Bone and with all despatch. Another 250 miles in the direction of the enemy airfields in Sardinia! The master of the *Cameronia* would again be Commodore. Ships were to weigh at 2200 hours and proceed according to diagram attached. Air attack was apprehended and a first degree of readiness was enjoined. Strangely, there was no mention of a naval escort.

When we hove up anchor, the bay was enshrouded in the drifting pall of the smoke screen; but there was wind and in the squalls a sufficient, if momentary, clearing for the movements of the *Cameronia* to be seen and followed. We had barely navigated the swept channel and taken up station abeam of the Commodore, and with *Clan Lamont* astern, when a surprising barrage of *ack-ack* gunfire was seen at some distance ahead on our course. There appeared to be a number of ships engaged: they were proceeding to the eastward and soon it was apparent that we were overtaking them. I expected an immediate signal of alteration of course from the *Cameronia* and was keenly on look out for it. But none came. I thought it strange that we should be steering into trouble, for the gunfire blazed and died away in sudden bursts of tracer that indicated air attack upon the convoy ahead. There was still time to haul to the northward or return to seek a precarious refuge under the smoke blanket in Algiers Bay. Then I realised that the Commodore would have his own orders—that had not been enclosed with mine. The convoy that we were approaching so rapidly seemed composed of small ships and had an odd formation but there was open water in it and it was towards this we steered. We had heard of a group of small fast ships called the 'moonlight squadron'—the *Royal Scotsman* and *Ulsterman,* the *Queen Emma,* and the *Princess Beatrix*—formed to relieve the larger and more vulnerable transports of the hazardous eastward passage. Would this be the 'moonlighters' and their destroyer escort we were about to join in company?

The weather was clear on the open sea. The sky was clouded over but, in the intervals of rain squalls, the moon shone through the rifts and laced brilliant patches on the ruffled surface of the sea. We were not left long in ignorance of what the unknown ships had been firing at. Some bright shaft of moonlight had touched our three large hulls and revealed us to attacking torpedo bombers. Just as we slid into position in the convoy— that strangely accepted us and adjusted speed to correspond with ours—the *Circassia* was apparently singled out for disposal. It can be confessed that we were not immediately at our working best under conditions of attack that we had not before experienced. The moment, too, was vexed by the added duty of taking up position in a convoy whose character and formation was as yet unknown to us. Although reasonably well-informed in the theory of defence by evasive action against attack by torpedo-bombers, we had not been practised and only a few of our D.E.M.S. gunners had done more than loose off a round or two at a towed sleeve-target. Upon sighting the four planes of the enemy as they came roaring in on their runs, we opened fire too soon and in consequence the Oerlikon drums were empty of shell when the two aircraft on our port beam closed in within effective range. But adequate defence in our novitiate was quickly provided. A neighbouring ship on our port bow—that, subsequently, we made out to be a fleet destroyer—suddenly turned towards the enemy spitting out a vicious stream of fire that had effect either to disrupt the airmen's aim or to discourage his attempt; we saw the track of one torpedo cross the

Atlantic weather: 1942

bow as we ported helm to correspond with the warship's action. . . . It seemed clear that the two operations of defence—evasion and counter-assault—could not adequately be served by one voice. On this voyage the R.N.V.R. gunnery officer who was to have sailed with us had been transferred to another ship, but I was fortunate in having a very capable and keen-sighted assistant in David Barclay, the Chief Officer. It was agreed that he should control the gunfire. We had, too, a third voice that was powerful in communications—C.P.O. Stagg, D.E.M.S.—who was eager to restrain the gunners' untimely enthusiasm. It seemed a good working party, with the helm and the engines under my hand. We were proceeding at fifteen knots and had still a little speed in reserve. It was understood in the engine-room that a double ring of the telegraph was the signal for 'all she'd got'.

When our immediate enemy had retired, there was opportunity to take bearings of the ships around us, all pressing on—to the eastward. I was still inclined to think we had joined the 'moonlight squadron' for—in the fleeting clear intervals between squalls—we could observe no outline of customary appearance. The nearest ship was the destroyer that had taught us our lesson. (Our ears were still ringing with the scream of fury she threw at the Heinkels when they came in on their run. *Room-pa, Room-pa, Room-pa,* increasing in crescendo to a high-speed tenor note!—whilst our Oerlikons were silent and the gunners cursing as they reloaded!) . . . No signals had been made. I thought it a curious experience. It recalled to me the remark of a military Commando officer whom I had taken to the Torch landing a month back. He said Commandos never made signals: they were trained to anticipate. It seemed that something like this was in progress, but my instruction was to keep station on *Cameronia*—and that we did.

Within half an hour we were again engaged. The moon was high in the nor'west and it could be reasoned that attack from the belly of an almost full moon could be expected. We heard the drone of the burdened planes as they came in from that quarter and were in good alert. Through my binoculars I could see the leading Heinkel of two that approached us curve in from the cloud and skim low down, almost on the surface of the sea, towards us. A shaft of moonlight touched him and revealed the beauty of his form, a swift shining silver bird whose only menace seemed to be in the roar of his twin engines and the undeviating line of his approach. At about seven cables range he dropped his left-hand torpedo. At the same moment we opened fire with all port-side weapons. In the din of it I heard the spotter call, 'Torpedo. Red. One hundred and five.' (105° on the port bow —a position difficult of evasion, as the enemy intended it to be.) By the book I was advised to turn away, to run with the track of the missile to evade it: but in convoy, that cannot always be done. At three cables, the *Cameronia* was in my way for that man-oeuvre. We turned towards. It may have been the accident of a bad shot or as the result of my double knock on the engine-telegraph that increased our speed a turn or two, but the torpedo passed harmlessly fifty feet astern.

Our guns had not been silent this time as the Heinkel banked after dropping his torpedoes. As he turned almost in the face of our gunners and at close range, every gun on the port side of the ship seemed to find a target. Of that action I had but a swift side glance. The helm took all my attention. Our sudden spurt ahead had put us out of station; we had drawn up on the escorting destroyer on our port side and that had to be corrected. But I had, in Major Price, of the 105th L.A.A. Regt., who was beside me, a very competent professional commentator. In an even voice he reported our fire from Nos. 4, 8, and 10 ship positions to be hitting the first Heinkel as he swept up to us and roared overhead: black smoke was seen trailing, probably from one engine, and the fuselage and tail assembly had been hit. When last seen he was turning to the northward and losing height. The second Heinkel had apparently attacked the *Cameronia* on our starboard side and seemed to have met a hearty reception. When the action had died down, and it was possible to confer on it there were still some adjustments to be made in our plans for defence, but it was agreed that we had done better and there was even the reasonable assumption that we had scored a point.

The third attack began quite unexpectedly in a blinding squall of wind and rain. We had no early warning of the approach of the enemy that on this occasion attacked from ahead. In the height of the squall and just at the moment we heard the roar of bomber engines, the destroyer on our port bow suddenly altered course and swept across our bows—uncomfortably close. What she had seen or avoided was not known to us but, repressing sailor inclination to swing to port and give her room, we followed her lead to starboard and quickly found ourselves closing on the *Cameronia* that was maintaining convoy course. My old ship must have known my coming for she too bore off to starboard and gave us water as I corrected the swing of the helm. There was now full tongue in the convoy—a heavier note in the volume of gunfire than any we had previously experienced. What had been nearly lateral fire in the earlier engagements turned to the high-angle fire of heavier weapons. Busied with the heading of the ship, I did not observe the numbers of the aircraft that then swept high overhead. The Major told me they were bombers, not torpedo bombers, and their attack seemed to be directed against the starboard wing and rearmost ships. I did not see any fall of bombs, but one great Heinkel that may have been hit passed close overhead on what seemed a very steep descent . . . . As quickly as it had come up the squall of wind and rain died down. The bombers had gone. It was quiet moonlight again and the ships, darkened and silent, were pressing on eastward.

We had been in anticipation of almost non-stop attack with every sea-mile we advanced the closer to the Sardinian airfields. Strangely, this did not occur. The intervals of rest and peaceful steadied progress towards our harbour grew longer as we steered past Cape Bengut. Towards morning, and when the stars high in the east had begun to pale, there was a long interval in which the enemy seemed to have relinquished his purpose. Never was the coming of daylight more eagerly awaited for we could admit to some weariness after the night's long contest.

It was during the uneasy half-light, the moon low and obscured, and in a brisk squall of wind and rain, the *Cameronia* was torpedoed from the air. We did not see the Heinkels coming in against the convoy from a southerly direction. It was still murky there, for the dawn was breaking high and the bombers flew at very low altitudes—almost on the sea surface—and with the dark of distant mountain ranges behind them. The laboured sound of their engines we knew and could recognise, but the true direction of that stuttering drone is not too easy of establishment by the ear at sea. One enemy plane grew in the darkness and roared overhead seemingly in almost perpendicular ascent and exposing his great dark shape to our fire. We had no success. Oerlikon gunfire, that seems so vicious and stabbing as it leaves the muzzle, is disheartening in defence when the tracer droops and fades . . . behind the target. We were learning another lesson—that the 'aim off' has to be vastly increased with the nearness of the target. Our sense of frustration as the great bird flashed overhead undamaged was deepened at that moment by the shock of *Cameronia's* misfortune. She was torpedoed on the starboard quarter—on the side away from us—and again, as with the *Strathallan,* there was no great shock in our ship at the moment of explosion.

Word flies in the quarters of a ship. As I watched the stricken vessel slow and stop and fall out of line, listing to starboard and with her casualty lights glaring, I could sense the excitements and concern amongst our own crew when the news went round. Like me, many of our men had served in her and many had relatives on board. For a brief space of time—as the convoy swept on to the eastward—our good routine was disorganised. From below and against orders the men of the crew crowded the foredeck and there was clamour and shouting. But I had not the heart to rebuke them for I too had my moment of excitement and anxiety and depression when we passed on and left that cherished old ship in her distress. (She did not sink. Under her own steam, limping on one engine and seriously flooded with sea water, she made port at Bougie: seventeen of her men were killed and 33 wounded. She was subsequently repaired and returned to further great service. Captain Kelly was promoted C.B.E. for his gallant conduct of affairs.)

★　　★　　★

With two Commodores retired from passage operations I was in no way eager to step into directive activity. But something had to be done for the convoy was approaching a position off Ras Afia at which by my sailing orders an alteration of course would have to be made. I had not the knowledge that the other ships were similarly routed and felt that the impending change of course should at least be made public by *Circassia* in such a close assembly of speeding ships. (The *Clan Lamont* had long since detached, routed to Bougie.) It was still half-light when we approached the pin-point on the chart and, with some hesitation, I made the signal for the alteration. It was accepted by the other ships and we turned in order and formation when our executive was made. So! It was apparent that we were expected to signal our intention and movements!

With the broad of day now come there was light and opportunity to scan the composition of the convoy. We were not, as I had thought, joined up with the Moonlight Squadron and its escort, but centred in a fighting force of His Majesty's Ships! As I turned my telescope on them, one after another, it was with consternation I made out the flag of a rear-admiral worn at the foremast of our next astern! I had long thoughts of how to remedy my indiscretion, then signalled to her: '*Please read my signals as informative.*' There was a long pause before a reply came through and I had unhappy visions of being thought a forward fellow. But when the reply did come from Rear-Admiral Harcourt in H.M.S. *Aurora* it was reassuring and supporting. It read, '*Fully understood, stop. Can you improve upon present speed please?*' I said I could, and we did, and it was left to me to make the necessary signal for that acceleration to the force. Throughout the remainder of the passage and until arrival in the swept channel off Bone harbour—where the *Aurora* sped ahead and guided me in—I was permitted to continue in my self-appointed task.

We arrived at Bone on the afternoon of the 22nd December and were quickly brought alongside to disembark troops. The celerity of that proceeding was unusual, but the reason for quick despatch was plainly evident in the appearance of what had at one time been a sleepy and pleasant harbour. Of modest compass, there was not one structure on the long breakwater quayside or one building on the higher ridge to the westward of the fairway that did not lie in blitzed and ruined condition. Jerry had been busy here since 'Torch' was lit, and the port had taken a cruel battering. When the Sea Transport Officer boarded us to assist in disembarkations, he was urgent that the ship be cleared of the military before sunset for the nightly air attack was due to begin very soon thereafter and the harbour would be blacked out. The state of the quayside would not allow of trucks to be used for unloading baggage and the heavier equipment. Troops would disembark carrying small-arms and light kit.

The landing of our men was almost a 'front line' operation, for foothold on the quay was more than merely hazardous. The rainy season had made of it a ruddy quagmire, ochred from the many mounds of mineral ore that studded its length and caverned by great bomb-craters in which the gathered deep water lay rosy under the westing sun. In groups and parties, Indian-file, and with the leader probing a long pole, the men scrambled and slithered and splashed, picking a passage under the crumbling walls of the quayside sheds and the twisted wreckage of dock cranes and shipping plant. It was, of necessity, a slow proceeding. Nor was the offshore unloading of the heavier military gear effected with dispatch, for the French barges were of decked construction, did not carry much, and were few in number. The ship was far from cleared when the wail of a siren somewhere announced the laying down of a smoke screen and work was suspended. We had known it was to be laid, and had been instructed to contribute to it; we were not, however, to use our weapons 'unless directly attacked' in the course of the anticipated air-raid.

The sounds of war (as of storm and sea-incident) when heard from an arm-chair in comfortable quarters have the curious effect of prompting the mind to activity—however fatigued the body may have become. It can be said that on the bridge I had walked all the way from Algiers to Bone and I welcomed the inactive part *Circassia* had been given in whatever the doings and alarms of the night. But, always, there is the review of events every shipmaster knows, to come between a tired body and its rest. Had everything been ordered and arranged, or was there not some small but important provision overlooked? To begin at the beginning is a good sailor maxim, and every incident of the passage was passed in review as I snuggled down and longed for sleep. Then came our present circumstance to urge its claim to consideration. Were we fully prepared for whatever might happen? 'Not unless directly attacked' were we to open fire. But what could be 'direct' attack in the foul asphyxiant smoke-blanket that bedded the ships and the harbour? No. It would be right to leave the tired gun-crews to rest in shelter near at hand as I myself was doing. 'The separation of ship's personnel during air attack' was, I remembered, the subject of a Trade Division circular. Did I need to stir and search through my littered files for it, or could I rest in the knowledge that we had been spaced apart in the ship and warned against congregation. 'Precautions against Fire on Shipboard' was another foolscap in the instructions: but I could draw assurance from the sound of gushing water at the deck-hydrant near my door and the thought that fire parties had been organised. . . . What was that again about the potatoes? . . . Oh yes. In the early morning H.M.S. *Dido* had signalled, 'Can you spare and supply ten tons potatoes on return Algiers, please?' . . . It was known to us that, in operations, the Navy was for a time on short commons. But with our experiences of the night so vividly in mind, I thought the words 'on return' singularly encouraging! . . . I drowsed uneasily. We were to do nothing unless directly attacked. Perhaps it was the droning of the enemy's bombers that lulled me to fitful slumber.

Many times during the night the bombers struck a note that brought me from my chair and quickly on deck. There was the moment when a stick of bombs thrashed in the waters of the fairway not far from us, but unseen in the dense black cloud of the screen: the midnight incident of a bomb-burst on the open spaces of the quay and sufficiently near to spatter our starboard top-works with the red mud of mineral ores; the early morning alarm when, by reason of a wayward puff of wind, the screen had thinned and the landward ridge across the harbour could be made out—with two great fires ablaze on the heights. That called for hurried 'action stations' until the draught had died and we were blanketed again. Several times too, the defences of the port and the guns of the naval ships opened up with a thundering barrage. I thought it strange that we could see no gun-flash from the nearby ships although the crash of fire was deafening, and guessed at some form of anti-flash device being used. From the absence of tracer one could also surmise that director or predictor fire was in operation from some central post. I could now understand the port commodore's instruction to keep our fingers off the trigger. What could we do but advertise our presence and position by throwing coloured tracer through the murky screen that enveloped us?

Perhaps it was in welcome of difficulties we knew and understood on the open sea we persevered in renewed effort to 'clear the ship' when daylight came. We were ready in good time and sailed at noon. The passage to Algiers was made without incident. The *Dido* accompanied us there, but she did not get her potatoes. A north-east gale had sprung up, suddenly as it does in the Mediterranean, and the unsheltered waters of the bay where we anchored was no place for suburban delivery. . . . We sailed again at nightfall in a convoy of sixteen ships bound home.

Chapter XX

GARELOCH FOR ORDERS

In the spring of 1943, on return from a fifth voyage with reinforcements for North Africa, I was instructed to bring *Circassia*
alongside at Yorkhill Basin in the Clyde to have her reconditioned. This was not unusual. The circumstances in which we
had been operating precluded the normal routine of upkeep at
sea and we had fallen somewhat from a proper standard of good
order. Repairs too, a lengthy list, were needed after six months'
service in the stormy winter season. But this, as I learned when
we made fast in the basin was to be no 'wash and brush-up' for
continued trooping service. The ship was to be converted to become an L.S.I.(L.). There were to be substantial alterations and
it was in no cheerful spirit I watched the construction gangs
stream up the gangways and clamber on board, all burdened with
cutting tools and welding apparatus, and start in at once to tear
pieces of my handsome ship away. I did not know then what
were the functions of a Landing Ship, Infantry (Large), but it
was clear from the haste of the working gangs that we were required to be fitted and equipped at short notice. What our duties
in the ship would become when conversion was completed
seemed uncertain. Perhaps, as was the case with the *Transylvania,* the ship would again be commissioned under the White

Ensign, and with no place in her for me. Would it be for me another period of beachcombing from ship to ship—on relief duty—or might not the high authorities turn to scrutiny of my yellowed birth certificate and, kindly enough, suggest retiral? I was downcast. But my fears were happily resolved with the arrival on board of the Sea Transport's technical officer, bulky with plans and blueprints for the work in hand. He was an old acquaintance with whom I had been associated on many other constructional jobs in Clyde waters. From him I learned that, with the scale of seaborne landings growing to huge proportions, it had become necessary to employ more and larger merchant ships in Combined Operations. The practice of requisitioning and commissioning such vessels as units of the Royal Navy was now discontinued and those converted to become L.S.I. remained under the Red Ensign with their Masters in command. As far as he knew of it, I was expected to continue in command of what would become a Fleet auxiliary when he had completed the alterations.

Over a pipe in my cabin, Mr. Mackinnon talked of his plans. We were to be fitted to become a 'SNOL' ship, the headquarters of a Senior Naval Officer, Landings. Yes. We would carry troops . . . commandos, he thought, and—in addition to our own merchant officers and crew—he was to fit accommodation for about 30 officers and 200 men of the Royal Navy whose duties would be to man and operate the flotilla of landing-craft and to control operations on the beach. He was also to fit fourteen L.C.A. and they were to be carried or slung from special davits and transverse beams, each having its own electrical hoisting and lowering gear for speedy operations. At this point I realised the need for entry in my own private dictionary of 'officialese' and reached for a notebook.

'L.C.A. What's that,' I asked.

'Landing Craft, Assault,' he said, and I wrote it down. 'Square-ended and flat-bottomed boats. Twin engines. Speed about six or seven . . . may be more. Length over forty feet. Carries about thirty-five soldiers and their gear. Three of a crew.'

I turned the figures over in my mind. 'But where', I asked, 'are you to get "sideboard" for fourteen craft of forty feet even in all the length of *Circassia*?'

I think Mac enjoyed my puzzlement as he sat there sucking at his never-absent pipe-stem. 'Oh. That's easy,' he said. 'Double-bank 'em. One above the other. Seven a side.

Seven a side? Double-banked? I thought of the hard weather we had recently experienced. A brief calculation made out that there would only be sixteen feet freeboard from the keel of the lowermost craft to water level. Not much clearance in a rolling ship, and the craft could not be stowed inboard in bad weather. 'Looks to me like "stand by for replacements",' I commented, 'like asking for casualty.'

He agreed. But that was the scheme, he said, as he unrolled the blue-prints and pointed out the alterations that were to be made. I had difficulty in recognising my ship in the plans and elevations, but the play for inches in strapping the doubtless un-wieldy craft to our upperworks was skilled and ingenious. In a margined box-print on the plans there was detail of the depart-ments and officers concerned in their approval and execution. I noticed F.O.A.S.C. 'Foasc'. I pronounced it with relish, as I fin-gered my pencil. 'Foasc, eh?'

My friend grinned. He said I would need a bigger note-book. 'Foasc', he added, 'was our ruling authority now. He was Flag Officer Assault Ships and Craft.' I pencilled it and was about to put the book aside. 'Just a minute,' he said, 'better put S.O.U.L.S. down too.' He fumbled with papers in his satchel and produced a communication from 'Souls'. It was a question-naire form from the Senior Officer Unallocated Landing Ships regarding the lifting capacity of the ship's derricks. I had much to learn in this new assignment.

Conversion was to me a sore experience. No sailor likes to see his fine ship torn apart, however urgent the necessity. Almost within sight of Fairfield Yard, in which with so much skilled thought and care and craftsmanship she was built, *Circassia* was undone and transformed. From day to day, I hardly recognised her when I saw her masts and funnel towering over the dock-sheds as I came down the Pointhouse Road of a morning. So much had been taken away, so much added on: the masts festooned with novel aerials to serve strange purposes, the funnel adorned by an upright T-piece to heighten the hoist of signal flags. Daily, our trim deck-planking was ploughed up and in no time at all strange new mushrooms of structural steel grew there to provide us platform for augmented armament. The swimming-pool was built upon to provide a multi-post for wireless mysteries: the elegant dome above the lounge was shorn away and an armoured house built there to protect the secret life of Combined Operations. A great tower arose on the bridge over my head, dedicated to the new protector—Radar Location—and armed sentries had to be posted there from the first installation of the base-ring to preserve its secrets. On every visit, I was sure to find some new device installed and new familiars exulting in its potency. It was the I.F.F. that brought me up—all standing—to a realisation that I must go to school again and learn at least some rudiment of what seemed a new profession. I.F.F. ('If Friend or Foe,' is a small complicated instrument that identifies a distant airplane). At Sherbrooke House, a new Naval Establishment across the river, its mystery was explained to me and a group of the ship's officers. I thought it strange to be schooled and instructed by a cinema film there and marvelled at its interest and sufficiency.

The completion of our re-fitment was evidently a first priority and was carried out without halt. On a bright day in early June we were inspected by Rear-Admiral Warren who was F.O.A.S.C. himself. He thought we had shaped up reasonably well. We were to proceed to a mooring in the Gareloch where our flotilla of landing craft with their crews would be embarked. Thereafter, we would be exercised at sea.

*　　*　　*

One cannot pretend that sailors are ever of the elect amongst people who claim early rising as a crowning virtue, for it is clear that only the daily routine of shipboard life has included them in so exemplary a congregation. But most seamen would,

I think, give preference to the early morning hours when the first cup is sipped, the first pipe set alight, and the first reflective survey of the day's engagements is made. In June and in home waters, 'B' time (which is Greenwich date plus two more hours of daylight) is at its working best, for sunrise comes happily then as an invitation to be up and alert and abroad. Yes. Certainly the best hour of the day was come when I stepped on deck to stand under the windbreak of the *Circassia*'s bridge and look out-board over the Gareloch. . . . The fine weather that had attended our entry on the evening before was still unbroken. There was little wind, but a nip in the morning air gave promise of a northerly breeze before long. We had made the ship fast to an Admiralty buoy that lay fairly close inshore off Blairvaddick, a blameless swinging berth, and out of the way of passing traffic: but somewhat too close to the beach for my liking. It was not that I had fears of the depths, but rather that the road back to Glasgow ran too near for peace of mind and that gave me con-cern. With the best intention in the world, it is almost impossible to devise a scheme of leave and liberty acceptable to a merchant crew. Inevitably there would be the daily list of absence over leave to be attended to and the difficulty of retaining substitutes on board to assume the delinquents' duties was not a happy prospect. Security too? I knew we were engaged in some as yet secret operations and had been warned that no letters from the ship were to be posted on shore. But what powers had I to pre-vent a free man in the ship from his correspondence? The most we could do had been to post a warning notice in crew's quar-ters and hope for some response to it. It seemed to me highly probable that the Navy had not yet fathomed the limitations of the Merchant Shipping Act. We would have our difficulties there.

When I came on deck, the tide was on the turn and the odd circumstance of canting so close inshore under the brow of Ben Airdhe was novel. As the ship turned slowly inward, the slender jack-staff on the stem seemed to be pointing out to me—slowly as though loath to let them pass across the bows—the beauties of the loch-side that I so well remembered. It inched over the ribbon of the road that ran down the hollow from Rhu, pointed along the gentle rise that led to Shandon and beyond, then called my attention to a jetty newly built at the Gully Bridge that I marked at once for future use. Traffic was already whirring and rumbling on the roadway—a long convoy of military trucks carrying munition from the new port at Faslane. High up on the hillside, a burdened locomotive on the West Highland Railway panted under the stress of its load and threw white steam into the Whistler's Glen. To our berth, the sun was long a-coming although good daylight was abroad and we lay in darkling glassy shadow under the hills. But across the loch on the Rose-neath peninsula the house windows were warm and a-glint in sunshine and, in the north, Argyll's 'bowling green' had all its tortured peaks aglow.

I had known the loch in many aspects. In less exciting days, to be ordered there was almost a penal sentence for a ship, frequently but a prelude to sale abroad or to the indignity of the shipbreaker's yard. But its sheltered waters had often provided anchorage for many worthy vessels 'laid by in ordinary' to await better times during recurrent trade depressions. These were days of stagnancy in the loch when the ships seemed like islets in the broad of it. Only they moved when turned by the tide or lay athwart in high winds with anchor cables strained hard and high. There was little life in them then and small sign of occupancy. Once or twice a day the old *Lucy Ashton* paddled amongst them as she plied up or down on her scheduled occasions or, at the week-ends, a cruising yacht might show white sails there as she tacked through the lines of the silent ships. . . . But Britain's wars had never sent ships to cower in sheltered harbourage and the loch was thronged now by active shipping.

As a late-comer we were not yet brought into the activities of the force we were to join: Force 'V' was its name in my note-book, now paged voluminously. Alongside at Glasgow, we had been converted, fitted, stored, watered and fuelled. Only our landing craft and their crews remained to be embarked and we would then be ready for the period of exercise and training. But there was not yet any sign of our reinforcements and I could take a student's interest in the nearby ships that were included in the group to sail with us. H.M.S. *Glengyle,* wearing the flag of Rear-Admiral Philip Vian, under whose orders we were now entered, could easily be identified, but the merchant ships—all clad alike in 'Home Fleet' grey and showing no nameboards or numbers, presented difficulty. Only by recognition of some particular in build, in rake of masts or set of funnel, could I make a reasonable guess. The *Ascania* could be nothing other with her strong upstanding build fashioned to meet North Atlantic weather: the *Durban Castle* and the *Derbyshire* (like *Circassia*) intended to voyage with the flying fish were of less massive construction. *Batory,* a Polish ship recruited to our aid, had Continental embellishment broidered on her prow and funnel, and the long length of the Dutch *Marnix van St. Aldegonde* marked her out in any company. With the absent *Llangibby Castle* and H.M. ships *Hilary, Boxer, Bruiser, Thruster* and *Ulster Queen* we formed the small force whose purpose and destination was as yet unknown to us in the merchant ships. But 'hush-hush' and 'top secrets' cannot command one's private thought. We had North Africa firmly in our hands. To what next field would we be required to urge that slender jack-staff on the stem? Europe, somewhere?

My reflections were checked by the shrill sound of a bos'n's pipe in *Glengyle* that lay the nearest to us. It was now seven and for her the day's operations were astart. At sunset on the evening before we had heard her bugles sound off the day and had noted that she had Royal Marines embarked. Unlike us, she was fully equipped with landing craft. We had heard that she had already seen service on the beach at Diego Suarez in Madagascar and it was with interest I raised my binoculars to see what business was afoot. I was rewarded by gaining a good lesson in setting commandos afloat from an L.S.I. (L.). Other than the first shrilling of the bos'n's pipe there were no high words of command although I could mark the crews scrambling into the craft and the swift but unhurried embarkation of the Marines from the 'sally ports' on the ship's high deck levels. The commandos were fully armed and many carried additional burdens whose purpose I did not then know. Suddenly, at some sign I did not see, or word I could not hear, all the lower craft on the side nearest to us were lowered swiftly and steadily to the water, cast off and formed line ahead on passage towards the Narrows: the upper bank was as quickly lowered then and joined the snake-like line of sea-hornets. From the far side of the ship similar groups had been sent away and all joined in some manoeuvre or formations, guided apparently by a flag signal-man in the leader. There were twelve craft. About 400 armed men sent off, outboard the ship on a mission, well within five minutes. It looked simple, but we would have much to learn in attaining to that efficiency.

It was a busy day at our moorings when the naval flotilla party joined. Embarkation was no problem for they came along-side in their L.C.A. complete with hammocks, baggage, and equipment, and were hoisted swiftly to the sally ports on deck. Berthing took longer, for it seemed not clearly understood that the ship was still a troop transport detailed to accommodate a military force of over two thousand officers and men. The Navy had its own ideas of priority that had to be mildly contested by the Sea Transport Officer responsible for the ship's conversion. There was also a puzzle for me to solve in this new admixture of the ship's company. When the working day was over and the attraction of the beach prevailed, there was confusion at the gangway. Our merchantmen, being solidly independent, re-sented any questioning about warrant for a run ashore. When mixed groups of merchant and navy men gathered at our one regulating gangway, the naval P.O. was suspicious of a protean act in a temporary exchange of clothing with our civilian crew and held up the despatch of the liberty boat. This provoked resentment on the part of the navy men entitled, and vulgar torrents of abuse from hotheads of our merchant crew. Never quite adequately defined, the matters were glossed over in some way. We settled down, but in the five days period of tests and training in the Gareloch, I longed for a sea course as far from the S.M.T. buses on the Glasgow road as possible. Only there, I thought, could we tune the ship and her heterogeneous manning to some form of concerted efficiency.

Seldom was a wish more happily fulfilled. On the fifth day, when we had gained experience and a modest dexterity at the shipboard handling of the craft, I was given the programme of more extended operations. We were to leave the Gareloch and embark troops off Gourock, then proceed to practise offshore landings on the lower Firth, Brodick, Lamlash, Inveraray, Loch Fyne. These were the familiar names of our ports of call on the training schedule. In the duty room of the Naval Control at Gourock, I watched the neat little 'Wren' fluffing out her papers and carbons to put my orders on record. As she settled down, I wondered if she thought any more of the job than just routine employment. How could she know that she was tapping out a perfect ticket for an old sailor's journey, a warrant to revisit the scenes of happy peaceful days when he was young?

* * *

We did not earn any palms for performance in the task allotted to us in the training period but, at least, there were few admonitory signals in the great file that lay for reference on my desk. When at Brodick the S.N.O.L. embarked. He was Captain Ian Black, R.N., whom I had previously met whilst *Circassia* was being re-converted at Glasgow. As so often my good fortune in war companionship, I found him a helpful friend, possibly amused at my ignorance of naval practice in a ship but tolerant of, and indeed at times impressed by, our unorthodox merchant ways. He brought my orders for exercise 'Stymie' which, appropriately enough, was to be carried out off the Ayrshire coast between Western Gailes and Barassie Links. He had news too that gave me some momentary disquiet. I surmise that my eldership amongst the merchant masters in Force V was the reason for my appointment as Vice-Commodore of it, but the new incumbent confessed himself a very inexperienced leader as he pored over the many puzzle pages of 'Stymie'. Captain Black aided me at once. He had had a part in mounting the offensive for which we were in training, as also the exercises we were engaged in carrying out. From him I learned much. There were many novel and, to me, inexplicable terms in the type-script and these he translated—that '(sim.)' was non-existent, 'falbot' a marker, amongst other navalese. We were to weigh at 2315 hours that same night and would be engaged on operations until daybreak. Together we considered the weather. It was not promising. The wind had hauled to the westward and that would make of the Ayrshire coast a lee shore. Whilst I thought of the sea's condition and the rainy misty weather as it would affect the ships, S.N.O.L. had his misgivings about the state of the beach and the possibility of damage to the landing craft that could not quickly be replaced. 'Stymie' seemed a good word for the project.

I shall not linger over our first attempt in landing operations. The weather did not improve. We proceeded as instructed, could not land our men on account of the considerable sea in-shore, and recall was signalled. But our experiences were not wholly negative of character. Simulated minefields in the Firth of Clyde that, as I was told, reproduced the known conditions on a certain foreign beach, were said to be successfully navigated. A naval trawler towing a dim blue light that represented a whole force of minesweepers made rendezvous with us, and was said to have swept and buoyed a channel in which the ships formed rigid 'line ahead'. As an introduction the experience was stimulating. In the early morning we returned to our anchorage.

On the night following we repeated the exercise—this time with reasonable efficiency. When crossing from Brodick Bay to Lady Isle, we came under very realistic air attack from a squad-ron of our own planes. Our ack-ack gunners and their weapons being safely policed, we made no reply to the float lights that were showered on us but the S.N.O.L. acting as umpire, con-sidered that the 'enemy' had set us afire on deck, just beside the petrol storage. In that emergency, we manned our fire-fighting apparatus, gas masks and all, and exercised the merchant crew. We did not badly, but a following drill that called for a smoke screen did actually set the ship on fire. Possibly we were inexpert in operation of the C.S.A. (Chemical Smoke Apparatus) with which we had newly been equipped, for it took a turn of its own and set a merry blaze on the poop deck. I am afraid I forgot for the moment the avoidance of imaginary minefields and turned the ship head-on to the wind until the substantial and unsimulated flames were extinguished, but I did remember to acquaint the following ships with our abandonment of station. Captain Black's expert naval signalmen, that he had put under my orders, were very quick to pass the word. We landed the commandos without serious incident, recovered the craft, and returned to Brodick Bay. S.N.O.L. considered that we had 'holed out'. We went to that green on two subsequent occasions, then were ordered to proceed to Inveraray in Loch Fyne.

I had not sailed Loch Fyne since, as a rambumptious boy of about twelve, I worked a very leaky and decrepit cutter of five tons round Ardlamont Point. I was not quite so cocksure and confident as then, when we led *Ascania* and *Derbyshire* through the narrows at Crarae, but we arrived at Inveraray on time. It was no 'token' force we embarked there, but the shock troops of the Canadian First Division whom we were to transport overseas towards a distant objective. They had been in training for many arduous months on the rugged Argyllshire mountains and on the beaches of the loch. It is perhaps invidious for a sailor to comment on the relative merits of the soldiers he embarks, but at least he may express his likings. As I watched the embarkation, I thought there was something very special in the bearing and the action of the boarders. At Inveraray it was no simple dockside movement of marching up broad gangways that was practised by commandos. The 'play for inches' of which I have written in connection with our fitment of the landing craft, had necessitated the discard of our accommodation gangways. But, spaced apart and in series, steel rungs had been welded on the ship's hull to form long scaling ladders. Towards these, the miscellaneous barges and craft from the lochside converged, and with incredible swiftness the sunbronzed men raced up the long flights. They were self-contained too, every man being burdened by his own personal kit and weapons: there was no confusion, no running back again for mislaid belongings or equipment. With the Canadians we engaged in many exercises. At the last practice landing on the Ayrshire coast we put them on shore in marching order at 2 a.m. on a rainy morning to face a thirty-five mile walk to the temporary barracks at which they would be held until the ships were ready for sea again.

With over two hundred naval shipmates aboard, it was well we had the advantage of a shake-down cruise; for, when we returned to the Gareloch to await the next turn in the adventure, there was reasonable amity below decks between the lions and the lambs of our large joint manning. It would be invidious to mention *who* was *who* in that connection, for there was nationality and its ancient grudges in the admixture. The merchant crew were Clydesiders to a man and the bulk of the naval party came from the South of England. It was only natural that there should be claim and counter-claim, but it was the comparison of service that provoked most of the controversy. The naval seaman was envious of the merchantman's greater wages and had his understandable gibe for the 'danger money' in current effect; he saw preference too in the statutory comforts of the fo'c'sles as compared with the bare troop-decks in which he had to sling his hammock. On the training period we did not long have troops embarked and doubtless, seeing idlers amongst the catering staff, he had his ideas about the sharing of shipwork. On our part, we were inclined to look upon the navy men as passengers, not dissimilar to the drafts we had so often trooped aboard. We did not know then that we would be teamed together for nearly two years.

Our relations with the naval officers were good, but it was undeniable that many juniors had reason for complaint about their quarters. With a view to the carriage of large bodies of commando-trained troops, Sea Transport had 'bunked' the junior naval officers too closely together. Most of them were R.N.V.R. But, in 1943, the R.N.V.R. had come of age. Many of its officers were in command of fighting ships, others had proved invaluable in service of the amazing variety of scientific instruments we had now at command. The friendly tolerance of the 'Wavy Navy' that had been a feature of the first World War had given way to a wholesome respect and indeed admiration in the second. The officers were entitled to raise a voice on matters of accommodation in the ship, and it was unfortunate that nothing could immediately be done to relieve the pressure. I had no recourse, pending official instruction, but to abide by the 'Memorandum of Equipment' in which their nests were specified. . . . The division of authority was quite another matter, and there were points upon which argument arose. What was done by or in the landing craft when away from the ship was in no way my business, but it was as well to be agreed on the manner of their approach when returning alongside. The flotilla officers and cox'ns were all young and impetuous, which is as it should be for such a special service, but they had their way of boring into my ship with their awkward squared bows as though they were still at initial training on the solid masonry of H.M.S. *Dundonald* at Largs. There were too many bumps and bruises, not all confined to the lighter craft, and I thought it opportune to read a riot act concerning such over-hearty boardings. It was at length agreed that craft making alongside should come under ship's orders and, for a time, the old-fashioned hand megaphone was used. Old-fashioned merchant-ship profanity burst from it on occasion, for the eye on the bridge could see and the voice was raised. We had not the polished art (that later we learned to practise) of leaving comment and criticism to more private moments, and the young R.N.V.R.'s resented such public admonition. But there was understanding as we and they toned down in the course of exercises.

The control of D.E.M.S. in disciplinary matters was another source of argument. 'Dems'—we made that word to describe the gunners supplied by the Department for Defensively Equipped Merchant Ships—were signed on Ship's Articles in the same way as the merchant seamen, but at a nominal rate of pay. To serve the augmented armament of the ship, their numbers had been vastly increased. About half of the seventy ratings had served in the ship before her conversion as an L.S.I.

and experience of Operation 'Torch' in North Africa and subsequent moonlighter passages on that coast had proved their resolution and good marksmanship. Having that in mind, I was inclined to overlook such minor faults as untidiness in dress and occasional departure from the accepted patterns of uniform behaviour, but it could be agreed that their standards in that respect invited criticism when the larger body of naval ratings was embarked. Commander Stephen Norris of the naval party was the 'bloke' whose word was law with the navy men on proper dress. He foresaw difficulty in a slackness I thought more apparent than real, and there was point in his contention. But I was far from agreement on a strictly naval control in the matter. I would take measures through Lieutenant Cleare, R.N.V.R., who had newly been signed with us as the ship's gunnery officer. It was my business to work the ship if attacked and Dems came under my orders for that purpose. Smilingly, the Commander concurred: but it can be doubted if it was wholly our ship measures that brought about the gunners newly trim appearance. I learned that—on 'liberty days' when we lay anchored in Loch Fyne and the Gareloch—the regulating P.O. at the gangway was under orders to refuse transport to any naval rating or Maritime R.A. gunner improperly dressed. The sumptuary act included such improvements as hair-cutting and facial lustration that, in merchant ship practice, I was powerless to impose! . . . By such adjustments and the quick establishment of a mutual liking, we steadied up together to serve a useful purpose in Combined Operations.

*   *   *

I had thought that Marymount, a villa on the brow of the hill above Gourock Pier, would be the place for Convoy Conference, for such assembly before sailing was usually held there. But there was reminiscence of the briefing before 'Operation Torch' in the summons to attend on board Admiral Vian's flagship, H.M.S. *Hilary*, then lying off Greenock, to be served with final instructions. Recalling the proceedings in *Narkunda* before sailing towards Algiers, I was in expectation of no more than a general instruction in convoy procedure and the receipt of 'Sealed Orders'. Certainly the great bulk of the files for Operation 'Husky', that we took on identification and signature, were as yet reserved for study when at sea, but there did not seem to be the want of confidence in the shipmaster's discretion that was notable in the North Africa landings. Perhaps our small numbers, (we were only twelve merchantmen in a much larger group of naval officers), and the probability that we were already well vetted by close association, had something to do with a new and gratifying trust in us. We did not need to guess and whisper this time. We were given the target at first glance, for there on the bulkhead of the operations room was the wall map of a sandy bay on the south-east coast of Sicily with our lines from seaward converging on Chiappa.

Chapter XXI

OPERATION HUSKY

UNLIKE the typescript of normal sailing orders, the great Volumes I and II of Operation 'Husky' were fully printed in letter type, illustrated by maps and diagrams, and clipped together in sailor manner with cord and toggle. In constant and attentive reading I had admired their lucid phrases, clear directions—even what came to be known as 'The Child's Guide' to operations, doubtless propounded for such civilian combatants as I. I had thought that everything and every step had been covered in it, and was surprised when, two days at sea and fine weather our portion, S.N.O.T. delivered to me a final message from the Admiralty. (Yes. That is right. The Senior Naval Officer, Transport, was Lieut. Adams, R.N., whose duty was to act as a link between the Navy and the merchantmen in the ship. His adenoidal description—that was very far from application to a very alert and helpful officer—was later altered to N.L.O., which is Naval Liaison Officer.) The envelope was addressed to the Masters of Allied Merchant Ships, it was marked 'personal' and was signed by Admiral of the Fleet Sir A. B. Cunningham, C.-in-C. of the Allied Naval Forces in the Mediterranean. It began—'The operation you are being called upon to undertake has as its object the assault and capture of the Island of SICILY as a base for future operations against the AXIS powers.' Its concluding paragraph was:

This is a great operation, the greatest seaborne attack that has so far taken place in history. It may have a decisive influence upon the course of the war. A great part of its success is entrusted to the well-proved steadfastness and seamanlike skill of the Merchant Navies of the Allies, whom I am proud to have under my command in this momentous task.

Between these two paragraphs there was brief detail of the magnitude of the assault, of great Task Forces converging upon

Sicily from Bombay and the Middle East, from Alexandria and Tripoli, Malta, North Africa, the United Kingdom and—non-stop—from the United States of America. The strength of naval and air support was briefly indicated. There was reassurance in Para. 17.—'The maximum possible air protection will be given to shipping. It must, however, be realised that much of this protection will be given indirectly by attacks on remote enemy air bases to prevent his aircraft from taking off the ground. It should not therefore be entirely judged by the number of aircraft actually visible over convoys and anchorages.'

Seldom has an inspiring message been more happily composed. One could take confidence from it, or that I thought as, on D day minus 1 and about 65 miles southward of Malta, we made exact rendezvous with the slower munitions and store ships of our joint convoy. All were not there. We did not need to count them for we had already learned that K.M.S. 18 had come under submarine attack and three of its ships had been torpedoed and lost. We had had early news of the casualties. In contrast with our ignorance of events on former convoy passages, our newly-installed Communications Branch could even pick the starters in the 3 o'clock out of the air. The news of the sinkings aroused special and apparent concern amongst the senior officers of the Canadian First Division on board. In this connection, I take the liberty of quoting from a friend's good book. Colonel Dick Malone was Brigade Major (Second Brigade of the First Canadian Division) and was on passage with us. In his book—*Missing from the Record*—he writes of the incidents:

Personnel and equipment of all units had to be dispersed throughout the entire series of ships. In the event that one or two ships were lost on the way we should still have sufficient types of personnel and equipment on the remainder to carry on. We did lose three ships by torpedoing off Gibraltar. Quickly we checked our loading lists to see what had gone down. We had lost some of our 25-pounders, some of our anti-tank guns, the General's caravans . . . but worst of all, included in those ships had been our entire complement of wireless vehicles. It was a bad bit of luck and left us with only small pack wireless sets as means of communication with our troops when on shore. There were many such problems one could wonder about while walking around the deck of the ship waiting for D day on the coast of Sicily.

The ships and escort of K.M.F. 18 were not the only vessels in sight as we approached the rendezvous south of Malta. The weather was exceptionally clear and almost one could see an active and living reproduction of the diagram plate, called 'Mickey Mouse', in the chart of the course marked 1200 hrs. D day minus 1. On that plate in 'Husky' instructions, the red lines that indicated the projected daily estimated positions of the many forces and convoys converged upon a pinpoint on the chart.

As we steamed on in the forenoon of 9th July and joined formation with the ships of our sister convoy, the masts and upperworks of distant vessels grew on the horizon on both sides and abeam: to starboard the Forces from Alexandria and the East, to port the overseas armadas from the United States. The spearhead, so long in the forging, at last was pointed.

Almost as though the windy gods thought our fortune in the weather too good for us, it worsened just after we had met together. In the sudden way of the Mediterranean, a moderate gale was aroused and a heavy westerly sea arose quickly when in the evening we rounded the westernmost point of the Maltese islands and set course for the beach on Sicily fifty miles away. A force of British cruisers joined us there. There was much signalling and radio telephone asides between the ships and it could be surmised that the state of the weather caused grave disquiet amongst the senior officers. Within *Circassia* there were opinions that the whole operation might be 'stymied' on account of the weather. The wind was about N.W. by N. force 7, but a plot on the chart of the beaches showed that the 'release' position to which Force V was bound would be—to a degree—sheltered by the high mountain ridge inland. There was, of course, the probability that the sea swell there would still be considerable and a broken surf on the beaches was to be expected. I held the opinion that the wind would lessen after sunset and this was later borne out, but it would be idle to deny that there was apprehension as night came on. What was to be done if a landing could not be made? There was no chapter on retreat in all the bulky pages of 'Husky'!

About one hour after sunset the wind decreased considerably. The sea and swell did not as quickly subside, but there seemed a sensible lessening in its range. We had the moon at first-quarter and even after moonset the weather was so clear that we had no difficulty in maintaining station by the eye. The Italians had developed an uncanny skill in laying contact mines in incredibly deep water. A field was rumoured to exist somewhere on our line of course. To meet that possibility, the convoy was disposed in two columns—a long snake-line of not less than six sea miles and H.M. Minesweepers *Cadmus, Circe* and *Hebe* had been sent ahead to sweep the waters in advance. The dim blue lights on their Oropesa floats, sheering on the surface, were comforting in the circumstances. We were the second ship in Column One with only the flagship, H.M.S. *Hilary*, ahead. On the starboard bow and leading Column Two was the powerful H.M.S. *Roberts*, a monitor mounting fifteen inch guns. For a time we had smaller vessels in company. They were the auxiliary landing ships and craft, flak-ships, tank carriers, tugs, and munition barges that had been spurred from the harbours of Malta towards their date and were labouring gallantly in the adverse wind and sea to fulfil it.

I had thought it possible that we would come under attack when, at about midnight, flares were seen low down on the horizon or landline ahead. It was known that the enemy had mounted several batteries of heavy artillery on the coastline in the vicinity of the target beaches and it seemed inconceivable that our progress and to what destination was unknown to him by this time. When the flares sprang up we on the navigation bridge thought that matters were drawing to some head, but the voice of the I.F.F. observer at that moment reported many aircraft he identified as friendly to us, in the direction of the land. The beams of shore-established searchlights suddenly streamed upwards in the sky ahead and we realised that our own assaulting aircraft were busy on their appointed task. How well that task was done, we in the ships, appreciated. A heavy and sustained bombing raid developed over the distant land and from the volume of defensive ack-ack fire, that we could see but not hear, it was apparent that the area was well alerted. But not a single searchlight beam was fingered in our direction and we steamed on in confidence that the enemy was otherwise engaged. The time was fifteen minutes past midnight: we were into D day and with H hour (which was the date for 'touch down' on the beaches) only seventy minutes away.

For some time the silence in the ship had been broken at regular intervals by a stout Canadian voice on the ship's P.A. system (Public Address). It came from the orderly room and was telling off the commando troops to take their places in the landing craft. It was firm, even, and unhurried. It said— 'Attention plaze. Attention plaze. Serial Numbers . . . go to Boat Station'. Then silence for a brief period in which, if one took a squint off from lookout ahead, a long line of dim figures could be made out on the decks below, a single file in which each man rested one hand on the shoulder of his next ahead. Lights had been extinguished in the troop decks so that the men's eyes should grow to the darkness. Long practised, this drill was found both neat and accurate in action. Recalling the substantial supper provided before 'Attention plaze' it was a comforting thought that our men were well fed and watered before embarking on their big adventure.

Very soon it became clear that our aircraft had a much more serious purpose than that of keeping the enemy searchlights upright and busy for our benefit. One of the first objectives of our Force's assault was the taking of the aerodrome at Paccino, a small hill town overlooking the bay, and by our reckoning it was over that point a major blitz was raging. As we drew on towards our 'release' position, recurrent tremors in the ship indicated the burst of heavy bombs on the shore line and we could now hear the *thudd* of distant great explosions. Considerable fire from the ground was erupting, but this did not last for very long. Just at about the moment we were signalled to

Clyde anchorage: 1943

anchor, it was seen that our air force had lit up a notable beacon for the fleets: a medium glare above the line of the shore, six or seven miles distant, grew quickly to an enormous blaze and we knew that the town or aerodrome at Paccino was furiously alight. The torch had been carried into Europe. Strangely, there was still apparently no finger on the trigger in the coastal batteries.

At 0039, 10th July (which was one minute early) we were told to anchor. This was a manoeuvre we had practised on many occasions during exercises in home waters and all with varying degrees of performance. The art of stopping, backing, and anchoring together in a group of closely-following ships is not one that is ever learned in commercial sailoring. Under normal conditions it could be a fairly simple proceeding—but not within the narrow ribbon of a swept channel. The ships were of many types, each with her own manner of idling when steerage way was lost. Some turned to the wind, others fell off and held the wind abeam. Although clear, it was now quite dark and only the bulk of the nearer ships could be made out. There was too the difficulty and delay of passing dimmed signals down the six mile line, for not all of the merchant ships were supple-mented, as we were, by expert naval signalmen. Despite the handicaps we brought up, as I think, in better formation than on any of the exercises and I heard of no collision. All was done in very complete silence, the anchors being payed out and not cast. Close upon the execution of the 'Anchor!' signal, the whine of our craft winches broke the long silence in the ship and the first wave of assault troops was lowered and sent away. The other ships were as prompt: their craft formed up on us as a departure point, their officers and cox'ns calling out flotilla numbers as they passed. Breathing a prayer, I thought the lines of plunging small craft looked insignificant and forlorn as they vanished in the darkness: but well I knew the great heart in them.

With our first wave launched and away, there ensued a period of apprehensive quiet and with all eyes bent in the direction they had gone. Paccino was still blazing fiercely and from that illumination glints were reflected on the masts and funnels of the nearer shipping. One wondered if some keen-sighted observer on the beach could not fail to discern strangers offshore and rouse an alarm, but nothing happened and we lay silently within effective range of his batteries. There was no one amongst the senior officers on the bridge who did not know the exact time of H hour but, curiously, no one seemed to re-member that it was still many minutes ahead. Again and again we peered through binoculars at the now darkened land ahead—for our bombers were at last inactive over the beaches—looking for sign of action that was not yet due for performance. Our impatience was tempered by the release of our remaining land-ing craft in which the second wave of supporting commandos were embarked, and that too was taken by the darkness; but for long in the dying wind we could hear the roar then the hum and the whisper of their powerful engines as they sped away at their best speed.

With the flotillas away, we turned active and busy within the ship mustering the remaining troops and arranging their gear and equipment for quick off-loading. We had carried in all about 2500 troops and, with 500 disembarked there was still the considerable 'movement' required to put the larger body on shore. For this, the instructions laid down a ferry service that was to be made by L.C.T. (Landing Craft, Tanks), and the larger troop-carrying barges. Where they were to come from could not easily be determined from the lengthy schedules, but one could guess at their inclusion amongst the fleet of smaller vessels that had, for a time, accompanied us from the vicinity of Malta. At three in the morning, the first of these drew along-side and, not without difficulty, the transfer of the men was begun. However well designed to land large numbers of infantry—indeed artillery, tanks, trucks—on the beaches, the vessels were not very well adapted to embark them from a high-sided ocean transport. Troops had to clamber down the ship's hull using the fitted rungs at the sally-ports or—with greater danger and mistrust—the 'scramble nets' that we had unrolled overside. The swell aroused by the recent gale was still con-siderable thus far at sea. On occasion, as the ferry craft surged in it alongside, the mooring fasts carried away, and the lighter vessel sheered off whilst new stern ropes were run out and thrown aboard: during that brief period, the side of the ship was black with men struggling to maintain hand-grip and foothold whilst awaiting a chance to jump with prospect of safe landing on the deck of the tender. There were some broken limbs amongst our men—whom we recovered on board to the ship's hospital—but casualties were surprisingly few. Operations were still governed by a partial silence, but at 0330 the 'SUCCESS' signal that we had so eagerly been awaiting came through in green lights springing up along the shoreline. The beaches had been secured and the R.M. commandos from the *Derbyshire* and *Glengyle* had taken the batteries with small loss. At this good news it was possible to accelerate the proceedings by the use of lights—discreetly shaded from the shoreward side.

Almost at the moment the green lights, on a point we thought was Castellazzo, had been displayed the lions of the Fleet woke up and roared. The hitherto quiet of the night was shattered by a first salvo from H.M.S. *Roberts* that lay three cables from the *Circassia* and heavy fire was joined by other warships. I can confess that I should have known better than to be on the bridge in trousers, shirt, a loose pyjama jacket, and without gun-fire plugs in my ears, but the night was hot and sultry and I was eager to listen to the sounds of conflict. The personal shock was wounding and painful and the blast like whiplash through my scanty clothing. The apprehension of awaiting a second salvo was even worse, for it was long of coming but continued at intervals that seemed to indicate direction by an observer on the land. We could not see the fall of shot until daylight came in; then we could make out large fragments of Sicily in the nor'west going up in dust.

As daylight grew and bearings could be taken we established our position and it was gratifying to find that we lay within a stone's throw (a fairly substantial one, I admit) of the spot in the Mediterranean that had been marked out for us in the great assault plan made so long before. The coast off which we lay was not quite new to me. In peacetime cruising voyages, one often deviates from the mercator line between ports, and on occasion I had steered close past Cape Passero to give the tourists a nearby view of a smiling stretch of Italian vineyard and pasture land. Almost right ahead of us there lay a small upstanding crust in the smooth white line of the sandy beach. Chiappa! In a hundred peacetime voyages one would never have remarked it. An insignificant brown crust, shaped not unlike the Old Man of Hoy. I recalled Convoy Conference in the *Hilary* when lying off Greenock before setting out. How the Staff Commander had so often tapped that position on the wall map with his pointer! Chiappa! We had made a good course into Europe.

But I had little time to follow upon retrospect and reflection. In the half daylight the escorting destroyers commenced to throw a smoke-screen around the ships and the land was quickly blotted out. In this protective screen the ships of Force V were signalled to weigh and follow the flagship into the inshore anchorage that had now been swept by the indefatigable mine-sweepers. It was a somewhat 'Snakes and Ladders' procession, we having to anchor and weigh again frequently. It could be surmised that these momentary halts were designed to hold us clear of the *Roberts*' range. She was still shelling some stubborn point far inland in the nor'west and the thunder of her big guns sounded perilously close. Although now equipped with ear protectors and adequate protective clothing, I found it physically impossible to restrain a nervous impulse at each succeeding blow . . . but noted that the naval officers who were with me on the bridge jumped as high as I. The weather had calmed. There were faint airs blowing from the land and the sea in the sheltered inshore waters were quiet. In these light airs the scent of lemon or orange groves could faintly be savoured though this was often overcome by acrid fumes when we passed through a patch, yellowish in colour against the white of the screen, that marked a position from which a salvo had been fired. The distance was not great and we had the masts of the *Hilary*, outstanding above the mist, to guide us.

Sunrise found us anchored close inshore off the Costa dell' Ambra and in sheltered waters. The smoke screen had been negatived and its vapours had wafted far to seaward, seeming to uproll as a window blind to reveal the great mass of shipping in the bay. The warships had ceased fire and lay quietly attentive to the movement when the distant munitions ships were ordered in to take up unloading berths under promising conditions. Far out at sea the destroyers of the Force could be seen patrolling in the rifts of vapour, on watch for the submarine attack that was hourly expected but, strangely, never engaged. On the land there was little sign of the night's invasion other than the crowded beaches and the long array of landing craft and L.S.T. stabbed into the sandy fringes of the shore. Above Paccino and at many points inland spirals of lazy smoke still uprose but these might have been normal on any day. From seaward we could not see the damage and destruction that the preparatory air attack had undoubtedly inflicted.

'Short stay' in sailor tongue has nothing to do with the period of a visit, but is the term used for being at anchor with the minimum of cable payed out. It is an insecure expedient, only employed in a particularly crowded anchorage and its feature is that steam must instantly be ready for emergencies. We were at 'short stay' when lying so close inshore and it was with growing anxiety I watched the incoming ships as they came to anchor so perilously near. An 'ammo' freighter let go just under *Circassia's* quarter. One is only allowed to collide once with an ammunition carrier and I was about to signal her to notify (in legal mercantile practice) that she was giving me a foul berth, when I remembered the only rebuke that so far I had had from Admiral Vian. That was at Greenock when we were attending Convoy Conference. I had offered a mild objection to carrying the paravanes—that are our protection against moored mines— in operation right up to the release position. 'What's wrong with that?' he asked. 'What's the odds about breaking up paravanes or having their gear foul an anchor? Paravanes are expendable . . . as we, you and me, and our ships all are . . . on this occasion.' But I was still disquieted as ship after ship was brought in until almost there seemed no way possible for our egress when we had landed out troops and their gear and reported ready for sea again. Curiously, Admiral Vian himself appeared almost as I recalled his naval point of view. I had often seen and admired a Flag Officer's barge, shining and immaculate and with the bowmen porting boathooks stiffly under the fluttering emblem of supreme authority in the area. But that was in peacetime and in harbour. I had not expected such a vision on the open sea and maybe under the guns of the enemy when I saw his barge snaking swiftly through the press of grey ships. Probably he was on a round of inspection for he did not come aboard but hailed us from alongside. He was satisfied to learn that Captain Black, our S.N.O.L., had already disembarked to join the beach forces on shore. From the Admiral's friendly manner, I took it that all was going well. I had the thought to speak of the congestion in my near vicinity. But no. We were expendable. I could find some way to hook or kedge my ship out of the press when we were ordered to weigh.

When anchored so close inshore we came within the working range of a military wireless set that had been installed near the navigation bridge. It was 'small pack', of the type that Major Malone considered so inadequate when he learned of the loss of equipment in the sinking of the *Devis*, *St. Essylt* and *City of Venice* off Gibraltar. By its agency, we learned that the wave of the assault we had helped to launch had rolled far inland before the sun arose. Paccino on the right flank and Solarino on the left had been taken and the Canadians were now well advanced on the roads towards Ragusa and beyond. The promise of paragraph 17 in the naval Commander-in-Chief's personal letter was well redeemed. We had air warnings aplenty whilst at the beach but no enemy aircraft were sighted over our place in Husky. Once, at about 1000 hrs. we saw concentrated shell burst in the air on a north-east bearing and concluded that a sister force was entertaining visitors on Barkeast beaches which were on the eastern side of Cape Passero, but that attack was momentary and did not extend.

The disembarkation of our remaining troops was quickly completed. *Circassia's* flotilla of L.C.A.—less one unit still grounded upon a beach obstruction—had returned from the adventure and was at once employed in ferry service much as we had practised it between our buoy in the Gareloch and the jetty at the Gully Bridge. It did not take long, but there was still the lengthier operation of unloading from our lower holds the bulk of miscellaneous troop and beach gear and equipment that was stowed below. We carried no heavy munition, but our lighter parcels—ranging from beach and roadway traffic signs (some of these were lettered in Italian), to cases of tablets for the purification of drinking water—made up in variety for what they lacked in poundage. As always, the military quartermasters had their second thoughts about priority and time was maybe lost in re-arrangements, but the work was carried on without serious delay.

It was not until almost the last barge was being loaded over-side that I recalled a promise I had made to Pipe-Major Esson of the Seaforth Highlanders of Canada: I was to see to it that the 'pipes and drums' of that fine Regiment were put on shore before we sailed. It was the least I could do in thankful appreciation of the many times the band had stirred our Scottish ship and crew by playing off the day at sunset in colourful 'Retreat'. It was not a simple matter to land the impedimenta, for there was opinion that a wartime regulation forbade the landing of regimental band instruments in operations. The pipes—the *Piobh Mor*—that could be disassembled and carried in hand, had gone, and might even at that moment be shrilling on the road to Ragusa, but the drums could not so easily be smuggled. Still, we had cased them up and one of the deckhands, facile with a paint-pot and sash-tool, had marked the case with the big drum in it—Medical Stores—and addressed to Colonel Hofmeister, The Seaforths. I think the letterer, who was a bright lad, may have heard the matters discussed, for, with the permanent O.C. Troops on board, there had been mild argument within his hearing. Quite uninstructed, he solved our doubts about the irregularity of the consignment by making it at once conform with orders and at the same time convey a heartfelt message to the troops who had sailed with us. Quickly, he lettered on the largest surface of the case that contained the big drum:

RETURN TO VANCOUVER, B.C., CANADA.

Chapter XXII

ACTION DEFERRED

In time of war idle ships are not popular in any scheme of naval direction. Valuable as they are in reserve, their supervision and berthage and protection are added responsibilities that the King's Harbour Masters are inclined to view without enthusiasm. Returned from the beach-head on Sicily to a congested and uneasy anchorage off the breakwaters at Valetta, the merchantmen of Force V were superfluous to requirements: unemployed now in the still great traffic between Malta and the new battle front, they took up space in the limited anchorage area (which was unprotected from seaward) and demanded attention that could more usefully be exerted in the urgent despatch of the smaller vessels and craft now largely engaged. Our part in 'Operation Husky', so long prepared and planned and exercised, was apparently concluded for it was in orders that all its many files of secret instructions were to be destroyed by burning and a certificate returned that this measure of security had been carried out. Force V had served its turn and it was some thing to know that the commandos and troops it had landed in the black of the night had forced the door. But we were empty now and such a large convoy of vulnerable transports lying-to in the open Mediterranean could not be allowed to remain there at risk. Permission to anchor was approved, but the signal was accompanied by an injunction to maintain steam in readiness for immediate departure. Further orders would be sent off to the ships.

We had opportunity in this waiting period to survey from shipboard the scars of the long siege the ancient city of Valetta had borne and withstood. The old knights had built well. It was almost inconceivable that so great and closely-joined a mass of habitations could live again after such a devastation, but amidst the ruin and the rubble the remaining battlements and spires and towers looked all the loftier and more proudly erect, outstanding from the huge mounds of shattered masonry. The Grand Harbour was obstructed by many wrecks, reminders of all the perils of harbourage under air bombardment, but channels had been cleared and an almost unending procession of storeships, fuel tenders, truck and tank carriers, ammunition ships, passed outward towards the distant front. The naval signal station, above the *auberge* of the Knights of Castile, damaged and in part destroyed, still functioned and from its high platform our signals had come. There, the flagmast, surmounted by the White Ensign, was gay with the hoist and rehoist of bunting whose messages controlled the passage of the outbound ships in the harbour below. We could see the watchers there at their posts, scanning all movement in the port and at sea. They would be in high spirit now—with the knowledge that the craft they were sending out to sea had the prospect of tying up at the quayside in the captured port of Syracusa instead of a precarious unloading offshore at the beach-head, and it was even rumoured that Augusta was also in our hands. Perhaps, as the signalmen peered out, they would now contrast the unhindered flow of traffic in the Grand Harbour with the isolation and emptiness they had known in the beleaguered years when only the sky was tenanted and that so often by the concentrated air forces of the enemy. It was almost at sunset when we received our new orders, brought out to us by a speedy picket-boat, and the sound of the bugles on the parapet of Saint Angelo came clear over the water as we hove up and headed eastward towards Suez.

After the stir and animation that had prevailed within the ship for so long, the emptiness of our decks now emphasised an absence of purpose in the voyage as the convoy steered south-eastward to the Canal. We had thought to turn west again when the landing was effected, to return to home waters and there embark the reinforcements that the campaign in Italy would require. But other considerations had pointed the jack-staff on the stem and where we would next be called upon to urge it seemed far beyond our speculations.

The Bay of Suez in July and August is a mean place for an anchored sailor. The port is one of passage and there are few amenities in the distant town to tempt the seaman to a turn on shore. Even the breathtaking beauty of sunrise or sunset on the colourful but barren plateau of Jebel Attakah, under which we lay, grew tiresome by constant and unvarying repetition and the passing of the days without word of further employment brought the fine spirit that had been with us in the days of action to a drab acceptance of our lot. The weather too was almost unbearably hot. For a time, an effort was made to combat the lassitude by promoting athletic exercise on the nearby sandy desert, but the dribbling of a football there did not long appeal. An attempt was made by Commander Norris (who had succeeded Captain Black as S.N.O.L.) to keep his naval party active by removal from the ship to tents in a camp on shore, but the heat there was even greater than with us in the Bay and the major plague of Egypt—the foul and noisome flies—quickly drove them back on board. There was news when the navy returned to the ship. Nothing official, rumour had it that the ships were being held for a landing operation further east when the sou'west monsoon, then raging in the Indian Ocean, had died down. Some days later support for this belief was enlarged when H.M.S. *Bulolo* anchored amongst us. Formerly a merchant ship, she had become famous as a landing 'ferret' and had played a leading part in many seaborne assaults of which she had been the flagship. In the rounds of ship visits that followed upon arrival we learned that we had become Force R and would be employed under Rear Admiral Peters. We would be exercised for a time with troops of the Indian Army in the Gulf of Suez. No arts of conversation could carry us on from that and we were left to speculate amongst ourselves upon the relative and tactical importance of the Andaman Islands or the Nicobars in the Bay of Bengal which were then held by the Japanese.

It was a relief to be at useful work again and there was a quick rekindling of an earlier zest when we engaged in practice landings on the barren shores of the Gulf. It was quickly evident that *Circassia* and the other ships converted in the United Kingdom were not well adapted to the carriage of native Indian soldiers. The domestic manner of cooking their own food, the aversion to sailor hammocks, the tribal habits in ablution and sanitation of the sepoys were not those for which we were equipped. Open cooking fires on deck, which seemed an expedient, were manifestly out of question in secret landing operations. The wash-places and appliances could not immediately be altered and high taboos were thus affronted for we embarked mixed battalions of Sikhs, Hindus, and Mahommedans for training. For a time we were makeshift in an odd routine (that included the provision of wire screens at the long cooking stoves, set up to segregate the sects in preparation of their foods)—but we did manage to accustom them to ship life, to amphibious operations and to landing on a beach that was simulated hostile by a variety of noisy fireworks.

Troops were mostly veterans of the campaigns in Eritrea and Ethiopia who had been retained in Egypt and the Sudan after Mussolini's legions had surrendered. They were splendid soldiers. Being lithe and agile, their footwork when embarking in a heaving craft alongside was marked by a surety few commandos could excel. Disdaining the iron rungs fitted as scaling ladders on the hull (which the European troops preferred) they swarmed on the 'scramble' nets with ease and were quickly all aboard. Once afloat and away, however, their soldierly bearing was not quite as strongly maintained for the *kali pani* (deep water) they thought unfriendly. In this connection, shipboard chatter had it that the flotilla crews preferred to carry the Mahommedans in their L.C.A. when the sea was rough, for they were said to be less prone to pay tribute to Neptune than the vegetarian Hindus and Sikhs! It was the practice to land the troops during the night or in the early hours of the morning. We did not re-embark them. They had to make their own way in the desert and over the hills to a rendezvous on the coast near Suez and were then barged off to the ship. In these long marches they were aided in communications by using 'walkie-talkie' wireless sets, which were then new to us. I had long known that Asiatics were credited with prodigious feats of memory but had not expected a somewhat simple-looking Jat sepoy of their Signals Corps to be thus endowed. His British officer was proud of the man and invited me to speak out from the bridge when the troops were mustered at Boat Stations. The only suggestion he made was that I should use short phrases and pronounce them in a tone of command. When the muster was dismissed an hour later, the signaller was brought up and repeated, word for word, all that I had said. While I could only remember the purport of my short address at the transmitter and had to rely upon a written memorandum for confirmation, the sepoy had recalled the sound of it. It was *that* he repeated, for I was assured that he knew little if any English!

Early in September we sailed to Bombay. The great rains of the sou'west monsoon had not abated nor had the gales and high seas gone down. It was clear that the time was not yet seasonable for a landing operation, wherever intended, in the east. We had sober thoughts of another distasteful period at anchor, swinging the tides, and doubtless far offshore in the harbour. But we were spared that wearisome assignment by being ordered to sea again soon after arrival. A considerable movement of troops was in progress and, with the *Ascania* for company, we reverted to normal troop transport duties between Mombasa and Colombo. Forces were being assembled in Ceylon—for operations in Burma, it was said—and the carriage of East Africans to a jungle-training centre on the island kept both ships busily employed until recalled to Bombay in November.

There had been changes in Force R since our detachment. Rear Admiral Troubridge had relieved Vice Admiral Peters, and there had been a new grouping of the merchant ships formerly attached to the force. Only three of the original L.S.I. were retained, but the convoy was supplemented by the inclusion of the *Winchester Castle, Empire Pride* and the Polish ships *Batory* and *Sobieski*. With the naval ships, H.M.S. *Glengyle* and *Karen*, we formed a compact group capable of a 'lift' of nearly 20,000 men. The naval party on board had been strengthened by Signals and Beach Control to bring the detachment up to operational numbers. *Circassia* and *Ascania* had been adapted to meet the caste requirements of the Indian Army. Thus equipped we engaged again in training cruises on the Malabar coast. In these exercises it became apparent that one of the objectives was to make shipboard familiar and tolerable to the native troops and, to that end, there was frequent exchange of the personnel embarked. From that policy the crews of the ships shared a dividend that did much to offset the monotony of the training programme, for the ships were regularly brought in from offshore to a berth at the sea wall to disembark and re-embark the drafts of the military. In this proceeding there was opportunity for liberty to be granted and the recreations of a pleasant port enjoyed.

Action seemed imminent when the ships, one by one, were placed in dry-dock to have the accumulation of shell and barnacle removed from the underwater hulls—a measure that would normally have been put off until next arrival in the United Kingdom. But the rapid growth of tropical waters had already reduced the speed of the ships and a cleansing was needful. When all had thus been groomed we were assembled in the bay for inspection by the naval commander-in-chief. Our state of readiness was remarked in a short address by Sir James Somerville that ended—as we thought—with the phrases that speed men out to do a task at sea. Even the lean British brigadiers who accompanied him on the rounds and who had watched our training exercises with shrewd appraisal had come to look upon the Red Ensign with a new respect. We could await final sailing orders with confidence.

When sailing orders did come they differed vastly from our expectations. The decisive conference of the great Allied powers had been held at Teheran and it was doubtless as one of its vital decisions Force R was ordered to point its jack-staffs west instead of east and proceed with all despatch to the Mediterranean. . . . Matters had not gone according to plan on the Italian front and there was the call for another seaborne assault there. Action on 'Operation Q for Query' was deferred.

Chapter XXIII

OPERATION SHINGLE

OUR 'tally' had again been altered and it was as Force P we arrived at Naples in January, 1944. There was then a temporary separation of the units. 'Operation Shingle' was to be mounted by the United States and the landing would come under American naval command. It differed from former operations where a lengthy sea voyage preceded the beach assault. Wherever this landing was intended, its target could not be at great distance from the Bay of Naples for it was apparently to be engaged without full employment of all the large troop-carrying L.S.I. The vast flotillas of smaller beaching craft could be *combat-loaded* in port before sailing and thus eliminate the transfer of seaborne men and their weapons, their tanks and trucks and trimmings, on arrival off the beach-head. But it would still be necessary to secure initial foothold there before the mass landing and for that the American rangers and specially-trained combat troops (the equivalent of our commandos) were still employed. Three large L.S.I., being self-sufficient in beach landing craft, were detailed to launch that spearhead of attack, and the *Winchester Castle, Circassia* and *Ascania* were detached from Force P and placed at the orders of the American Admiral. The other ships of the Force were retained by Admiral Troubridge for a simultaneous assault by British troops whose target beaches were not then disclosed to us. The ships thus detached were instructed to engage in exercises with the great flotilla of Allied smaller ships and craft then assembled within the Italian coastal ports that extended from Pozzuoli in the west to Castellamare. In that period of preparation we became familiar with many strange vessels that had newly been designed for seaborne assault. The conspiratorial form of initial surprise attack, using L.C.A. on the naked beach, was still the opening gambit, but experience gained in the Far East, in North Africa and at Sicily had promoted the use of larger Trojan Horses that could beach themselves on the enemy's doorstep and from hinged bows disgorge a sizeable force of armed men in tanks and carriers.

There were three main classifications in the invasion fleets, Ships, Craft and Craft Vehicles. All were lettered on the bows to indicate their purpose and so many were the varied employments that a sub-division into brackets was common. The initial prefix was letter 'L' for Landing: 'S', following, indicated a ship of over 200 feet in length, and 'C', for craft, a vessel of lesser size. 'V', for Vehicle, may seem an odd misnomer for a buoyant craft, but there were many types of amphibians engaged—designed, like Cancer, to be equally at home on sea or land. These ranged from maritime armoured tanks weighing twelve tons and capable of navigating at three knots in smooth water to DUKWS, Jeeps, and Terrapin, of a light and handy character. It was the concluding letter of the label painted on their bows that indicated a vessel's purpose and capacity, and the whole alphabet seemed hardly large enough for necessary tabulation. 'D', for Docking, was a sizeable ship, containing within her lengthy hull a sufficient tanked basin having removable watertight doors at the stern by which ingress and egress of maritime ship casualties could be controlled. Often there is danger and hardship in bringing a damaged vessel to port for repair; it seemed a sensible if unusual proceeding to sail a fully-equipped dry-dock towards the area of not unexpected disaster. 'F', for Flak, bristled with anti-aircraft weapons, whilst 'G', for Guns, was a quickly mobile strong point that could be brought into action close inshore where her battery of 4-inch guns could be impressively employed. With most of the assembled vessels we had no great difficulty in recognising their part in operations and the manner of playing it, but one long and curious craft marked 'R' aroused much speculation as she came to anchor amongst us. Even such experts as Captain Norris and Lieut. Cleare (the latter our ship's D.E.M.S. Gunnery Officer) could not quite divine the purpose of 'hedge-hog' rows of upstanding pipes on her long foredeck. That they had to do with rocket projection seemed obvious, but the manner and volume in which they could be fired from a built-in structure—that could not be ranged or trained—was productive of lively argument.

The majority of the ships and craft assembled in the harbours and in the bay was American but many were under the White Ensign. In addition to the descriptive lettering on the bows, all had serial numbers and it was in pride and wonderment we noted numerals mounting to nearly a thousand. Wherever the assault was intended there would be a great host wading in from the sea on D day. Having completed our exercises with the fleets off the Volturno River and in the Gulf of Salerno, we returned to Naples to embark 'Combat' troops of the 3rd. U.S. Division and—on the 20th January—were summoned to a final conference before sailing on operations.

It was right that these formidable new landing ships and craft with their fearful devices should be serviced and com-manded by young men, and youth was the essence of the gathering at Naval Headquarters in the Via Partenope. Or so I thought as we sat together in what may have been a university classroom there and glanced around at my fellows in the enterprise. All were young and many very young. On board his ship the Master is not often reminded of his years. By custom he is known as 'the Old Man' whatever his age may be and the adjective has only the significance of an admitted seniority. But, seated again on the students' bench and with platform and rostrum fronting me, I had not the familiar ship atmosphere to establish me in such youthful company. What was I doing in a gathering like this and what fellowship had I with these eager young men in the anticipation of adventure? I felt oddly out of place, somewhat miscast for even a minor part in the enterprise.

Before the conference began, and as a measure of security, we were called upon to examine the credentials of each neighbour to left and right. Possibly Rotarian in origin, it was a friendly form both of challenge and self-introduction. On my right, there was no need for recognition for my brother officers from Force P sat there, but on the left, a young American officer who could not have been more than twenty proffered his identity card. He held it out rather shyly, almost as though he thought the action an intrusion. I had no such official document to offer in return but he accepted the signal that had summoned me to the meeting and confidence was established. There was opportunity for a brief exchange of courtesies whilst the wall maps were being unrolled and the charts displayed. In the open American manner of losing no time in the welding of a new friendship, my neighbour came quickly to number me amongst his intimates. He seemed slightly in awe of my ship's tonnage and confided that he was only a small-boat sailor. But she was a good boat and he was proud of her. His vessel was an L.C.S. (Landing Craft, Support) and he was happy in praise of her power and capabilities. She was of very light draught and he was hopeful of using her armament in an advanced position on the beach-head. . . . No. Not long. He had only been in the Navy for about sixteen months. . . . But he had sailed small boats . . . oh . . . ever since he could remember. . . . Yes. He was from Boston—but how did I know that? . . . Oh. Accent, perhaps, or some turn of the words. Yes. I knew Boston and had many friends there. I too had sailed small boats on Boston Bay. Did he know—recalled from our confidences by stir on the platform, we gave our attention to the business of the meeting. But I was strangely fortified. I liked the lad's friendliness, his good manners, his interests and enthusiasms. I did not feel so very old or out of place or alien now in this community. There might be a call for Bartimeus. I could 'get by' in such company.

As we had surmised, 'Shingle' was to be a near exploit. It was to be launched behind the German front on the night of the 21st–22nd against the towns of Anzio and Nettuno, only one hundred miles distant by sea from Naples. The landing would be made at two in the morning of the 22nd on a strip of marsh-lands of the Littorio Maritimo that lay twenty-nine miles due south of Rome. The beaches there had a favourable gradient of 1 : 80 with very few outlying and submerged rocks, but the whole area was strongly fortified. The lecturer, a young naval commander of the United States Navy, paused in his restless pacing of the platform, took his hands out of his pockets and referred to his notes. He seemed unsure of how many dangers to disclose, for eager young eyes were focussed on his, but went on to speak of beach mines and a retaining wall that ran east between Anzio and Nettuno and on which many strong machine-gun posts had been identified. On the rising ground inland the enemy had established heavier defences, said to be 150 to 205 mm. artillery that could range the beach and transport area, but it was not known with certainty that the batteries were continuously manned. A number of mobile guns, mounted on rail-trucks, could be served from the railway that ran parallel with the beach near Anzio. An important objective of the 'rangers' who were to be landed on that 'Yellow' beach would be to secure the mouth of the tunnel where the railway under-ran the grounds of the Villa Borghese. In continuation of his text, the lecturer disclosed the area of the British simultaneous landing on the beaches west of Anzio and that brought him to detail of our part in the operation.

H.M. Ships *Royal Ulsterman* and *Princess Beatrix* with the *Winchester Castle* were to land troops on this beach and capture Anzio; L.S.T. in great number would transport men to the central 'Red' beach and take Nettuno; *Circassia* and *Ascania* were the only large vessels to be employed on 'Green' beach, the most easterly in the assault, where we would be centred amongst the smaller landing craft and our duty would be to land the first two 'waves' of the assault. With the *Ascania* we would have a post of distinction on the eastern flank—outstanding amongst the small craft. As the lecturer turned his page on that, the unwarlike thought occurred to at least one of his listeners that there we would be a mountain of a target for the enemy's heavy batteries if we could not clear before daybreak.

When the general outlines of the operation had been made clear, Admiral F. J. Lowry, U.S.N., who commanded the sea operations, had some hard words for us concerning the exercises we had already engaged in offshore. He admitted the adverse circumstance of a sudden N.E. gale in the Gulf of Salerno that made difficulties, but added that adverse circumstance was exactly what we were all in the war to overcome. From his flagship, U.S.S. *Biscayne*, he had formed a poor view of our abilities. Delay, due to bad weather or other causes could be met by a decision to retard H hour: a general signal could be made to that effect . . . but the sequence of the assault must still be maintained. What had caused him grave concern in the course of the exercises was that so little initiative and resource had been shown in preserving the serial character of the operations: it would be fatal to land the men or material out of turn so closely was the one linked with the other. We would have to do better. He concluded with a reminder that this would be no exercise, no ranging shot with opportunity to fire again.

We—of the larger transports—had no definite knowledge of the incidents to which he referred. Having speed in reserve, we had been able to meet without difficulty the strong head winds in the Gulf when we exercised, but the smaller craft had perhaps been pressed beyond reasonable limits.

*   *   *

In convoy, the 'rate of overhaul' is an easy calculation, for the standard speed of the other ships is known; but the 'rate'— by which is meant the interval of time in which a fast ship overtakes a slower vessel proceeding in the same direction—can be an alarming consideration in the black of night when the speed of many strange vessels that come suddenly in sight is a matter of guesswork. That was our experience when, being within the narrow limits of the channel that minesweepers had newly cleared for passage of the assault fleets, *Circassia* and *Ascania* had to be snaked past countless ships to gain place at the tapeline and at the scheduled date. I suppose there could be sound reasons for the order that held us at anchor until nearly all the other ships had sailed. But the 'last shall be first' was quoted to apply in our case, and it was now needful to press on with dispatch. Before sailing from the anchorage under Nisida, we had spent the bright morning hours watching the procession of other ships and craft with their escorts passing endlessly out to

Merchant gunners at the 'ready'. (George Anderson, A.B. and Lawrence Halcrow, steward, of the S.S. *Highlander*; both commended for gallantry in action: August, 1940)

sea, timed for departure in groups and convoys of equal speeds towards an almost simultaneous arrival off Anzio. Now, with vision alarmingly restricted by a dark and moonless night—and all ships unlighted—it was with less enthusiasm we numbered our consorts in the adventure as we overtook and passed them in the mine-swept channel that was not even marked for margin. I would confess to great anxiety in the course of that short midnight passage, for it seemed so much a negation of every standard of prudent navigation that I had learned to trust. All seamanlike precaution except keen lookout and the sudden use of helm was denied to us. With our date and position at the beach-head so firmly insisted, we could not slow down or stop; nor could we swing wide for clearance into dangerous water that had not been swept for mines. Continuously, we had to shave past the smaller ships and craft—so small and almost indistinguishable, like drift-wood on the dark of the sea, as made out suddenly from a high bridge. Often we were bullied by Yankee loud-speakers (almost in the way a Bronx taximan does in crowded traffic) when our displacement wave threw its crown of spray and broken water over someone's low look-out. Only one factor was favourable—that we were all heading the same way. It seemed in the manner of a miracle we touched nothing on the passage. What Captain Grattige of the *Ascania* who was following our movements at two cables distance astern, thought of our wavy progress I could only imagine. But I think that he too, when he had mopped a heated brow after anchoring quietly in a position within open range of the German artillery, would thank God for the relief.

In the darkness we could not see the land that is there a low-lying plain extending to the foothills of the high Lepini ranges. But there was no sign of activity on the bearing where we knew the land to lie. Occasionally, a dim blue horizontal flash caused apprehension that the enemy was alert and manning his heavy batteries, but quickly it died away without incident and we were left to guess at nothing more deadly than tramway traffic on the distant Anzio-Acciarella road that was the primary objective of the American 'ranger' and 'combat' troops—the equivalent of our commandos—then embarking in the ship's landing craft. We had learned by now that silence in offshore operations served little purpose and could even be a dispiriting burden to carry into assault and the embarkation of the G.Is., stepping into the L.C.A. at deck level and in readiness to be lowered away, was marked by high-strung jest and 'wise-crack'. At Number Two, which lay housed near the navigation bridge, there was apparently a former elevator attendant amongst the armed men. The similitude of the operation of lowering the craft to his civilian employment prompted him to recite in sing-song the detail of ladies' intimate garments that were to be found at 'the fourt' floor' of a department store. What would be found at the basement he did not say as the craft went down the high side of the ship to the sea alongside. It was a noisy proceeding perhaps, but the lads were in good spirit when all were water-borne. Although the sky was overcast, there was little wind when the flotillas were released. The sea was calm and, as they moved off towards the beach, their passage could be clearly traced by phosphorescence, stirred by their displacement. Again, as at Sicily, the thought occurred to me—how pitifully small and impotent the flotilla looked for such a great enterprise.

We had not seen any aircraft on the passage from Naples nor, during darkness, had our instruments disclosed any activity overhead. But from something that had been said at the conference, there was a vague expectation that—as at Sicily—a blitz would be in progress when the fleets had assumed position off the Anzio beach-head. I remarked on this to Captain Abbott of the U.S. Navy, who, as Senior Beach Officer, had sailed with us. He said that an aerial bombardment had already been launched . . . but not in the assault area. It had been made at about sunset as a diversion to keep the Germans busy, at Civitaveccia nearly thirty miles to the westward. He added that we would bombard the beaches ourselves very soon and it was then our argument about the Rocket Ships was finally determined: we learned that it was the ship that was aimed at the target and not the projectile. The rocket was not quite a secret weapon, but it had not before been used from seaward in land-

ing operations. Captain Abbott, who had attended trials, was
enthusiastic. Before he disembarked with the second wave of
attacking troops, he said there would not be one live crab left
on the beach area after five minutes of the barrage!

Whether a crustacean survived the barrage was unknown but
could well be doubted when fire was opened at H hour minus
ten minutes. We had experienced heavy naval gunfire before
but nothing comparable with that short and sudden fury on the
beach-head. Until it opened up, there had been silence and no
sign of movement amongst the ships in the Transport Area offshore. Only the 'Reference Vessel' that was anchored ahead of
us made an occasional spark in the darkness, flashing letter 'W'
on a screened arc seaward as a guide for rearward craft in the
swept channel. In our position we were over-distant for close
observation of the beach assault and the first we knew of it was
a curious sound not unlike the rending or tearing of hard canvas.
Then followed the explosions of the war-heads on impact with
the ground and the bombardment was instantly at full-scale. The
din was not that of naval salvoes with the intervals necessary for
re-loading: it was continuous, and the flights of the rockets,
that were fired in groups and series, seemed to hold some
definite pattern combing the whole beach area with terrific
intensity. Heavier explosions, that rocked our ship at nearly four
miles distance, may have been the blowing up of sea or ground
minefields. All through the brief period of action the rocket
ships—whose number we could not make out—emitted smoke
or chemical vapour. As suddenly as it had begun, the barrage
ceased at exactly three minutes to H hour.

After such an awakening it could be expected that the enemy
would be alerted, and it was with apprehension we awaited
action from the distant great guns in the uplands. There was no
general order to lay down a smoke screen, nor would that have
helped, for by now the great assembly of shipping offshore must
have been sighted behind the flame and smoke of the bombardment. Any shell fired into the area would find its own target.
But there was no flash or sound from the land: only from the
westward, where Anzio lay, was there the low reverberation of

continued gunfire. The flames from what were apparently scrub fires on the coast above tidemark died away; all was quiet again and one could put binoculars aside, rub tired eyes, and wonder at a miraculous immunity. It seemed reasonable to think that the enemy had again been surprised.

Whilst there was now movement amongst the ships near to us, we were scheduled by the instructions to a period of awaiting events. The invasion craft were timed to move forward at intervals of ten, twenty, thirty minutes after H hour, and those within sight of us in the darkness could be seen to heave up and depart—their places being taken up by the rearward groups. Ours was now the lesser part of housing the still considerable body of reserves who could not be disembarked until troop landing vessels became available. In that waiting period thought centred on the fortunes of the landing craft at the beach-head. Recollection of early exercises in Loch Fyne and on the Ayrshire coast where, at close quarters, I had observed the flotillas and the commandos in training, enabled me to visualise the hazards of the operation. Often I had watched the long column of L.C.A., steering in line ahead on a course that was roughly parallel with the beach, turn suddenly together to line abreast to stab into the foreshore and release the fighting men. How the commandos would run, crouching in small groups, to disappear with unbelievable celerity into the sparse cover of tufted dunes and marshland above the shoreline! But that was in training periods. Perhaps a few mild smoke bombs would be thrown at their heels to quicken the charge, or—in the night—cooperating planes would drop brilliant flares (simulating bombs) to expose and hinder. But no rocket barrage was then put down to tear the landing area to shreds and pock-mark the beach with deep craters into which sea water would quickly seep. We could expect damage here even if no resistance was met, for pyramidal stakes and other cunning obstructions under tidemark—even if shattered by bombardment—could still be sharp and ragged enough to rip apart the light plating of the landing craft. Propellers would doubtless be fouled too in the shallows of the beach for a new and classical expedient to arrest the progress of landing craft had been found at the Sicilian beaches. A 'Fleece', anything but golden, fashioned of teased hemp cordage was said to have been moored in quantity there. In the form of a long waft idling underwater, these fleeces could and did become entangled in the screws of the landing craft, halting them under the close range fire of defending forces.

L.S.I. No. 238 bumped noisily alongside after three in the morning. She had come from the beach immediately after landing her quota of assaulting infantry. From the lieutenant in command of her we had word of happenings there. The state of the foreshore when he beached his vessel was very bad as a result of the rocket bombardment, but there was no immediate opposition and he had been able to get the men on shore— although with difficulty on account of shell craters and obstructions. He thought 'Green Beach' was already secured. There was some firing on the left flank where there were a few buildings still upstanding, but otherwise the whole area seemed deserted. It was said that there was strong resistance at Anzio. No. He had not seen our L.C.A. Captain Abbott was on shore; that he knew, as orders had come from him. . . . The magnetic compasses in his vessel had gone all 'haywire' for some reason. Would we give him a bearing of the beach-head and a comparison with ours? . . . We were glad to do that, and within thirty minutes he had cast off with nearly five hundred men crowded on his vessel's narrow decks.

We were cleared of all troops before daybreak and the greater number of our L.C.A. had returned alongside. The officer in charge confirmed the former news that the beach had been taken without serious opposition. The assault force was reported already advanced to the Mussolini Canal some miles inland. Lieut. Prentice, R.N.V.R., the senior flotilla officer, was still at the beach-head with four craft—at least one of them said to be badly damaged and unable to put to sea. I was impatient to proceed. I thought our task at the beach-head completed and it was in orders that we could now sail towards a rendezvous at sea with the other ships of our force, returning from Anzio. There was not much time. As the whole operation was under

American command, Captain Norris had not landed from the ship; the part of Senior Beach Officer having been entrusted to Captain Abbott, U.S.N. In my impatience to get out and away before daylight—and German planes—came in, I protested about the delay to Norris. I suggested making a signal to the beach to expedite matters. In his disarming and smiling manner, S.N.O.L. reminded me that L.C.A. No. 395 was still His Majesty's Ship, and until we knew with certainty that she was a total loss it would be improper to do that. But a signal seeking information might be made, and that was immediately sent off.

As always, the growing daylight brought its tempering influence to bear on my impatience. I could understand that the loss of even one of His Majesty's naval craft could not be swiftly written off like the destruction of an army vehicle or any other combat casualty: there would have to be a painstaking survey on the spot to decide the possibilities of salvage—all for post entry in Lieut. Prentice's Log of the Operations that would subsequently be the important document in a Court of Enquiry. I recalled one remark Captain Norris grinned out. He said 'No ship is completely gone until she is under the water. . . . And sometimes, not even then.'

Perhaps my acceptance of the delay was prompted by an incident that occurred as I was pacing the bridge on tip-toe to heave up and get away whilst the going was good. It was still the grey before dawn and there was very heavy ack-ack fire going up from the Anzio area and the ships engaged there. The man on lookout at the stern called up that he saw an object on the port quarter. What it was he could not determine. A swift scanning revealed no more than a small dark object in the water about fifty feet away. It might be floating refuse from a ship in the area for we had noted, when at the anchorage off Nisida, how the waters there were strewn with empty cartons and boxes from the assembled ships. But this, as our binoculars revealed, was no discard of what might once have held chewing gum or corned beef hash. It was floating low and had horns: we had only to touch it or let it touch us . . . once. It was as well my impatience had put the anchor party on the fo'castle-head to stand by. We hove up quickly and shifted to a better anchor-age, reporting a floating mine to the Reference Vessel as reason for the change. (We learned later that H.M.S. *Palomares* and U.S.S. *Mayo* were damaged, and the U.S.S. *Portent* sunk, in some such circumstance on D day, the mines being probably cut adrift in night sweeping operations.) At this time there was heavy gunfire on the eastern flank where H.M.S. *Penelope* and the U.S.S. *Brooklyn*, having put observer planes in the air, were shelling the cross-roads inland to discourage reinforcement of the enemy in the area.

Daylight had come in broadly when our damaged craft at length appeared out of the haze and billowing smoke of the beach area. There were only three in the labouring group and it was soon made out that two were in damaged condition. Assistance was at once sent from the ship and the crippled L.C.A. taken in tow, but that was a long proceeding for both were badly holed under water and only the devoted effort at the pumps and indeed frantic baling by the use of tin hats had kept them afloat. Even when dragged alongside there was long delay before we could relieve the weight of water and hoist the battered remnants to the davit heads. Exhausted by his ex-tended efforts Lieut. Prentice reported on proceedings. They had, he said, 'touched down' at H hour minus 0001 minutes. There was no near opposition and troops had landed as planned. The beach was in a bad state but he was told that there was firmer ground on the dunes up-shore. Two craft were holed by under-water obstructions and a third was mined when backing off. One man was missing, believed drowned. Service regulations had been carried out and he produced a receipt signed by Captain Abbott for the hulk of His Majesty's L.C.A. No. 395 sunk at the beach-head!

Chapter XXIV

ON 'MONKEY ISLAND'

Upon return to base at Naples from the Anzio-Nettuno assault, we were immediately employed in the transport of troops across the Mediterranean, from North Africa and the Middle East to the Italian ports which were at that time in our hands. The stubborn resistance of the enemy in Central Italy, aided as it was by continuous and abnormal bad weather, demanded the reinforcement of the Allied armies at many parts of the front. We moved Americans from Oran, French colonials and 'Goums' from Algiers, British and British-Indians from Alexandria and the Canal Zone: southbound, we carried displaced persons recovered from the Balkans to Egypt and, on one occasion, a shipload of German prisoners of war. On these ferry passages we still retained on board the S.N.O.L. and a substantial number of the Royal Navy officers and ratings who had joined the ship in the Clyde. The L.C.A. and all other special Admiralty fittings were also undisturbed. From those and other indications it could be surmised that further beachhead operations were in course of planning and that we might again be called into shallow water at short notice.

Amongst the many useful heirlooms that the Royal Navy

had bequeathed to us in the conversion of the *Circassia* from armed merchant cruiser to merchant troop transport was the complete fitment of an upper navigation bridge upon the deck space commonly known as 'Monkey Island'. Originally—and when the ship was requisitioned by the Admiralty in 1939—it had been nothing more commodious than a bare expanse of roof-top to the wheel-house and chart-room. Its only furniture then was a light wooden screen protecting the standard compass, and the reason for that important instrument being placed there was positional—it being almost the only point in the ship from which a clear all-round view of the horizon could be taken. On peace-time voyages the deck was not often used by the Master or senior officers who preferred to have the steersman in plain sight at all times from a post on the bridge below. We had not then attained to confidence in voice-pipes and were perhaps dubious of an order being correctly acted upon unless one was there to see it carried out. In general, it was the junior officers who were 'fagged' to climb the steep ladder and attend to hourly comparisons of the compasses or to take bearings of distant land or sea marks. But the navy is expert with voice-tubes and has no doubts about the spoken order being quickly carried out. When the ship was being armed for her new duties, a post was required from which the commanding officer could see all around, within and outboard his ship, oversea to the horizon on all sides and upward into the sky above: from its height above water and under certain weather conditions, he might even be able to scan the undersea as well. 'Monkey Island' met these requirements and was strongly and skilfully adapted to this purpose of control. As protection for the vital spaces of the wheel-house, the forty-foot deck was encased in plastic-armour composition: a strong bulwark was erected round it and on its inboard face the many storm-proof telephones from the gun posts, lookouts, radar and wireless cabins, were installed. A voice-pipe of good proportions led straight to the ear of the steersman and another to the Master's cabin below. Flag lockers occupied the space at the after end with ample room for speedy signalling. In a sheltered corner a hooded chart table was fitted up. Much in the manner of a photographer with his dark head-cloth, one could dive at night for a quick look at the plot without fear of a temporary blind spasm when return to darkness was made, for the dim orange glow which was there installed was friendly to the eye. It was in all respects a comfortable ship post, well sheltered from the rushing wind by a cunning contrivance on the outboard face of the bulwark that shed the draught high overhead. Clamped to the deck in a central position, the Navy had left to me a stoutly-built, high-legged chair from which I could survey the whole round of the horizon.

My field of vision from the control post there was not always material nor was every thought constantly devoted to navigational problems and the maintenance of course and speed. It was a favoured spot for relaxation when all had been done, and, inevitably, reflections upon the events of wartime sailoring intruded, stirred up perhaps by some landfall in sight. There was the day when, for the first time in many years, the Straits of Messina had become again a friendly waterway and the Duce's boastful monument on the hill above the city of less significance than the still visible turbulence of ancient Charybdis. Or the stormy evening in the Malta Channel when, distant on the beam, the ship-like prow of the invincible islands fronted the western gale, recalling the long embattled convoys pressing on to their relief and sustenance. Or again, the rippled surface of the Galita War Channel that runs close to the Tunisian mainland had its many reminders in wrecks and stranded ships of the anxious days that followed upon the application of the 'Torch'. The bridge chair on 'Monkey Island' when the course was set and the day proved fair was an inviting post in which to indulge reflections.

*   *   *

In periods of relaxation aboard ship in wartime it is as well to have a constant reminder of peril in plain sight, for the normal atmosphere and the nearness of familiar sea furniture is apt to encourage the assurance and confidence that good fortune can always be enjoyed as at the moment. It is so on this stormy day in late March, although many on board may not be as content as I. Euroclydon, who has many other names, is blowing his hardest from the nor'east and the convoy is running before heavy seas in the Skerki Channel. We are on passage from Naples to Mers-el-Kebir and, in light trim, are making heavy weather of it. But the weather hazard is bearable if unpleasant and has the merit of allaying apprehensions of attack. A U-boat had been sighted in these waters on the day before, but the breaking seas now thundering on the banks is likely to discourage an attack. Still, German submarine commanders are not all dismayed by adverse conditions and we are maintaining good lookout. The object that has reminded me of possibilities is my life-jacket that hangs beside me, folded over the rail. It has become routine to carry it around—perhaps as an example to the many casual fatalists amongst the crew. It is of waistcoat pattern, of blue denim, and its supporting power lies in the kapok fibre quilted into it. Clipped to the shoulder is a small electric bulb and with attachment to a battery sewn into one pocket. Encircling the emergency garment, there is a length of stout cordage having a loop spliced in it by which one could handily be hooked from the water. The jacket is of the latest pattern and is approved by the Ministry of War Transport.

Observing it hanging there all ready for instant use in emergency, I am led back to thought of a bitterly cold day in the Afrika Dock at Antwerp where I had just joined my first ship, to begin a career at sea. She was the full-rigged sailing ship, *City of Florence*, and the date was in November, 1890. A beautiful ship, I thought, as I surveyed her from the dockside before climbing the gangway on board. But I was not allowed to admire her there. As quickly as the bustling Mate could have me change to working rig, I was given a job to do. Some large bundles had been delivered at the gangway and lay on deck. I was told to open them up. They contained lifebelts of the old pattern—slabs of native cork sewn up in cheap cotton duck. I was to count them and carry them to the sail locker in the aft 'tween-decks where, as far as I know, they were no further disturbed. 1890! A new regulation of the Board of Trade had made it compulsory at that date for all British ships to carry a sufficiency of such life-saving appliances for every member of the crew and I had counted twenty-eight. Before that time, I was told, it was uncommon for a ship to carry lifebelts: only the lifeboatmen on the coast used them. Curious that I should have come to sea at that important date . . . and that my very first ship employment was to stow my life-jacket away in a dark and inaccessible corner of the ship's sail-locker!

★　★　★

Piecemeal as the atmospherics permit, we are now learning a little of what has happened in the landing at Anzio-Nettuno. We know that the Allied forces are established there, where we helped to place them, but it seems that the footing is not yet firm enough for the march on Rome that was anticipated. The front there is proving difficult with the Germans dug in on the higher ground. We are picking out of the ether too the little scraps and oddments of information that go far towards solving the puzzle-picture of events subsequent to our exit from the beach-head. Not less than three British manned L.S.T. have 'gone up' in the minefields offshore and the full casualty toll of lesser vessels is not yet fully known. American losses are not mentioned but are rumoured to be heavy. H.M.S. *Janus* was sunk by air attack on D day and since then *Penelope* and *Spartan* have gone too. But, all for all, the enemy has a singularly light bill against us. As so often, he is driven to an exploit in *schrecklichkeit* to cover his failure in legitimate war action. The hospital ship, *St. David*, was bombed from the air and sunk on D day plus two. As an hospital ship on her Red Cross mission, she could not have been in the actual combat area, but anchored well offshore and she would certainly be showing all her peaceful distinguishing marks even although such indications would point the conflict in her near vicinity. It would be a sedulous respect for international obligations that held her there— immobile—a sitting target for the berserk *Luftwaffe*. We should have known what would happen. Had the German airman not already worked out the formula for such occasions? He had precedent. The *Ramb* in 1942, *Newfoundland* in 1943, *Talamba* and *Dorsetshire* off Cape Passero at the landing in Sicily, and now the *St. David* to mark another infamy in the calendar of 1944. With that knowledge, we should have known that it was senseless punctilio to paint up and illuminate and beflag a bull's-eye for the flying *herrenvolk*.

Pondering the tragedies of the *Talamba* and the *St. David*, I have the recollection that we did not have hospital ships off-shore at Helles and Suvla Bay in 1915. The wounded were largely transported to Mudros in troop transports and were there transferred. L.S.I. like the *Circassia* could have been specially useful in such a way at Anzio when the assault troops had been landed and the ships were routed to return empty to base. Landing craft would have been ideal for stretcher cases and the hoisting gear provide outboard elevators to every deck and corridor. I wonder if thought had ever been given to that?

★　★　★

Now that the instancy of combined operations has been stayed for a time and the ship's engagement changed to the slightly less warlike traffic of normal troop transport there has come a rift in the relations between us and the naval contingent remaining on board. There are frictions. Small matters in themselves perhaps, but significant of a disharmony that may lead to trouble. Relations with the senior naval officers are happily undisturbed. Captain Norris, who is now S.N.O.L., agrees that the dual character of an L.S.I. (L.) under the Red Ensign, yet partially manned from the Royal Navy, leaves over-much to the composition of difficulties on board without reference to any established regulations. Our books (the King's Regulations on his part, and Sea Transport Instructions on mine) do not agree. His junior officers who, in thought of beach-head operations, have patiently endured the crowding into communal staterooms, see injustice in the fact that the ship's merchant officers have each a room to himself with suitable accommodation for personal equipment and effects. On the lower-deck, there is the same impatience in regard of the better amenities of the ship's fo'c'sles where, by the naval way of thinking, our un-enlisted crew is revelling in high pay for doing but little. We have not now many naval P.O.'s left with us but doubtless those who remain are tired of 'living out of suitcases' in their temporary quarters—a corridor where they have to sleep on sea-mattresses on the floor-boards.

Victuals too, and as always, enter into the sum of discontents. Nowhere at the many ports we have entered since sailing from Bombay could adequate and suitable fresh provision be supplemented. Iron rations are all very well for emergency, but it is difficult to cite emergency in our now apparently unhindered progress from port to port.

It is a big and difficult problem that is unrelieved by reference to the Sea Transport Authority at the many ports of call. The transport seniors are all agreed that the matters are urgent but feel that nothing much can be done thus far abroad. Their business is to embark troops in the ship to full capacity and they point to our Memorandum of Equipment that certifies space in the ship for 248 officers and 2240 other ranks—and that is about the numbers, naval force included, they propose to embark for transport. Nor is it of any use to refer to N.O.I.C. (Naval Officer in Charge) for a ruling in the matter. We are patently hermaphrodite under the Red Ensign and all that can be done is to report to Admiral Troubridge as Chief of Force P, now distant and operating somewhere in the Adriatic. It is a vexatious circumstance that occupies much of my thought as I sit in the navy's high chair; but one that may be resolved by quite irregular concession and temporary agreement. Under war conditions, it is no small task to keep peace in a ship.

★　　★　　★

Watching the bearing of the high light of the Pharos at Alexandria as it grows and flashes on the sea-line ahead, I think of the commitments of a week's stay in the Egyptian port. Vile weather, in which we have lost one and damaged a second of our remaining L.C.A., under exactly the circumstance I had feared when the craft were shipped at Glasgow, has slowed the eastbound convoy from which we have just detached. Daylight has long since departed and we are marking time now off the outer channel buoy, not slowed—for enemy submarines are still reported to favour the locality—but maintaining speed and zig-zag whilst awaiting moonlight to steer safely past the many wrecks and obstructions in the swept channel.

My reflections date back to a few day's stay at Algiers on a former passage. It was at that port we had had the first opportunity since the days of our *Brutum Fulmen* at Bombay to give leave and liberty to the crew. I was prepared for the normal misdemeanours of men long held to shipboard, but not for the discovery that we had some infamous gangsters on our books. There was, of course, the customary procession of minor defaulters who had 'drink taken' and were incapable of duty or were absent without leave. These charges could safely be met by a small fine—with mention of reconsideration upon report of subsequent good conduct, but it was the long list of ship's property lost, stolen or missing that caused concern. Drugs had disappeared from the ship's hospital and many items were missing from the lifeboats' emergency equipment; the crews' bedding in large quantity seemed to have vanished into the slums of the Kasbah. Upon joining the ship each crew member was supplied with bedding, bed linen and towels and he had contracted to pay a modest sum if unable to return this ship's property on termination of his engagement. At Algiers in wartime, a bed-sheet for which the forfeit was ten shillings could be trafficked for five pounds or more, could it be smuggled on shore. The result was a dearth of sheets in crew's quarters that was plainly evident on inspections. Naive requests for replacements were not entertained—not at ten shillings—and it was thought that the trade might thus be discouraged. But the merchants in the fo'c'sle, deprived of the opportunity to acquire further personal stock, were by no means put out of the business and it was when a number of our reliable hands complained of the loss of the bedding for which they were responsible it became apparent that the system was expanding into a thieves' market. And there seemed to be threat and intimidation employed by the operators, for the older men whom I had known for years were curiously reticent when reporting the thefts, not alone of bedding but now of money, clothing, personal trinkets, cigarettes. No one would put a name to suspicion. Misguided perhaps, this misplaced loyalty was understandable for the old sea phrase has it 'A sailor a'fore a landsman an' a shipmate a'fore all'. But that would date back to the day when theft amongst shipmates was almost unknown. We had now a new breed to classify and examine.

I think the Essential Works Order of 1941 responsible for the infiltration of these undesirables. We needed men at that date and the Merchant Navy Pool supplied them. I suppose it was no part of the Pool's business to examine character too closely when 'called-ups' elected to serve at sea, nor would it be reasonable to bar the adventurer. Not all the adventurers were unsuited to sea life but most of them were only afloat for a term of service at higher rate of pay than in the armed forces and many of them were determined to exploit their new pursuit in every possible evasion of its duties and contempt of its traditions. The pitiful Tables of 'Fines and Forfeitures' under the Merchant Shipping Acts that was posted up in crews' quarters would doubtless provide light reading for the corner boys, skilled in the deceits of the waterfront of the greater seaports from which so many were drawn. Nor was the prospect of a bad Character Report on termination of engagement a deterrent to one who had no intention of remaining in sea service beyond the date of general release.

And now the clever villains have enlisted the rigid 'blackout' that is maintained on board from sunset to sunrise to further their designs. The incident that so disquiets me as we stand off and on the entrance to the Great Boghas Pass is that an elderly nightwatchman in the ship, of good character and known to be energetic and reliable, was found at daybreak the other morning lying unconscious on the outer decks. He had been cruelly mistreated and is still in the ship's hospital. He still persists that he can't identify his assailants and, without information, there seems little can be done to bring the case before a naval court in H.M.S. *Nile* when in the port—a revived procedure designed to meet the growing indiscipline in merchant ships employed in war service. It is not in any mood of pleased anticipation I look forward to a week's stay in Alexandria.

*   *   *

We have had a well-merited promotion in our ranks and Captain Barclay has taken on his duties without any unusual display of authority; but that is not a matter of wonderment. For long he has been Staff Captain in fact, even when his rank 'on the books' was that of Chief Officer. At Alexandria on our call there, instruction from the Owners bade me engage him in the senior post. The matter has been regularised. He has signed on again, this time at 'One Shilling a Month', and the other navigation officers have each taken a step up. It is a happy circumstance . . . but I am wondering if there was not a whisper about my advanced years in the Board-room? Whether or not that is the case, the new arrangement is exactly to my liking for I can now legitimately delegate an officer, in whom I put great trust, to attend to ambulant duties that sometimes I find exacting.

I cannot recollect when Staff Captains were first established in merchant ships. The appointment must be of comparatively recent date, possibly as a result of experiences in very large vessels during the First World War when the rigours of almost constant watch-keeping had seriously enfeebled many elderly shipmasters. Or would it be that social duties in the development of cruising voyages had called for it? The size of modern ships too! Looking outboard on the beam from 'Monkey Island' I see the *Monarch of Bermuda* keeping station with us in the northbound convoy from Oran towards Naples, 22,000 tons in her. In the early days, which both her Captain and I could recall, that tonnage would have made up no less than eight sizeable ships of the period, each with a Master and Mate to serve her. . . . Certainly, seafaring was a harder occupation then, but the insurance companies seemed not to insist that the Master should always be at his post when the ship was under way. I remember Captain James Horne of the *Loch Garry*, who would never dream of boarding the ship in a dock. It was for the Mate and the local pilot to have her towed down to an anchorage at the Tail of the Bank where, in the stately garb of tight frock coat and tall hat and an umbrella firmly in hand, he would come off to the ship only when he considered the wind and the weather favourable for setting sail! . . . Changed days.

*   *   *

Private and individual wireless sets are forbidden in wartime on board ship. It is thought that the passive reactions of an imperfect instrument—like the massed frequencies of electric razors—might give direction to the enemy. So, we have the system of broadcast rations, using only the ship's controlled and official reception and relaying 'this is London' at scheduled times of the day. Many amplifiers are fitted throughout the ship, on deck and in troop quarters, in public rooms and kitchens and in crew accommodations. As the same line is also used for 'Public Address' it is geared to a loud and standard pitch that cannot locally be modulated or switched off. Its voice can plainly be heard on 'Monkey Island'.

It is past six in the second dog watch: sunset is still aglow on the high peaks of the Sinai range and we are steaming steadily northward towards Suez, on passage from Bombay. We have just been listening to the day's important news—that Cassino has at last been stormed and taken and that the Eighth and Fifth Armies have joined forces in Italy. A small item of home news arouses conjectures. 'The British Railways announced yesterday that passenger services might be cancelled without warning.' . . . We had been long absent from a home port and only fleeting rumours of great preparation for an assault on the western coasts of Europe had reached us. It had been noticed too that when in Italian and North African ports, the great assemblage of invasion ships and craft brought out for the Sicilian and the mainland adventures had been gradually reduced, doubtless to swell the tonnage elsewhere available for a major assault. Force P is now widely scattered and only the *Winchester Castle,*

Ascania and *Circassia* are included in the convoy pressing northward. We had thought it probable that we too might be recalled from abroad to augment the 'lift' required in the vast project that was whispered, but the item in the news that the railways could not guarantee their schedules indicated that the date was near and we were unlikely to take part in it. . . . And now, the news concluded, London has turned to entertainment for forces overseas, and the loud speaker on the deck below blares out the 'plug' of the day—*Mair-si-doats an' Goat-sy-doats an' Dickle-ammsi divey!*—it goes!

It is curious that 'Soldier Song' has been of such little account in the Second World War, that there has been so little of marching rhythm in it. Probably the wrong start was made with the boastful insincerity of laundry operations on the Siegfried Line and that handicap was never overcome. It is not of solo singing at ship's concerts I am thinking or of the rousing old-time choruses that so often followed upon that. It is to soldier chorus my thought goes back, to the airs that had the spring of marching feet in them. . . . Tipperaray! . . . I can recall that chorus as I first heard it sung. Out of Dublin for Boulogne in the *Massilia*. I was Mate in her then and had all to do with clearing the 'tween decks of import cargo we had brought from India to make space for the H.L.I. (there were no regular troop fittings in the urgency of the call) and put them on the road to Mons. Tipperaray! The lilt of it! . . . 'Keep the Home Fires Burning.' . . . 'Pack up your Troubles.' . . . 'Give me the Smile I can keep for a while.' . . . These were the songs!

It has fallen dark and the wireless broadcast is over now. As though to remind me that the rhythm of 'Soldier Song' is not quite forgotten, a whistler somewhere in the shadows of the boat deck sets up a trill. Quickly he is joined by others—the Somersets, I think, Soon they are whistling together in fine marching spirit:

Chapter XXV

CASUAL PORTENT

On the sea wall of the long breakwater at Mers-el-Kebir, just abreast of where *Circassia's* gangway jutted shoreward, there was a large bronze plaque set into the smooth stone face. It commemorated the dead in an uneasy naval action of the war when, on the 3rd July, 1940, it was thought necessary by our naval command to damage or destroy the still powerful Vichy fleet of warships assembled in the port and thus eliminate a threat to further operations in the Mediterranean. As I remember it, the lettering was well-phrased, but it made sad reading for the crews of British troopships so often moored there when we and the French had reunited and were engaged together again. After the 'Torch Landing' in North Africa, the naval harbour and the adjacent mercantile port of Oran came under American direction. In frequent calls at Mers-el-Kebir to embark troops for the Italian front we had seen little of the French navy and nothing of its port administration. Only an elderly battleship, the *Lorraine*, represented them there. She was berthed at the extreme eastern end of the breakwater and we had come to look upon her much in the same way as we surveyed the great Cathedral on the mountainside that was one of the leading marks in making the land. Obviously an important and powerful ship, if dated 1913, she looked forlorn at her seaward position—hemmed in there by some form of protective booms alongside, her only companion a lowly 'gash' boat under her stern to load up with ship trifles and take them to be dumped at sea. But she was dignified and imposing and a keen watch was kept in her. Always saluted by the dipping of ensigns as the ships of her reconciled allies passed out or in, the courtesy was punctiliously returned by the slow and impressive lowering of the Tricolour. How she was manned we did not know for no

Rendezvous after Operation Bigot; August, 1944

great activity could be seen on her broad decks at any time. But every morning shortly after sunrise a long procession of her sailors coming from the town passed down the inshore face of the breakwater and, skirting the end of our gangway, made their way towards her. In late afternoon they could be seen returning. Possibly they were relays of 'libertymen', but as almost every man carried a small package or hand-grip, it could be thought that their routine was on a 'maintenance' basis and that their packages contained rations for the day. Often, I had watched the groups as they passed by on the quayside. They did not march in any formation as naval dockyard practice usually prescribes, but sauntered along as independent workmen do—choosing their companions perhaps for a word or two and some linked hands like pleasant children. But, for all I could observe, we might as well not have been there at all—moored alongside in their port. No one looked up at us nor did they ever seem to comment upon our appearance or our mission.

But it was different on the morning of the 7th June, 1944. Early astir for a stretch on deck and pondering the great news of the landing in Normandy that had been broadcast on the evening before, I was alerted by an unusual commotion at the town-ward end of the breakwater where, moored closely together, were the smaller units of the U.S. Navy that ranged from patrol boats to minesweepers and fleet auxiliaries. Shouts and cheering could be heard but it was some time before the participants in the demonstration could be seen rounding the angle of the sea arm. The white cap-covers with red pom-poms identified the crew of the *Lorraine* on the way to their ship, but the distant pattern was not that of sauntering groups and parties as on the day before. It was regular, and in lines of threes. The *col-bleues* had formed up in marching order to stride along the quayside and halt at every ship for a round of cheers! . . . It was a heartening and apparently unrehearsed proceeding, spontaneously projected. They cheered the American flotillas, then marched down the line of British and Polish transports. When they approached our gangway, it was '*Vive Church-eel*', '*Vivent les Anglais*', '*A nous la Victoire*', they roared out, doffing caps to wave in answer to our now crowded decks' response. In the uprising of so many arms, each buttoned by the white and red of their headgear, the plaque on the sea wall could not be noticed in the cheering moment!

With three of our sister ships of Force P and other troop transports we had been routed to Mers-el-Kebir to take part in 'Operation Phib-81-2' there being mounted by the United States Navy. We had come from Alexandria in the hope and expectation that we might be engaged in northern waters with the great seaborne assault we knew to be impending somewhere on the Channel coasts. A period of training exercises in company with American warships and the new naval L.S.I. of the U.S. forces encouraged this prospect. At night manoeuvres in the Gulf of Arzeu the Task Force had joined to practise a new manner of approaching the beach-head that, in some ways, indicated engagement in very deep water. We did not anchor as we had done on all previous landings, but kept the ships in formation by small adjustments of engines and helm when lowering the L.C.A. and sending the attacking troops away. Admiral Rogers of the U.S. Navy, under whom we served, may have had an idea grown out of experience in the Far East, but his purpose was not disclosed to us. We found its application difficult. Radar in the black of the night was of little use as the surrounding vessels were so many and so closely in company, and there were also the currents in the Gulf to complicate the varying drift of idling ships. Only after frequent trials was a reasonable efficiency assured and that was dependent on the accurate positioning of a distant 'marker' vessel.

The news of 'Overlord' in Normandy ended our hope of being there employed and opened up many avenues of wild conjecture about the location of the next exploit. Exercises were not immediately suspended, but a slowing down became noticeable and there was not the feeling of urgency that had marked their commencement. 'Operation Phib' as a title inspired many jocular comments and we were not greatly surprised when, in mid-June, there was a gradual dispersal of the merchant ships grouped with the U.S. Task Force that indicated some change of plan. With the *Winchester Castle*, *Derbyshire* and *Sobieski* we were detached and routed east to Malta. There was nothing in sailing orders that could be taken as a guide to next employment but some matters of repair and refitment were now overdue and the Royal Dockyard at Valetta was the nearest British port where such work could be undertaken. That we would continue service in the Mediterranean was hinted by the Routeing Officer. We were still three L.C.A. short of established numbers and he thought replacements would be fitted when at Malta.

As we headed out of harbour on sailing, we saluted the battleship at the end of the breakwater. It was noticed that there was great and unusual activity in her. The protective booms had been removed from alongside and storeships of small size were tied up where the great baulks of timber had been. The 'gash' lighter was not at its customary mooring under her stern. She seemed more fully manned too and some form of directional exercise or drill was in progress. The great fourteen-inch guns in the turrets were elevated from the sheer line of harbour housing and swung in impressive arc to seaward. Lying off and apparently waiting for a busy working party to complete the rigging of hoisting gear and platforms, a long low ammunition barge was held in place. The *Lorraine* was magnificently alive again and was preparing for sea action . . . somewhere!

Chapter XXVI

THE RETURN TO FRANCE:
OPERATION BIGOT

An excess of caution may have arisen from the political situation in Taranto when we embarked General Montsabert and his divisional headquarters. There was bad blood between the townsmen and the French troops withdrawn from the Italian front and encamped in the district prior to embarkation on an overseas adventure which, as rumour had it, was intended against Genoa. Facismo was not quite dead amongst the bare-headed youth of Apulia and Otranto and nasty incidents had occurred. There were all the elements for sabotage and spying in the ancient naval port.

Whatever the reason, we were not admitted to confidence and 'Operation Bigot', mounted by the United States Navy, was not as fully explained to the senior officers of the merchant transports when we attended conference as had been the assault landings on Sicily and at Anzio. The matters of Convoy T.M.-1's passage towards a secret rendezvous in the western Mediterranean was exhaustively considered and discussed, we were informed of our stations in its formation and of the measures to be taken for defence or protection, but we were not given the location of the assault area nor were we briefed on the manner of landing the French Army that was embarked in the vast assembly of troopships and naval vessels then anchored in the Mar Grande. We did not know where we were going nor what was expected of us on arrival at the beach-head. But no one asked questions for, included with our convoy forms and plans, there was the now familiar large sealed envelope marked 'Not to be opened until instructed by the Commodore' and it was confidently expected that precise instructions were contained in it.

We put to sea in the early hours of the 11th August, 1944, and in late afternoon were signalled to open the secret envelope. It contained a series of abstract charts of the Mediterranean showing the routes of many task forces and convoys from North Africa, Naples, Salerno, Taranto and Corsica, all converging upon a point off Cape Camarat in the south of France. There was no information of where or how troops were to be landed or disembarked, but study of the charts revealed that 'T.M.-1' was a fast 'follow up' convoy and was scheduled to reach the combat area on D day plus 1, which was the 16th August, 1944. On that date and when approaching the rendezvous I was suddenly called upon to take over the duties of Vice Commodore.

The assignment worried me. Certainly, I had acted in that capacity on several occasions but had then been fortified by written orders containing detail of the operations involved. I suppose a naval officer in similar circumstances would have made light of it and considered the signal to indicate a quick change of plan requiring a deployment that his knowledge of the operations could meet. But I had not that knowledge and there was not, that I could find, any page in 'Instructions to Masters, Operation Bigot' that gave me counsel in the matter. At the conference in Taranto a Vice Commodore had already been appointed and he would doubtless be fully advised and documented. But he was the Master of the troopship *Staffordshire* which was leading Column One on the extreme left of the convoy and I could see no escort ship being called in to collect his instructions and ferry them across to me. It was apparent that some alteration in the dispositions had been made at the eleventh hour for we were about to separate and the signal read that *Circassia*, on the extreme *right* of the convoy, was to assume Vice Commodore of a named group of six ships and lead them into the Gulf of St. Tropez.

We were at prayers when the signalman brought the message. I had stepped down from the bridge at the special request of General Montsabert who commanded the division of the French army embarked in the ships of the convoy. I would have preferred to remain at my post, for we were drawing near the combat area but the kind old white-haired soldier insisted and I could not deny him. It was, he explained, *'une occasion dramatique'* this celebration of the Mass by the *Armée du Liberation* on sighting the shores of France after long exile, and were not we of the ship his good comrades?

It was a solemn and colourful ceremony. A small field altar was set up on the fore-deck and the celebrant with his assistants wore the vestments of the Church over the stained battle-dress in which they had fought in Italy. The banners of the two French battalions we carried, paraded in a fanfare of trumpets, were brought to the altar to be blessed anew and the spectacle of the kneeling soldiers, browned and battle-visaged, rank upon rank occupying every inch of space upon the sunlit decks was impressive. Under the stress of great emotion, General Montsabert addressed his men when they had risen after the Benediction. His sentences that began so bravely became almost halting as he went on. From time to time he raised his arm in the direction of Cape Camarat that had grown out of the sea horizon whilst we were at prayers. Standing closely beside him, I could note tears in the old General's eyes as he spoke of long separation from *La France*. I too was moved and felt honoured by a modest part in the repatriation. All the while the ships of the great convoy pressed on in formation towards the distant land. It was a fine day of calm weather and the convoy, under the protection of a formidable escort steered straight courses. A flight of patrolling aircraft covered the area. There was no visible opposition to our advance; only, at a position drawing gradually abeam warships were apparently in action against some stubborn resistance in the Levant Islands. There was the sound of continuous heavy gunfire from that bearing, but the islands were as yet under the rim of the sea-line and the targets could not be made out. We were rapidly approaching the rendezvous position called 'C.A.' in latitude 43° 10′ North, longitude 6° 40′ East when I returned to the bridge.

To pick up a following of named ships out of convoy and set course and speed was no difficult task, but with the pinprick at C.A. on the chart almost underfoot it was in a mood of uncertainty I made the necessary flag-hoists when our group was detached. I had signalled the Commodore, seeking further instructions and telling him I had not the information of a point of landing. The reply was that we would receive orders from an American control vessel in the Gulf. The Gulf is wide and where the control was to be found was not stated. With that I had to be content as the ships of the convoy separated, the main group proceeding towards Cavalaire Bay which lies on the south side of the Camarat peninsula and our section standing on northward to the Gulf.

When we rounded the Salinas Beacon and entered the wide bay it was to find the whole sea area there jammed with shipping of almost every conceivable shape and size. It was apparent that a large convoy of munition ships had just arrived from northward and was taking up anchor berths, for the most of them were still under way and questing about for room amongst the naval assault craft clustered thickly off St. Maxime and St. Tropez. Where to look for a control vessel in such a congestion was something of a problem. It would not have been so bad had we been a single ship with liberty to stop and drift awhile until matters were resolved, but with five ships closing up in line astern and awaiting guidance, the only course one could take was to circle out to sea again, slow the convoy and await developments. At about two in the afternoon our almost continuous flashing of the daylight Aldis brought an answering spark from out of the mass of shipping and craft. The control was a small vessel and in little distinguishable from the surrounding craft. While due allowances could be made for her preoccupation with the control of earlier arrivals, her reply to our request for further orders did not bring any instant instruction that we could act upon, nor did the wording of it indicate accurate acquaintance with the purpose of our visit. We seemed to be an unexpected addition to the invasion forces and all the matters of the 'Condition and Capabilities' of our impatient circling group had to be communicated in long pad signalling. The information that two ships, the *Circassia* and *Batory*, were equipped with landing craft and carried the commanding generals and their headquarters of the French Army brought about a pause in the exchanges that indicated some consultation at the distant end. Finally, we were instructed to proceed to the head of the Gulf, anchor, and disembark there. A more experienced Commodore might have found some way of keeping the ships together in the passage through the confused assembly of shipping, but that proceeding seemed dangerous to me and I made signal to 'Act independently' and 'Anchor as convenient' when the general text of Control's instructions had been passed down the line. As a result, we were widely separated at the anchorage and further communication was difficult if not in some cases impossible.

In *Circassia* we found an anchor berth of a sort that was far from sailor choice at the extreme western end of the Gulf. It was close inshore, almost too close for my peace of mind (in expectation of a breeze from seaward when the sun had gone) and just off the mouth of a small stream at St. Pons les Mures. The land there was a low-lying valley fronted by a long sandy beach on which there was evidence of opposition to the assault landing that had been made on the morning of the day before. Three or four wrecked landing craft lay shattered and abandoned on the Plage and the upperworks of a larger L.C.T. showed above water almost under our bows. Heavy explosions resounded from the flats in the valley—at first alarming, but later recognised as the work of a mine-clearance detachment of American troops—but there seemed to be no other military activity in sight. On the southern side of the beach a small jetty, newly placarded by a large beach traffic sign 'P' seemed an appropriate landing place and helmeted G.I.'s were established there but we had not, as expected, been signalled in by the Beachmaster nor had Movement Control come off to board us in the press of shipping. In anticipation of immediate disembarkation troops had been fully equipped and loaded into the L.C.A.—all ready for lowering when the ship was anchored —and they had become restive and impatient under the restraint of such long delay. General Montsabert and his Divisional Officers too seemed to have lost the mood of high exaltation and expectancy that had been theirs at mid-day. It was far from the incoming of a pattern with their long-cherished dreams, and it was not easy to explain to them that the disembarkation of troops with the land so close aboard—and inviting—was not the ship's decision but that of the U.S. Beach Control. Unfortunately I could not now court the advice of a S.N.O.L. for Captain Norris had been transferred to other duties some months ago and no one had been appointed in his place. The senior naval officer on board was Lieut. Prentice (who had done so well at Anzio) but he was as perturbed as I at the absence of positive orders. He agreed to put off to the beach and investigate the situation.

On return he reported the jetty and nearby beach suitable for landing, but no one amongst the American troops in the vicinity seemed to be advised of the disembarkation of a French army. The beach was said to be cleared of mines but large areas further inland remained to be dealt with and that was the operation in which the U.S. sappers were engaged. Beach Headquarters at St. Tropez had been informed by telephone of the ship's position. . . . The period of awaiting further orders was enlivened by long signal contact with the *Batory* in which General de Lattre de Tassigny (Commanding French Army 'B') was embarked, and it was probably as a result of his protestations we received orders to disembark all troops and equipment in late afternoon.

Just after sunset, our smooth despatch of the soldiers was rudely disturbed. A group of square-tipped Heinkels came over, strangely from seaward, and bombed the crowded transport area with sudden intensity. Attack was not unexpected and a barrage was immediately set up, but the enemy was high and out of range to all but heavy-calibre guns. Our best defence seemed, as so often, to be the smoke screen and we were quick in providing that blanket; but before our vision was blotted out we had a glimpse of a squadron of enemy bombers coming in from the N.E. and an amazing volume of tracer fireworks from the anchored ships in the Gulf curving and falling far below their altitude. Loud above the din and rattle of the barrage, there was the frequent crash of bomb explosions: a burst sounded perilously close in a direction we knew an anchored ship to lie and another—a full stick and of sharper intensity—from somewhere near the jetty where we had disembarked our troops. After that, the enemy seemed in no mood to linger; the barrage diminished and died down. We ceased smoke raising, but it took long for the vapours to dispel in the calm of the weather and give us sight of our neighbours again. We became suddenly aware that the smell of the encircling fumes had changed from the all too familiar acrid pungency of chemical smoke to the unmistakeable tang of burning timber. It had become quickly dark and in the rifts of clearing smoke there was a bright glow in the sky that we thought to come from ships afire. When visibility had improved it was seen that the wooded heights above St. Tropez were ablaze and pouring dense volumes of black smoke into the Gulf. Lieut. Cleare, at his station with me on the bridge, thought the Americans were throwing ammunition away and the widespread fires on shore the result of the 'bonus action without hope of dividend' on the part of the many liberty ships in the Gulf, and was caused by the incendiary tracer they had expended in the fruitless barrage. In the murk of the forest fires we took a halting signal from the ship anchored close-to. She was the *Essex Trader*, loaded with Army vehicles and ammunition, and had been hit during the raid by fragmentation bombs: there were casualties amongst her troops and crew, many being seriously wounded. Could we send a doctor on board? That we were about to do when one of our L.C.A. returned from the landing jetty with bad news. A bomb or bombs had burst there whilst the troops we had just landed were moving off at the exit from Beach 262. Some had been killed outright and there were many wounded. There was no Field Aid Post near at hand and troops were already on the march to the Route Nationale 98. It was requested that we re-embark the wounded. In prospect of such a duty, we could not spare a surgeon for the *Essex Trader*, but it was possible to signal the *Batory* and ask her to send assistance to the stricken ship. One could always count on Captain Dechaikowsky.

Transport of the wounded from the beach area did not prove difficult, despite a scarcity of stretchers and the immediate need to extend our limited hospital accommodation into cabin quarters. The ease with which we could hoist the landing craft to the level of the hospital deck made rapid progress possible. It was a new experience to be thus suddenly converted to an hospital carrier, but the duty was quickly met by Major Macgregor, the Senior Medical Officer, and his two assistants: even Dr. Laurie, our gallant old retired practitioner who had signed with us as ship's surgeon, rolled up his sleeves to bear a hand in a branch of casualty that he had not likely undertaken since the last Great War. Amongst the wounded were some American sappers but the majority was French. Three were dead when brought aboard. Their broken remains were laid out in seemly fashion on the after hatch to be returned to French soil in the morning, but we had no Tricolour to cover them. This omission was repaired later by a thoughtful signalman using flag 'T' of the International Code, reversed.

Shortly after midnight we had met all our commitments and the thought of departure brought up its many knotty points. A light westerly wind had sprung up to dispel the lingering scud of the smoke screen and turn the still billowing drift from the forest fires to seaward. The ship had not swung inshore as I had feared she might. For that I was thankful, but the manoeuvre to turn her head to seaward when we got under way again presented, as at Sicily, no small difficulty. I had been over-ambitious in anchoring so close inshore, and withdrawal—having a wreck under the bows and concentration of shipping under the stern—would provide uneasy moments. It was with this in mind and in the failing light I studied the disposition of the ships astern and pondered a course of action when the anchor was aweigh. I might have to ask the unfortunate *Essex Trader* to heave short and snub ship to northward when the time came. That could give me sufficient arc to cant to seaward. There was little hope that the press of shipping would be relieved by any sailings before morning. The whole length of the Gulf was bright with the working lights of the ships, actively employed in transferring overside to landing barges the huge munition of the invading armies. The urgency of that task was patent in the omission of 'blackout' and that acceptance of the risk of air attack so lately pressed in the area.

Of the five ships with which we were grouped only the *Batory* was within signal sight. She reported good progress in disembarkation and, through her, it was possible to communicate with the others. Not being equipped, as we were, with L.C.A. and being berthed at greater distance from the beach, they were dependent on beach transport craft and were not yet fully disembarked, but there seemed no good reason why we should not all sail at daybreak and only an official permit to get under way at that time was wanting. But who was to grant the warrant for departure? We had had no direct communication with the naval authority on shore and when, after long probing, we did raise the U.S. Control Vessel, it was to be told to await further instructions. No one but myself seemed to be interested in the return of the empties, but, coming from the established Naval Control, I could accept the signal as a Good-night salutation and go below.

My period of attempted rest in an armchair below was uneasy. We were still in a second degree of readiness in anticipation of renewed air attack. That did not come; but the old bad habit of introspection, fed by the indecisions of the day, persisted throughout the night to keep me wakeful. It was the contrast between the ordered and precise direction of the landings on Sicily and at Anzio and the perplexities of Operation Bigot that came uppermost in my mind. One could understand that a beach landing would not always go according to plan, and the switch from left to right that had urged us into St.

Tropez was probably dictated by the fortunes of D day in which we had not been occupied. But that should have been foreseen, the way it was in 'Husky' the way it was in 'Shingle', and the matters fully explained at the Convoy Conference in Taranto harbour before we sailed. . . . *Hutt!* It was time for another pipe and a turn on deck. . . . But there still to ponder the uncertainties of our arrival in the Gulf—the apparent ill-advisement of the Control Vessel in regard of our place and purpose in the job o' work—and the casual manner of our reception in the landing area! . . . It all summed up to the chancy conviction that the time was not yet ripe for the launching of a French army to the assault! . . . None of my business anyway. A glance outboard at the now moonlit anchorage reminded me of the sailorwork that would be needed to extricate my ship from the press of surrounding vessels when we came to sail again. There was a new and disturbing scrap of information to be considered. When reporting on the air attack at the beach-head, our flotilla lieutenant said he had been warned by an American engineer officer that the area where the *Circassia* lay anchored was the most heavily-mined water in the Gulf ! The U.S. sappers had not the duty to sweep the anchorage. How could they know of mines there? . . . But there was evidence—the half-submerged wreck under our bows. It *was* curious that the inshore stretch of water was unoccupied by the smaller vessels who could have found a depth of water in it suited to their needs. Only the shattered wreck. . . . Maybe. . . . If we canted the wrong way when the anchor left the ground at departure?

How amazingly the difficulties, so gravely pondered in the darkness, are illuminated and in part dispelled when the morning's daylight comes! How foolish I had been to don a thinking cap and indulge in gloomy foreboding—for here was the broad of daylight again, with calm weather, and the water space in which to cant the ship when getting under way seemed vastly and miraculously enlarged although nothing had moved in the darkness. I would not have to edge my bows into suspect water, nor would I have to ask our crippled neighbour, the *Essex*

Trader, to give us a helping hand at departure. In the welcome clarity of the morning light I saw a better way to handle the situation. Preoccupied by independent action at the beach-head, I had overlooked the fact that the *Circassia* was still Vice Commodore of the group (however lightly the duties of that office had been served by her) and I could initiate a movement. It was neither prudent nor necessary for us to lead the other ships of our section to sea in the circumstance of an obstructed fairway channel. We could all join company and form up in convoy when in more open waters and clear of the assembled shipping in the Gulf. Quite properly, I could instruct Captain Dechaikowsky in the *Batory* to heave up and get under way before we did when the time for departure came. If the windless weather held—and it looked like doing that—we could back astern into the berth that she would then have vacated and there gather way for the turn to seaward. It only remained now for the U.S. Control Vessel to spark up and send our sailing orders. She was not in sight at daybreak and there was evidence that she might elsewhere be fully engaged. A large convoy of L.S.T. and munitions ships had come in with the dawn and appeared to be directed towards St. Raphael and the north where, as we had learned from beach-head gossip, the American forces were steadily extending the field of operations.

On this D day plus 2 there was little sign, other than the ships and their traffic, to indicate the surge of battle for foothold on the coast. There were no sounds of it and only far inland, up the valley towards the foothills of Les Maures, was there sky sign of combat in the swift circling of aircraft that our instruments identified as friendly. From this it could be guessed that some airdrome or landing place in the area was in our hands, a supposition that the absence of enemy bombers from the air above our packed mass of shipping did much to encourage. The forest fires above St. Tropez had petered out but there were spirals of heavy smoke ascending in the still air from two vessels among the ships. A third, a liberty ship, had been beached off La Pilon and lay listed there in shallow water. These were probably casualties from the air-raid of the previous night, for we had not seen them there when we came in from sea. At beach-head P where we had landed our troops, the jetty had been destroyed and only its machinery—a futile old hand-crane—jutted out drunkenly above water. But the grapes of wrath had not altogether disrupted the housewifery of the little dwellings at St. Pons les Mures. In one of the tiny gardens there a hopeful village woman was hanging out clothes to dry in the warming sun.

*   *   *

I had often thought of our small part in landing operations as not unlike that of the urchin who rings doorbells then legs it for the nearest friendly entry. For so often we had sailed from the beach-head with only the knowledge that we had completed our task and it was rare, in subsequent service at long distance from the field of that action, to learn of what had happened in the area after we had put to sea. But 'Bigot' was different. We urchins did not have to run far or fast, for the port of Algiers claimed us for 'stand by' duty throughout the firm establishment of the new front in southern France. Berthed at the extreme end of the Musoir du Sud, with the white city in which the 'Torch' was lit outspread on the hills above us, we learned of its flaming progress northward through Europe. Not since Torch and Sicily had we disturbed the flag-pins on the big war map in the Operations room and they were rusted on its discoloured surface when we came to pinch them out and advance the line northward to Aix, Argentan, Grenoble, Vichy—and westward to Toulon, Marseilles and Port de Bouc. In normal circumstances, a merchant transport's wireless installation is sealed when in port, but, with us, the navy's all-hearing network—built into what had once been a swimming-pool—provided us with almost hourly bulletins concerning the amazing upsurge in France towards the Rhine. Nor was our swift acceptance of the news confined to the official communiques. In some way, little items of special interest to the 'Circassians' were picked out of the blue. With sorrow we learned that gallant old General Montsabert—who won all hands and hearts aboard when he sailed with us—had not survived. And there was a special day when we knew that the aged French battleship—the *Lorraine*—after signal service in the bombardments of the enemy on the coasts—had led triumphantly the Allied fleet into her own familiar home port of Toulon. Whatever purpose was served by the remaining ships of Force P being held at Algiers seemed to be negatived in early September. In our hands, the great port of Marseilles was at last in working order: there would be no more need for beach-head operations. L.S.I. had served their day in the Mediterranean and we sailed for home.

Upon arrival in the Clyde on the 14th September, 1944, it was without surprise we learned that *Circassia* would revert to her normal occupation as a troop transport. But it was with much regret we parted from our naval shipmates who had sailed with us for so long. Captain Allen brought the news as we lay anchored off Greenock. He was the senior and now the only remaining S.N.O.L. who had been attached to our group of merchant ships in combined operations from the date of its inclusion in Force V for Sicily. He had not sailed with us in the *Circassia* during operations but friendly contact had been established on the many occasions of joint conference and endeavour. It had fallen to him to wind up naval matters in the now disbanded L.S.I., a duty that he entered upon with enthusiasm. It had doubtless been hard for him to endure the tedious periods of 'stand by' whilst so much was doing on the distant fronts—and now, for him, there was the prospect of more active service. He thought the 'flotilla' would still be held together in some form of inland water service in the Low Countries. 'Mudlarking' he called that and he was eager to adventure in it. Whilst the officers and men of our naval party were packing and lashing up there was time for the careful drawing of a cork. (Veuve Cliquot, '35 I think—almost the last bottle of my bonded cellar from the sumptuous days of my vanished *Transylvania*.) The 'sun being over the fore-yard' and the ship in harbour, that was the right proceeding. There was talk, but no valedictory magniloquence. We had completed our workmanlike jobs together in reasonable harmony. But all were agreed that uncommon good luck had always attended the *Circassia*.

When the Navy left us it was in 'Commando fashion'. There was the *p-r-r-r-rupp* (with perhaps a special flourish) of the bos'n's pipes as the men with their baggage, equipment and etceteras were summoned to the L.C.A. to embark in the craft for the last lowering from the ship they had served in. They were in high spirits in prospect of 'a spot o' leaf' before setting out on another adventure. From the bridge and for the last time I spoke 'Lower aa-way' in the loud hailer and they were quickly gone. . . . The ship looked strangely lean and narrow with the empty falls dangling overside and the landing craft that she had nursed for so long gone away into the rain and mist.

Chapter XXVII

BEACH OPERATION IN REVERSE

NOVEMBER is not the time of the year in which one can indulge a hope of clement weather in the vicinity of Ushant and I came away from the routeing office at Glasgow in thoughtful mood after having been briefed for the voyage. The sailing orders that Naval Control had made out for me contained some matters that aroused anxiety. Refitted for normal transport duty, the *Circassia* was to proceed to the Baie de Morlaix on the Breton coast, anchor there in an exposed position, and embark 2000 Senegalese troops from barges alongside. They were to be taken to a West African port. It was to be a beach operation in reverse.

Morlaix! I had no knowledge of it, nor had the Naval Control, and the office held no large-scale chart of the bay and its approaches. The general sheet of the channel showed only a rock-studded creek and indentation on the coast-line eastward of Ile de Bas. But a copy of Admiralty Sailing Directions (Channel Pilot, Part II) was dug out from somewhere and in it I read:

Baie de Morlaix is entered between Pointe de Bloscon and Pointe de Primel about five miles eastward; it is encumbered with islets, rocks, and shoals, and access is difficult. . . . Plateau des Duons consists of numerous above-water and sunken rocks and extends south-westward from Le Pot de Fer and lies about three miles W.N.W. of Pointe de Primel. Tour de Duon, a white tower in which is a small room where shipwrecked mariners could find shelter, stands on the highest rock. . . . Numerous other rocks and dangers, the positions of which can best be seen on the chart, lie within those described, but no vessel should attempt to penetrate further into the Bay without local knowledge.

'Without local knowledge'; it was not a good prospect at the best of times, and November was hardly the season to make experiment. In the text there were other references to Tours de Sauvetage and it seemed almost that shipwreck was a common feature in the area. Pilotage was mentioned, and the local men were said to be 'usually found fishing off their station between Ile de Bas and Primel'. With Brest only lately stormed and taken by the Americans and much of Brittany still in a state of unrest, would the fishermen-pilots be returned so soon to the ways of sea commerce and put off at the summons of the 'pilot jack' at the fore? I thought it unlikely. But my main concern was not with the problems of navigation; these could be met and dealt with when the time came, and with the charts outspread for guidance. It was the imponderable state of the weather and what appeared to me a dubious prospect of embarking troops in an open roadstead that presented a vexed question. *Circassia* was no longer a landing ship designed for operations on the beach. The L.C.A. and their powerful hoisting gear had been dismantled and put on shore, and Senegalese levies could hardly be expert in the employment of the scramble nets that were still retained. The occasion would be one for the use of substantial transit lighters or barges of some sort, difficult to hold alongside in a rough sea or swell. I spoke of this, pointing out that no alternative was laid down in my orders. What was to be done in the event of a strong onshore wind prevailing, and our inability to carry out the movement?

'That would be your decision,' said the Routeing Officer. 'If the weather is against performance on the coast, it's up to you to cancel the proceedings and get out to open sea again. In that case, you would carry on to Plymouth for further orders. You will have a destroyer from Devonport with you on the coast: you could make your signals through her.' He glanced out of the high windows at the Square, before writing out the amendment to my sailing orders, and made hopeful remarks. It was a day of rain and mist, but it was not stormy: autumn weather, perhaps. I did not feel quite at ease in thought of my demur . . . but it was as well to have it all there in black and white.

We made a good passage to a rendezvous in the swept channel eastward of Lundy Island where we were met by a destroyer of the Channel Forces. The glass was still low and unsteady when we rounded Land's End and crossed the Channel in darkness, but the weather was moderate with a S.W. wind and almost incessant rain. Daybreak, if wet and cheerless, gave us sufficient sight of the landmarks to keep within the charted fairway and we anchored in what seemed a good position in the early fore-noon. . . . I had been unduly apprehensive. Our berth was well sheltered from the S.W. wind by the trend of the land about St. Pol and Roscoff. There seemed no reason why the embarkation should not proceed as planned. We had all day to get the troops on board and I could look forward to departure before nightfall. Enemy submarines were reported in the area and we would offer a sitting target but our escort had remained under way outside the fairway buoys and had signalled that an 'asdic' watch would be maintained whilst we were anchored. All seemed well.

The port was under American direction and it was not long after anchoring when the Embarkation Officer came off from the shore to make arrangements. He was Colonel Forsyth of the U.S. Army Transport Staff. We had met him before when he was stationed at Glasgow. It was soon apparent that he had found Movement Control at Morlaix not as smoothly depart-mental as at the Clyde. There were difficulties. No! The ship was in a good position—almost as far inshore as he had hoped we would come, for there was the matter of the tides in the river to be taken into account. No! It was money, francs or dollars, that was the trouble. The Senegalese demanded arrears of back pay before they would consent to be embarked and there was no money in the coffers of the newly established Comptoir Militaire in Paris. Of the 2000 troops we were ex-pected to 'lift', only 500 had received their money and the rest refused to embark unless they also were paid off in full. He thought the Senegalese were probably ex-prisoners of war who had worked with the Germans in the occupation. The American Army had clothed and fitted them for the voyage, but they were troublesome and unreliable and the High Command was

Cape St. Vincent and Lloyds Signal Station on Sagres Point

anxious to get them out of the country at any price. He had been in telephone communication with H.Q. and thought it likely that the U.S. would take over the commitments and pay the troops. Meantime, the men who had been paid were embarked in two 'Z' craft, now probably stuck in the mud of the Morlaix river and awaiting the tide to float them off. He added that there were only two periods of tide each day in which the river was navigable. The next tidal period would be at about 11 p.m., but that would be in darkness. Would I be willing to remain at anchor overnight and sail when troops were embarked in the morning? . . . Off-hand, I could not answer: there was nothing in my orders about the 'economics' of the movement but I was firmly instructed to arrive at Plymouth not later than 4 p.m. on the following day to supplement with British troop-details and passengers for Lagos and Takoradi. . . . The arrival of the 'Z' craft alongside brought about a break in the conversation and I welcomed the opportunity for reflection. It seemed that this too 'would be my decision'.

'Z' craft are long and narrow. When brought alongside the hull of a high transport ship, it is with difficulty they can be held there by warps that are, of necessity, led almost overhead to the ship's inboard bollards. As the crowded craft lumbered into position and tied up, it was quickly apparent that they would not lie in sufficient quiet and steadiness for long. The ship was head to wind and the increasing breeze, now considerable, caused her to sheer in wide swings, setting the craft to fret and plunge dangerously. This situation was relieved by the clever action of two American P.C.-type auxiliaries. Although small in size they were possessed of great power. Pinching into the broadsides of the 'Z' lighters and spurring vigorously, they held them firmly alongside and the transfer of the men was quickly in progress. And not only were they able to hold the 'Z' craft in position, but the pressure exerted corrected the tendency of the *Circassia* to sheer in the wind: the sea surface on the port, the embarkation, side became quiet as the proverbial mill-pond. . . . If we could be made to lie as quietly as that, I saw no reason why we should not complete the embarkation during the night. The port side would then be again the embarkation side and shaded lights, blanked to seaward, could be used with safety in the blackout. Although the barometer was still low, and falling lower, there was not yet any unmistakeable sign of a gale force. There would be opportunity, at any rate, to get the men on board and we could remain at 'stand-by' to sail with the first appearance of daybreak. By signal, I consulted the destroyer's captain and he concurred. Colonel Forsyth was heartily in agreement with my proposal when I told him of it. He anticipated an objection from the local seamen who manned the 'Z' craft: in the darkness, they would not be happy in handling such long vessels in the tortuous windings of the river. But the task would have to be undertaken: 'Z' craft were built to be put ashore anyway. In some haste, he checked up on the embarkation he had made and saw the craft cast off. He said they were the only two serviceable ones he had since the landing in Normandy and they would be needed for the midnight movement. In one of the useful P.C.'s he returned to the shore to speed the arrangement, leaving us to sheer and fret in the wind again. A second anchor was let go in an effort to steady the ship.

When he had gone, I wondered if I had been rash. It would have been so easy to say 'No' and claim warrant for that in the amendment to my sailing orders. As the afternoon grew on, the wind increased and heavy squalls whitened the waters of the bay. The rain had ceased between squalls and there were even shafts of sunlight that played on the broken water over the many shoal patches. We were still sheltered from the full blast of the S.W. wind but out at sea it was apparent that a heavy sea was sweeping up-channel. The narrow stretch of open water through which we had made passage to our anchorage, bordered by shoals and rocky islets looked sufficient sea-room for exit, but how would it look at night-time—if the need arose—with the buoy lights extinguished and the sea-marks obscured? Ruefully, I reflected that we were almost in the position I had envisaged in the routeing office at Glasgow! But it was not now 'up to me to cancel the proceedings and get out'. I was committed: I had lost the opportunity, and could only carry on in the hope that the wind would not haul to the N.W. Before sunset, the destroyer signalled the text of a 'Gale Warning' she had received in code. The northing of the wind was indicated in it—a message that added to my uneasy reflections.

It was nearly midnight when the 'Z' craft returned alongside, their open decks crowded with a strangely silent manning of seasick soldiers. Quickly, they were lashed-up and the P.C. vessels put into position. The lee anchor was hove up and an additional scope paid out on the first—that had held so well. The manoeuvre worked well again: with mounting confidence I watched the tugs exert the strain and hold the ship braced and steady as they had done during the day. All now depended upon the anchor and its cable holding and I blessed the circumstance that had so lately placed the ship in the Govan Dry Dock where the ground tackle had come under a very thorough survey. It would be tested here, but we were lying in a good position if the strain proved too great, heading nearly on the bearing of the open channel where a dimmed sternlight of the destroyer showed her in readiness to give us a lead out to sea.

Colonel Forsyth, wet through but in high spirits, had not resolved all his difficulties in this concluding lift of the undesirables. It was late in the afternoon when he received final instructions to pay the recalcitrant Senegalese on United States account, and the disbursement had not been completed by 'tide time'. There was reference to a curious scene at the dock-side in Morlaix. One of hesitant embarkations in the 'Z' craft, of coaxing and argument; of subversive oratory by the men's leaders—the witch-doctors, the Colonel called them—being countered by the display of American dollar bills at the shoreward end of the gangway! He said the whole affair was almost like the milling at a racecourse with unsteady bookmakers endeavouring to portion out the odds. Curiously, he said, the French military officers who were supposedly in command of the Senegalese took no part in the proceedings. He thought we would not find them of any assistance on the voyage; but the white *sous-officiers,* who spoke the language, were helpful. Of the 2000 personnel we had hoped to embark, only 1500 had been brought on board. Nor was the whole matter concluded by transport of the late arrivals. Not all the men from the 'Z' craft had received their dues. About 300 had come off on the personal promise of the U.S. paymasters that they would receive their money on board the ship before sailing and that commitment would have to be met.

I had hoped that the matters of embarkation would quickly be concluded once troops had been transferred from the craft alongside and when over an hour had passed with little sign of it I took opportunity for a look at the confusion and congestion below. Added to monetary difficulties there was the misdirection caused by the babel of strange tongues and the scene recalled to me much that I had read of the almost forgotten 'slave trade'. Drenched during passage on the open decks of the 'Z' craft many of the 'blacks' had stripped off their new and treasured uniforms to dry wherever they could be hung, whilst they themselves stood about or crouched or lay as nature made them. They were strangely quiet, but their great sombre eyes followed one's every movement with resentful intensity. There was already a noisome stench in the troop decks; much of it from the steaming glistening bodies, but most from the evidence of seasickness that had been their general condition on boarding. A few white sergeants were making some effort to direct the men towards less crowded quarters, but there was no French officer to be seen amongst them and it was obvious that the *sous-officiers* were themselves disheartened. A desk had been set up in a central position, and the U.S. pay staff were seated there, striving to complete the payment of the troops. There was commotion there, and clamour in many tongues. Long difficult names were shouted out to bring the payees to the counter and there was outcry and argument about the relative value of franc and dollar. A man in civilian clothing seemed to be busily employed by the Americans to translate for them the enquiries made. This he did, speaking in rapid French to the white sergeants who, in turn, made curious throaty noises that were apparently understood by the Senegalese. I learned that the civilian was a local man, a *maquisard* from St. Pol de Leon, whom

Colonel Forsyth had found invaluable in advancing matters in the port. The colonel said this assistant spoke English well, but with a Scottish accent! In peace-time it had been his business to sell onions, and he had tramped the Lowlands and the Highlands on that employment!

I was glad to return to the better air of the bridge again and to learn from Captain Barclay that there was no serious change in the position of the ship and the state of the weather. But there was a definite indication now that a change would not be long of coming. The glass had steadied and with a trend to rise. There was a brightening in the windward sky and the rain in the squalls was colder: it seemed likely that before long the wind would shift into the N.W. and blow hard from that point. In that case, we would be on a lee shore and it might be necessary to slip anchor and seek the safety of open sea. In that sudden event, the 'Z' craft alongside could prove a danger to the working of the propellers when getting under way and the drag that they would exert on the lee side of the ship might complicate the turn to seaward for there was little sea-room between us and the shoals. Despite the protests of the embarkation staff, it was decided to send the craft away whilst there was still opportunity for their local crew to make for Port Neuf at Roscoff. It was my intention to put to sea at the first approach of daybreak and have done with the harassment of the lengthy business. If the 'battle of the dollars' continued beyond that time, . . . well, . . . we could carry the Americans through the channel gale to Plymouth—a suggestion that was not received with enthusiasm by Colonel Forsyth and his tired officers.

Happily, there was no need for that. Before the day broke, the long-expected shift of wind came roaring at us around the promontory of Roscoff. Strangely, it did not bring with it the dreaded onset of the channel seas. Had our signal for a pilot been answered when we entered the bay, we could have been spared many hours of apprehension. 'Local knowledge' would be familiar with some curious twist in the tides or in the figuration of the outer banks that still sheltered the anchorage from the full destructive force of a N.W. sea. Out to seaward, the change in the wind had brought about a furious maelstrom of storm-lashed angry waters, but at our berth it was practicable to bring one of the faithful P.C. boats alongside to embark the tired but triumphant financiers of the movement. We sailed in time to round the breakwater at Plymouth in accordance with the sailing orders.

Chapter XXVIII

RUSSIAN EPISODE

IT was well known that rumour stemming from the victualling department in the ship was not lightly to be dismissed. Upon arrival in a home port, an astonishingly shrewd guess as to the nature of our next employment would often be whispered in the quarters of the cooks and stewards. While the deck and the engine-room could do no more than indulge in speculation, the galley newsroom had material grounds upon which to base opinion, for it was its duty to attend to food storage for the projected voyage. It was perhaps from the negatives in the store lists they drew conclusions. Let them be ordered to prepare for unloading a surplus of *atta* remaining over from an eastern voyage, they could gather from that discard that we were not bound east again for a term, because *atta* is staple diet for Indian troops. Then, the storing of any large quantity of dried or cured fish would rule out the possibility of a trip to Australia, for the 'diggers' have a rooted objection to fish ration in any state or savour. There were many signs to be observed and interpreted as soon as the provision trucks came wheeling down the quayside.

But when we lay at the embarkation sheds in K.G.V. Dock at Glasgow on return from our long voyage to the east, the commissariat was at a loss. The dusty bags of *atta* had been unloaded and that was that: an unusually large consignment of fish—fresh, cured, and dry—had been stowed in the chambers and we could not therefore be bound to the Antipodes. Beyond these negations there was no clue, no indication of whence we would head out on the next voyage.

It was then that the deck department took cross bearings from a substantial consignment of Admiralty goods addressed to the Commanding Officer, H.T. *Circassia,* and marked as being despatched from the Naval Depot at Priddys Hard. The Sea Transport people placed the twenty-three bales on board and requested that the supply notes be signed and returned. Supply notes in wartime betray all the signs of urgency in that they are not often decipherable. Beyond some indication that the scrawl was hurried hand for 'Special equipment, merchant transport' there was no clear description of the content. We had not indented for any special equipment, and it became necessary to break out a bale and open it up for investigation. It contained Arctic clothing: there were sheepskin jackets, fur waistcoats, fearnought trousers, heavy woollen underwear, long sea-boot stockings smelling of fish oil, mittens, fur caps with perspex visors and ear-flaps, sea shawls. In some bewilderment we sewed the bundle up again. But the contents had been seen by the seamen who assisted in the examination and the word 'Russia' was breathed throughout the ship!

There was nothing in the news of the day (March, 1945) that would indicate any need for a British force in Russia at that time. Certainly, Mr. Churchill, President Roosevelt, and Marshal Stalin had met at Yalta in February and 'reached agreement on joint military operations' but any purpose to be served by embarking British or American troops for the far north was difficult to envisage. I doubted if armed forces would be sent, but there was the possibility of a Mission for I had lately seen Captain Grattige, just back from the Crimea and the Middle East in the *Franconia* he now commanded, and had learned of that adventure in diplomatic voyaging. Our state of uncertainty was relieved by the visit of authentic Russians to the ship as she lay in readiness two days before sailing. They were military officers and 'advance party' of a lift of 1700 men of the Soviet Army.

These were ex-prisoners of war who had been retrieved from the Germans in the surge of our advancing forces on the Continent and were to be embarked for passage to Odessa in the Black Sea. When that destination was known, I could foresee little need for our new Arctic equipment and concluded that Priddys Hard had a standing order in respect of ships intended for all Russian ports: the consignment was untouched throughout the voyage.

We sailed from the Clyde on the 10th March, 1945, in a medium-sized convoy that was happily remarkable for its diminished destroyer escort. This seemed to augur a confidence that the enemy's U-boats and aircraft were not now in much strength abroad. Off Gibraltar the convoy was dispersed and in company with the *Duchess of Richmond*, also bound to Odessa with Russian personnel, we spurred ahead at our best speed. It was a new experience to be slipped from the leash in Mediterranean waters and an order that had just been issued did much to lessen the tensions of independent sailing. We were empowered to use again our navigation lights which were extinguished at sea in 1939. In the long years we had almost forgotten the gleam of lights on the waters and the friendly glow from the mastheads, and the red and green of port and starboard looked dangerously bright after such long disuse. The *ping* of the zig-zag clock was stilled as we steered on the voyage for it was no longer necessary to twist and turn on our courses from point to point. The weather too was unusually fine for the time of the year and it was pleasant to be cruising in company with a ship we knew so well.

Our Russian shipmates, or at least those on the lower decks, were smiling and apparently contented with conditions in the ship. They seemed well disciplined, were cleanly, and kept their troop-decks in good order. They were unarmed and no military drill was prescribed, but it was noticeable that they were never exercised in any form of physical training that was customary with troops on an ocean transit. With their officers it proved difficult to form acquaintance. It was not quite the barrier of language that held us apart, for one can smile in many tongues, but it was early evident that they were averse to any public show of friendship and particularly so when one amongst them was within sight or hearing. Amongst ourselves, we spoke of this one as 'the Commissar'. He was younger than most of the Russian officers and spoke colloquial English well, although with many unnecessary flourishes that betrayed a shallow knowledge of it. We were always unsure of his rank: the insignia he wore suggested a junior of some branch, yet he seemed to have a superior standing amongst the others. Being the only known English speaker amongst them, he was much to the fore and was undeniably useful in liaison duties. With experience of many seaports, I had no difficulty in classifying the 'Commissar', as we came to call him although we had no knowledge that he had that rank. He was of the same type as the tradesmen's 'runners' who frequent merchant ships immediately upon their arrival in a foreign port to solicit business in chandlery or ship supplies, bunkers or butcher meat. He had the same manners of approach, the same oily geniality, the eager appearance of helpfulness in all the matters that might burden an incoming shipmaster. I would admit him friendly enough, but he seemed to frown upon any such approach on the part of his colleagues.

The Russians were not the only contingent in the ship. At Glasgow, we had embarked a sizeable group of British Red Cross executives and helpers intended for duty on the return voyage from Odessa. At that port, when we had disembarked the Russians, we would re-embark with British or American ex-prisoners of war who had been liberated by the Russian Army. It was anticipated that many of them would be in rags and very likely in poor physical shape and, to relieve that distress, Mrs. Giraud and her staff of capable ladies of the Red Cross had brought on board a substantial stock of clothing and comforts to be distributed. The permanent military staff, under Colonel Arthur H. Hope, the O.C. Troops, had also been enlarged to meet the situation and we had thus a considerable body of 'details' accommodated in the ship. The most that could be done in the way of entertainment for their leisure hours was the provision of cinema programmes in the only place available, the troops' recreation hall. These shows—there were three a day—proved popular with the Russian troops, even if they were to them only an appeal to the eyesight. They could not have enough of the glories of Hollywood.

It was not long before 'the Commissar' brought the Russian Colonel to my quarters to lodge an opinion. The grizzled old soldier spoke his piece—a few short sentences—and, that being apparently a form of verbal shorthand, the younger man made long translation of what he was supposed to have said. He had objected that his men were endangered by being crowded together in the recreation hall and asked that the programmes be discontinued. . . . 'If we were attacked by the enemy,' he was reported to have said, 'it would be very difficult!' . . . I pointed out that that was a matter for him to regulate, there was no obligation on the Russian's part to attend the entertainment. There was a large crew in the ship and there were also the civilian passengers. I said it would be undemocratic to deny these others their pleasures on the voyage and so could not close down. . . . I wonder if the grim old colonel understood English. Perhaps. It is possible, for I thought I saw the faint trace of a smile on his face when the interview was concluded. It was noticed that the Russians did not attend in any numbers after that. The show was not forbidden to them but another pastime seemed to be encouraged. Our salvage of old discarded charts and the pasteboard of empty boxes was drawn upon to provide card-sheets for the artists amongst them. The portraits of Stalin and other Soviet leaders were not ill done either. These, they mounted on rough scrap-wood frames to be carried in procession when they had landed in their homeland.

But not all were eager for that day of repatriation. A space in the troop-decks had been allotted to the Russians for use as an orderly room and throughout the voyage it had been busily engaged. What went on there we never learned, but it was thought the soldiers were subjected to frequent interrogations there, for they seemed thoughtful and, in some cases, even gloomy when passing out of it. As the passage lengthened and the ship approached the Dardanelles, there was the same appearance of anxiety on many faces. It was Major Nicholson, the troops' Welfare Officer, who first remarked it. He had previously been in charge of a camp in the south of England where the Russians had been assembled before embarkation. He thought that few of the ex-prisoners would be sent on leave or to their homes when arrived in Russia. They had seen something of another way of life, and could not be set at large to speak of it. Perhaps he was right. We passed through the Straits in the darkness and, at morning muster, some men (the numbers were never known) were reported missing. There was a rumour —which could not be sifted—of men having been seen to slip overside, fortified by ship's lifebelts, when we had slowed and stopped off Chanak to take on the Turkish pilot. It could be possible for resolute men to make the shore there, for it is close aboard at the narrows. A rigorous search was made throughout the ship when the men were missed but no trace or information could be found. Under normal circumstances an enquiry would have been held, but the Russians were against such a proceeding. The only suggestion made by 'the Commissar' was that we should immediately call in all lifebelts! Our legal duty was met by an entry in the Log.

We arrived off Istanbul in the morning and anchored to obtain further instructions before entering the Black Sea. The Turkish Port Authorities exercised no restraint on our movements for we were a merchant ship on her lawful occasions. But the matter of the missing Russian soldiers had been officially reported and steps were taken. Not long after we had anchored, an ancient gunboat lumbered out and took up a berth in the vicinity. No one but Captain Shergold of the *Duchess* and myself were allowed to go on shore and that only on a visit to the British Consulate.

The Consular Adviser, a British naval captain, had an odd circular route mapped out for us—a detour to avoid floating mines which had broken away from the vast minefields laid down by the Russians, Germans, Rumanians and even Bulgars. Every depth of less than 100 fathoms was suspect, and the limits of the minefields were not known. But until we approached the delta of the Danube our route would be in deep water and floaters drifting south on the constant current would be the menace for which a good lookout must be maintained. At a point on the northern coast a Russian guardship was stationed. From her we would each receive a naval pilot who would take the ships through the swept channels to Odessa. It was agreed that we should continue together until within sight of the guard-ship. The *Duchess,* having better speed, would then proceed ahead and enter port before the *Circassia.* It was thought un-likely that port facilities such as tugs and harbour pilots would be available at Odessa. But ships had been there since the ice in the Dniester had broken up . . . and had come away again. The captain was cheerfully optimistic when he bade us good-bye. That the menace of floating mines required constant and serious consideration was made plain before we left Turkish waters. The Turks had netted the northern entrance to the Bosporus in a peculiar pattern of boom defence that I had not seen before. It was set at a 'shedding' angle and, over on the European side, there seemed to be a catchment of sorts in which some naval craft were—at our moment of passing through—engaged in dismantling an ugly monster. . . . Any doubts we may have had about the incidents of the night were dispelled by a feat on the part of a Russian soldier when the *Circassia* was clearing the northern exit of the Bosporus. We had just discharged the pilot and were getting under way again when the cry 'Man overboard' was raised. It was not then possible to turn the ship and the man could be seen swimming strongly in the direction of the pilot's launch that had turned towards him. We saw him picked up but, as the launch continued its passage to the shore, I had no inclination to return to claim the man: the swift current running there called for all my attention.

Odessa was largely in ruin. It had been subjected to assault on all sides and from the air in the course of incredibly bitter fight-ing for possession of it. The extensive harbour was littered with wreck and obstruction and the long breakwater was breached and open to the sea. Where the shattered masonry of the break-

water had been blown in the bombardments could not be cal-
culated and it was somewhat in fear of finding it we sounded a
careful passage towards the only sea-face where a ship of our
size could lie. As the Consular Adviser had surmised, there were
no tugs available and we had also to use our own ship's boats to
run hauling lines to the quay. But we did have the help of a
capable harbour master who assisted in berthing the ship.

It would have been unreasonable to expect a cruelly-stricken
city to extend a civic welcome to its warriors returned, but I had
not thought our entry on what was certainly a humane mission
would be met by sullen and ill-disguised hostility. It was curious
too that the rounds were opened by a medical man—the Port
Health Officer. It is right and proper that the good health of all
on board an incoming ship from abroad should be documented
and attested for the guidance of the Port Authority and there can
be no question about firm compliance with such an international
regulation. But there is international courtesy too and that was
never in evidence at Odessa. Storming into my day-room without preliminary, he handed me a questionnaire in which the
text was wholly in Russian-Greek letter. I indicated that I could
not read it and he called a lady in to translate the questions, then
left abruptly. Naturally I offered the interpreter a seat and the
business of filling up the form proceeded. She was a woman of
middle years, obviously under-nourished, and of sad expression.
She spoke good English brightly and her accent was cultured.
Perhaps that was her fault. For when I was about to write down
that I knew of no unusual preponderance of rats in the ship, the
uncouth disciple of Hippocrates returned, to pour out what
could only have been a torrent of abuse directed at her. Had I a
vicious cur to chasten, I could not have used more passionate
accents. In silence then, the paper was completed and I bowed
the lady out.

It was in this same atmosphere of suspicion and distrust all our
proceedings at the port were conducted, nor was it noticed that
the Russians we had brought out of captivity were welcomed
home. Disembarkation proved a dispiriting and lengthy
business. Not for our pleasant Russians was there a quick-step

on the quayside with banners fluttering and the pictures of their leaders proudly displayed. No! In small groups, sometimes in ones and twos, as they came down the gangway, they were accepted by officials who were mostly heavily armed, and marched off to a receiving shed. When they were gone and the duty fell to us of clearing up the troop-decks in preparation for the return voyage, there were many portraits framed in scrap-wood to be swept aside with other refuse and dumped at sea.

Chapter XXIX

THE LAST CONVOY

I HAD thought the Commodore was bound to do something about it for he had made no signal to authorise such an outburst, in whatever happy abandon, on the day of Victory in Europe. The rattle and display from the ack-ack armament of 'Pennants 14', which was the rearmost ship of the port outer column, was still singular but it might prove an infectious outbreak in the circumstances throughout all the ships of the last K.M.F. convoy to be sailed from the United Kingdom in the war. Sure enough, the daylight Aldis from the guideship stabbed out a reproof and it was with interest I scanned our interception of the message. It read—'To Pts 14 from Commodore. Suggest cease fire. You may yet need a few rounds.'

The occasion of the *feu de joie* was the official ending of the war in Europe and the date, Tuesday 8th May, 1945. When we sailed from the Clyde some days before, it was in expectation of victory at any time. Berlin had been stormed and entered, Hitler was dead, and the German armies in Europe had surrendered. It was known then that the surrender on land was complete but the situation on the high seas was conditioned by a phrase in the Admiralty Signal addressed to all ships at sea— '. . . and although resistance has ceased in all areas where the German Government is still in touch with its remaining forces, precautions on the voyage must not be relaxed.' There was no knowing what final vicious injury the dying beast might yet inflict. Many U-boats were still at sea, and that the fangs were not quite drawn was indicated by an intercepted SSSS from a torpedoed ship off May Island on the morning of the 7th May. It was curiously in the pattern of Britain's wars that this should end, as it had begun, with the sinking of a merchant ship. . . .

The *Athenia* on the 3rd September, 1939 . . . and the *Avondale Park* on 7th May, 1945!

Thus, the progress of the last convoy into the Atlantic had been governed by all the precaution of a war voyage. Bound south towards the Mediterranean, one would have thought that the direct route could now be taken, and this belief was encouraged by the convoy's passage down the Irish Sea and westward in the Georges Channel, but when we had passed the Tuskar and skirted the Irish coast, it was towards the old war-route in about 18° W. we steered. Zig-zag courses were still maintained during daytime and at night all lights were extinguished. An escort, reduced from the usual five frigates to three, kept station ahead and on the beam. At times one or the other would be detached to investigate a stranger on the horizon, possibly in the hope that she would turn out to be a surfaced U-boat flying the black flag of surrender and for which we had been warned to keep lookout. The weather was fine and the visibility exceptional, but we saw nothing of the enemy. The official message that the war against Germany was ended came through in the early morning of the 8th May, a time when the decks were deserted and only the watchkeepers were about: it aroused no excitement for it was discounted by earlier broadcasts. But in the morning the full significance of the signal was realised. Zig-zag was not resumed and the Commodore made a wide alteration of course to head the convoy towards a landfall near Cape St. Vincent—a point on the Portuguese coast that few Allied merchant ships had sighted during the war years. There was expectation that the convoy might be dispersed as the day wore on, or that at least the faster ships would be detached to proceed independently at better speed. But the Commodore made no further signal and we were left to guess at the date of general release. As customary, we were all astir at the early morning alert, for routine persists in a ship, and when Lieut. Cleare came to the bridge to test out the controls it broke upon me suddenly that his rounds had no longer the importance of instant readiness attached to them. He and his D.E.M.S. gunners could happily stand down now to become a 'care and maintenance' division in the ship.

Care and maintenance? As daylight grew and the familiar superstructure of the ship took shape and colour after darkness, it was with a newly critical outlook I studied her appearance. In the war years it had not been possible to maintain her in the fine condition that was our pride in the peaceful days of commerce. Such upkeep demanded a constant renovation of dingy and blistered paintwork and there were, in war, many factors that weighed against 'shipwork as requisite'—a phrase that used to be of daily entry in the mate's working Log. Amongst these handicaps, there was the shortage of paint supply, but the principal restriction was much more fundamental and curious. To clean off a 'fleet' of steel plating before the application of a pristine coat of new paint, chipping hammers would come thunderously into use and the din a betrayal of position to an enemy listener underwater! We could not afford to hammer our plates when the stinging bees were swarming at sea. It was with a jaundiced eye I surveyed the rusty scuppers, the patched and blistered bulkheads, the makeshifts and extemporisings that had for so long been apology for 'shipwork as requisite'. But *Circassia* was not in singular case. As the sun came up above the sea-line and brightened the outlines of our sister ships in the last convoy, it could be seen that all were as weather stained as we. For the most part drab in some shade of grey, patches of red lead —or of golden rust—gleamed in the morning sun: discoloured ribbons on the broadside marked the places where cargo lighters and tenders had bumped and rubbed along the length of 'boot-topping' on windy days at the anchorages: a newcomer, brought in from far abroad, still showed traces of the original standard war scheme for merchant ship colouration in the dingy yellow of her upperworks. But there was uniform colour in the flags we wore. The small war-ensign at the gaff that, day and night, we had flown on sea-passage for so long, looked ragged and smoke stained. We could do better, and the six-yard Red Ensign—a legacy from the ship's Admiralty service—was hoisted in its place. It was then that Pennants 14 proclaimed her joy and independence. When that outburst was stilled by the signal from the Commodore, there began the rounds of interchanging messages between all ships and the flags seemed more vividly colourful and fresh and gay as they fluttered in the light wind.

Inboard, we were embarked with suitable personnel for the gaieties of an Occasion. On recent voyages we had not transported any large regimental or corps-detachments. Details and minor reinforcements had been the most part of the nominal rolls. But now the character of our embarkation had advanced a little further towards the ship's peace-time role, for we had many ladies taking passage with us to Naples. Added to drafts of W.R.N.S. and W.A.A.F. with some Red Cross and an E.N.S.A. party, we carried the large secretarial staffs of British commissions for Italy and Austria. The brightly modish attire of the civilian ladies mingled with the blue and khaki to emphasise the gala atmosphere of the crowded decks, exactly as though we were again abroad on a festive cruising voyage. They were well squired too, for the R.A.F. was in strength aboard and certainly not wanting in the social duties.

But receptions and gaiety and rejoicing can be tiring in time to an elder at the feast. After church, and when the schedules of entertainment for everyone on board were running smoothly, a quotation from old Karl Baedeker occurred to me:

> At this point the Glacier is reached, and a rest is taken.

*   *   *

'Monkey Island' has been vacated on this early afternoon. There is not now the pressing need for such a high lookout, nor for the state of readiness that had marked the days before. The watchkeepers have stepped down to the bridge below to find relief in the longer distance it affords for measured paces from one wing to the other. The only other tenant of the deserted deck is the duty quartermaster, on lookout for signals. I notice that he is trim and newly shaven in honour of the day, but he fidgets at his post beside the Aldis and his gaze is more often directed at the festivities below than towards the ships of the convoy; he will be in hope of joining the revellers down there when his watch is over. And who shall blame him? For this is the day that he and I have worked for throughout the stormy years and signals cannot now be of vital importance. Likely enough, the Commodore in the guideship will have reached the glacier too, and we shall not hear from him until after tea.

The war has been a long traverse: nearly six years of it. But the wheel has come full circle now, to find me where the opening of 'Envelope Z' had found me—out at sea in the Atlantic. I had not thought to be afloat and at my ease at the end of it when I broke the seal of the first 'lettered' message in my cabin in the *Transylvania*. . . . I think of my trusted shipmates who were with me then. Many are gone now, sunk in her when she was torpedoed in 1940. Others have returned to sail with me from time to time until merited promotion was theirs. Mr. Macdonald, who brought me that first 'lettered' message, survived the loss of the ship. A thought of him, now in naval service at the Clyde base, promotes a link towards the harbinger of today's good news—the last of the 'lettered' messages. Curious he should be David Sproat, to whom in 1917 I passed the order to break wireless silence and send out the distress call when the *Cameronia* (the first of that name) was sunk under us in the eastern Mediterranean! Much troubled water has swept over our bows since then and it is strange that we should be together again on this day of victory achieved.

*   *   *

I had lately read J. L. Hodson's *Merchantmen at War* and the taste of that good book still lingers. He thought well of us. But were we as gallant as all that, or merely stubborn in defence of our ancient livelihood? Who knows? I could not say. Except for the first year of independent sailings across the Atlantic, my lot in the war had been in service of troop convoys that were in general heavily protected. Only rarely did we sight an active enemy and often our speed and sharp helm power enabled us to evade him. I had not known the bitterness of the Russian passage nor had I experienced the long-drawn odyssey of a seven-knot convoy in the Battle of the Atlantic. The tragedy of the open boat I knew only from hearsay and I had not often the oppor-

War damage; an incredible condition in which the oil tanker M.V. *Lucerna* made port at Glasgow and was there repaired for further sea service

tunity to observe the bearing of my fellows in adversity. In all my voyages I had been incredibly fortunate. . . . No. I could not say. . . . But a recollection of Halifax in 1942 brings the thought that Hodson could be right. . . . Bitter winter weather there and the snowdrifts banked high in the dockside streets in a succession of icy blizzards. On my way to the hospital I passed a vacant lot at the waterfront on which the relics of ship disaster in the Atlantic were ranged in row and row. These were ship's lifeboats, the open boats in which the survivors of merchant convoy sinkings had made the land on Nova Scotia. Sea-salt and the snow had whitened them to the semblance of stones in a graveyard, with here and there an iron-grey prow or sternpost upstanding in the drifts. Perhaps only a sailor could build for himself a realisation of the agonies the men in these frail shells had known as they tended sail or laboured at the oars to reach the shore. At the hospital, where I had gone to visit an old shipmate who had come through such an ordeal, the ward in which he lay was overbedded by the many victims of exposure, frostbite, gangrene, lying pitifully under the sheets as derelict as their craft in the boat-yard. I was told that not many would ever be fit for seagoing again. They had paid a hard price in defence of a livelihood. . . . Yes. There was gallantry enough.

★　★　★

A number of war taboos seem to have grown up of themselves without any special regulation in the ships. I cannot recall that the disuse of 'house flags'—the distinguishing emblems of the shipping companies—was ever officially decreed. But from shortly after the outbreak of war until now, few if any were ever displayed at the masthead. It may well be that the towing swivel fitted there for the operation of kites and captive balloons made such a display expensive in torn bunting, but the flags were not worn in wartime. Now, on this great day, some have appeared again, probably run up on the same wires that tethered our now discarded balloons.

The *Corfu,* that is our guideship, is thus decorated by the colours of the P. and O. and has also an important symbol at the fore—a flag not usually hoisted except when leaving or entering port or when ships are forming up in convoy. It is a white burgee (or broad pennant) and has a blue St. Andrew's cross superimposed. It denotes a naval commodore embarked in her, Vice-Admiral Sir Malcolm Goldsmith, one of the retired flag-officers of the Royal Navy who volunteered for sea duty with the merchant convoys throughout the war.

I surmise that on first introduction the Commodore would not be as warmly received in the merchant ships as later when he came to form his opinion of our abilities and we to recognise the skill and sailor wisdom that was embarked to help us in the early days of convoy practice. For it was new to the master to have a senior sailor on deck to be consulted on the matters of the voyage. 'Commodore, Sir!' did not come very trippingly to the tongue of one who, officially still in command, had yet to heed another's voice in ship control. In the smaller ships the matters of berthing accommodation could be productive of irritations when the ship's officers might have to be double-banked in small cabins to make way for the naval signalmen attached to the naval officer's staff. That this apparent hardship was dictated by the need to have the signalmen as close to the flag halliards and the Aldis as they could be berthed was not always appreciated. But how quickly the atmosphere of constraint and diffidence gave way to confidence and understanding as the saving plan of convoy operations became familiar! There was never 'fuss and frills' with our important shipmate. Perhaps well-tailored in service uniform when he stepped on board, it was not long before he was at his ease, padding about the bridge in a shabby old sea-suit or a duffle coat the same as that worn by his signalmen. Often, the shining new 'brass hat' of a Commodore, R.N.R.—that was now his rank—was quickly replaced by an older favourite, its twin embroideries on the peak of it tarnished and faded, that possibly he had last worn on the quarterdeck of his own flagship. . . . No. It was not long before he had established himself in the merchant ships and it will be long before his influence amongst the merchantmen is forgotten. Hodson mentions in his book that twenty-one Commodores of Convoy had

gone down with the ships they sailed in. A gallantly high per-
centage in a group that cannot greatly have exceeded a hundred.

I recall a meeting with the Nestor of them all. At New York
in 1942. His was a friendly visit to the *George Washington* as she
lay at the Chelsea Piers. We had met before and he had heard
that I was in port. I was not in good shape, nor was my ship.
We had just arrived after an anxious trial voyage from the U.S.
Navy Yard at Philadelphia. Both my ancient ship and I had
lately come from the surgeon's hands, and whilst I was progress-
ing towards recovery my ship was still unseaworthy and groan-
ing her multiple complaints in almost every joint and pulse. The
visit of the old admiral put me stoutly on my feet again. Who
was I to feel downhearted at the infirmity of my single ship
when here was a sailor of my age smilingly recounting his long
days of effort in battling the Atlantic, then at its tragic worst,
with a convoy of fifty or sixty ships to bring through?

★　　★　　★

The last convoy has been dispersed, and we are an independent
ship again. The order came before sunset and was marked by
prudent detachment, with the faster ships released in the order of
their potential speed. We were then approaching a point off
Cape St. Vincent at which a wide alteration of course was
necessary to head for the Straits of Gibraltar. The freedom of
the seas established now, we had sighted many homeward-
bound vessels steering on opposite courses and the Rule of the
Road was better served by independent action.

How quickly the old habits, so long restrained, return to the
commercial sailor! It has grown dark, for the moon is not yet
risen and there is little twilight off the Spanish coast. Darkness,
black darkness, has been our portion for so long that the novel
vision of lights at sea again requires a second thought for reassurance. Perhaps curiosity or an urge to extend the unusual features
of V.E. Day is responsible for an excess in the unauthorised display of lights on deck from which the quiet sea takes reflection
and shimmers in the unwonted glow. . . . We are all 'libertymen' now and I can find no serious grounds for reproof when

the cloistered planks of the bridge and even 'Monkey Island' are invaded by passenger groups from below in quest of communal excitement. Maybe it is as a contribution to this, the junior officers so often man the Aldis and flash out a 'What ship?' as the homeward-bounders pass by on their lawful occasions.

Communal excitement! I recall the tremendous outburst of the London crowds in November, 1918, for I was on leave there at the time and saw the massed emotion of a people express itself in frenzied rejoicing in victory. But there were quiet places too. I think of the dim interior of St. Martins-in-the-Fields in which I had sought retirement from the tumult and the swaying multitudes of Trafalgar Square. The phrases of the Psalm of Thanksgiving after Victory at Sea, which the R.A.F. padre had intoned this very morning, flow in with that current of thought. . . . We had need of thanksgiving.

> The waters had drowned us and the stream had gone over
>   our soul;
>   The deep waters of the proud had gone over our soul.
> The Lord hath appeared for us: the Lord hath covered
>   our heads,
>   And made us to stand in the day of battle.

Chapter XXX

UNFINISHED BUSINESS

EVER since V.E. Day the Commodore's reproof to an exuberant ship in the last merchant convoy of the war had often occurred to me. 'We might yet need a few rounds' was the memorable admonition, quite obviously a hint of unfinished business still to be attended to by the ships engaged in overseas transport. It called for no great speculation to recognise the only combat area in which such transport would be most heavily engaged and it was as well to keep our powder dry and our D.E.M.S. gunners up to strength, even if 'care and maintenance' was now their only immediate duty. When we sailed again from the Clyde in July, 1945, the question of when Japan would totter and fall as Germany had done was uppermost in our minds. For we were bound east again and, before sailing, I had had a communication from an almost forgotten correspondent. S.O.U.L.S., who is Senior Officer, Unallocated Landing Ships, was again interested in the lifting capacity of *Circassia's* working derricks and, this time, there was enquiry about cooking arrangements for Indian troops. Memories of Bombay—to which port we were routed —were revived as I completed the questionnaire and I thought that 'Action Deferred' in 1943 had now its possibility of achievement.

This was confirmed when, after a fast and uneventful passage, we came within sight of that port. Bombay has its own special way of presenting its civic and surrounding beauty to the in-comer by sea and at no time of the year is this more manifest than in early August when the great rains have become inter-mittent and, between squalls of the petering monsoon, the visibility is enhanced. There is first the growing into view of the high serrated ranges of the Western Ghats, resolving from watchet outline to a deep and frowning indigo as the land is closed. The rim of the sea horizon ahead, that has been clear-cut for so long, becomes dentated and irregular when slowly, one by one, the lesser islands and the towers and domes of the city uprise. It is not long then before the masts, the funnels, the top-works of the shipping in the bay and the coastal sea-marks appear jutting out of the sea rim in measured progression. As we came in on such a morning, it was difficult to find anchorage, so many were the ships, large and small, berthed in the outer roadstead that now seemingly extended beyond all former limits at the Prongs and Middle Ground. It was noticed that nearly all the ships had a distinguishing number painted on their sides and we learned soon that we had become 'P.(9)' in 'Operation Zipper' intended against the Japanese occupation of Malaya. When we had disembarked the military drafts and details, together with the many civilian passengers brought out from the Clyde, the ship remained alongside for some days whilst refitting for the carriage of Indian personnel. That completed, we hauled off to anchor again in the outer harbour and there remained awaiting further orders.

The change in the monsoon is not the best of weather for riding out that unsettled season in what is practically the open sea. Anchorage there is completely exposed to the heavy sou'west swell that still persists and it is vexed by the run of swift tides. In consequence there was little traffic with the shore, for boat work was hardy and indeed highly dangerous at times in the sudden uprising of the sea. But there were occasional days of moderate weather in which ship visits could be made and the news of day be discussed with our fellows. Naturally, it was the bearing of the news broadcasts on the prospects of the impend-ing assault on Malaya that prompted these wet uncomfortable journeys in a heaving motorboat. That the operation was in suspense at that critical date seemed obvious, for there was little sign of urgency in the preparations: beyond refitting and numbering the ships, the naval authority had apparently lost personal interest in us once we were ticked off and cleared to the anchorage. Newspapers were hard to come by at such distance from the shore and the wireless programmes conveyed no more than a reading of headlines. . . . But we were stirred to the depths by brief disclosure of the atom bomb affright on Hiroshima. We did not lower a boat that day, but went silently about our trifling ship-duties—not understanding, and somewhat in awe and fear of this adoption of a weapon we had thought only invoked by the classic gods.

Japan surrendered on the 14th August. India was probably more greatly excited and relieved by the defeat of the Japanese than by European victory and acclaimed V.J. Day with oriental lavishment. Bombay, long habited to communal display, be it of welcome or relief—or temperament—was in high festival mood on the official days of holiday. Viewed from the offshore anchorage, the city never seemed more regally fair nor its harbour more colourfully enriched by such a vast assembly of decorated ships. At the dockyard anchorage where many naval ships and craft were berthed, a glorious symbol of the return to peaceful days was proudly displayed: the Jack was hoist at the prow of all His Majesty's ships again.

What effect the surrender of the Japanese would have upon 'Operation Zipper' was of course the subject of wide conjecture. Knowledge of the situation at sea when Germany collapsed prepared us for a post-war period of alert, for no one knew how far or how quickly the writ of a discredited emperor would run. The 'nips' were known to be still in fighting strength in Malaya and the islands; the creed of *hara-kiri* still obtained and, as many thought, they were unlikely to accept defeat. When the celebrations had faded, it was soon known that the landing in Malaya would be carried out though there might be a further period of stand-by until the weather in the straits had calmed sufficiently to ensure the success of beach-head operations. But if there had been a plan for mass sailing of the ships from Bombay, the new situation had altered it. A number of the troopships were detached and routed to other Indian ports for embarkations, a measure that may have been designed to relieve pressure on the railways in the vast movement of troops. *Circassia* was amongst the ships thus disengaged and we sailed independently to Vizagapatam in the Bay of Bengal. In that old pirate's lair we embarked the Kumaon Rifles and a Gurkha battalion and sailed towards a rendezvous at sea with the main assault forces on the 31st August.

'Zipper' was a prudent and leisurely proceeding, in some ways resembling 'Torch' in its wide diversions. We seemed to be controlled from somewhere far ahead. It could be conjectured that policy dictated the tangents of our course towards an objective or it may simply have been that the clearance of enemy mines in the approaches took longer to effect than had been thought. There was the same exercise in manoeuvre to slow the speed of advance but, this time, no signals were made to exercise weapons or to cloud the convoy in chemical smoke. Instead, Rear-Admiral Martin (curiously known as the Chong Captain) kept us up to the mark by a form of signal quiz in which *Circassia,* not specially learned in war dates, earned at least one mark for being the first to signal 28th February, 1900, when the day of the relief of Ladysmith was queried. (I was standing off the Bluff at Durban in the *Australia* on that date and remembered it.) . . . On the evening of the 7th September, with the high northern peaks of Sumatra in sight to southward, the broad formation of ocean convoy was narrowed to two long columns before entering the Straits of Malacca. At daybreak of the following day speed was reduced and we found ourselves trailing within distant sight of the battle-fleet in which only the *Nelson* and two or more aircraft carriers could be made out in the screen of lesser vessels: a huge ship on the horizon that we could not identify proved, later, to be the French battleship, *Richelieu.* Throughout the daylight hours it could be seen that there was considerable flying 'off and on' the aircraft carriers. None of their planes came near us but it was observable that their flights were solo or in pairs and not the massed squadrons that might indicate a counter to enemy opposition. We augured well from that circumstance and steamed slowly and confidently during the night. The plan of operations to land the liberation forces in Malaya was aimed at a long front extending from north of Port Swettenham in Selangor to Port Dickson in Negri Sembilan, a distance of over forty miles. Both of these ports are small and have only modest facilities for coastal traffic, but they were at road- and rail-head and so of advantage for quick deployment of the Army. A good road runs between the ports at a short distance from tidemark and it was towards a central position called 'W' beach on this long front that the group of ships in which *Circassia* was included was ordered.

When we arrived at our point of release in the early morning of the 9th September, we found the Navy in undisturbed occupation of the beach at Morib. We had not known our destination by that name, but a large beach-sign set up on the foreshore lettered 'W' confirmed our navigations. For some hours we had been steaming slowly in a swept channel the mine-sweepers had cleared and marked by 'dan' buoys. At the anchorage which was easily recognised by the bearing of Bukit Jurga— a solitary conical hill on the inland plain—a full-sized turning-buoy had been laid down. It carried a large blue flag and on that, lettered in white, we read, 'Zipper Sports Ground.' We did not see point in this inscription until later in the day, for we anchored nearly at the turn of high water and the beach appeared to be all that was desirable for the quick boatage of burdened troops. A fringe of gleaming white sand backed by mangroves and the high fronds of jungle palms lay invitingly extended as far as the eye could follow. To the north of us a group of L.S.T. was beached in line abreast almost as though berthed in a ship-yard and already tanks, trucks and mobile field-guns were rumbling ashore from their yawning hinged bows and crushing down the palms and jungle growth that obstructed passage to the inland highway. When we anchored, infantry landing craft were quickly in attendance to be loaded to the gunwales with cheerful sepoys. All seemed well and there was prospect that

the ships would be cleared and ready to proceed to Singapore—
if that port had been entered—before nightfall.

But we had not taken the ebbing tide into consideration in
that pleasing expectation. As it drained away, extensive shoals
and mudbanks intervened between us and the firm of the
strand: the L.S.T. at the northern beach listed drunkenly when
they were left high and dry on the uneven runnels of the banks:
the landing craft, that had set out so jauntily from alongside the
troopships, were soon in difficulty and signalling for instructions
to beach-head H.Q. on shore. Landing operations were suspended for a time. With the sun rising high and baking the
shoal-heads to some appearance of foothold, orders were apparently given to the landing parties to get overside and walk. It
was now clear that the 'sport' referred to on the Zipper flag was
aquatic. Burdened by full battle equipment, the men floundered
in the mud and water on the long journey to the distant beach.
By our reckoning they had upwards of a weary slogging mile
to trudge before reaching firm ground and there seemed to be
many runnels and water channels to be crossed neck-high. One
shuddered to think of what would have been their fate had the
beach been held in any strength by a resolute enemy!

In these circumstances, our airy anticipation of being quickly
disembarked was dashed. There were only two tidal periods of
the day in which the troops' landing could be accelerated and
even then the rising tide did not immediately advance matters to
full-scale employment of the transport craft, for we had to wait
until they had floated off the mud-banks before returning alongside for another draft of troops. It was D day plus 3 before we
were finally cleared of all landing personnel with their baggage
and equipment. . . . Happily for me, the delays brought about a
meeting that I considered a perfect award for long sea-service.
On the southern sector near Port Dickson there had not been the
difficulties of wading the troops ashore, operations had been
quickly concluded there and my son David, who was the naval
Beachmaster in that area, had concluded his task. Sailing north
to another assignment, he called in at Morib to board us for a
while and have a word with the 'Old Man'. We celebrated the

end of our wars together out there. I thought it almost a Kiplingesque episode when later, as we were heaving up, I saw the frigate *Nith* in which he had taken passage creaming off north to Rangoon whilst we were turning southwards towards Singapore!

★   ★   ★

R.A.P.W.I.'s are Released Allied Prisoners of War, Indian. It was quickly to embark these cruelly mistreated unfortunates we were ordered alongside upon arrival at Singapore. This employment had been foreseen before our departure from Bombay and *Circassia* was well equipped to meet it. Although we could not accommodate serious hospital cases, the ship was adequately stored and serviced to care for the walking wounded, the hungry and debilitated ex-prisoners from the jails and prison camps. The Red Cross in India had stored us amply with clothing and necessities and had provided a staff to supervise the issue. The ship's permanent staff had been augmented by additional Indian medical officers (one of them a mental specialist) and the numbers of medical orderlies had been increased. As first aid, we could be useful.

Damage and destruction in the city was not plainly discernible when we felt our way gingerly through the wreck-studded sea-channel to the docks at Tanjong Pagar, but once moored there the extent of our 'denial to the enemy' of the use of quays and docks and warehouses was plainly visible. Not many bricks stood one upon the other as a result of recent Allied air-raids and Japanese war material that littered the quays and sheds was blasted far and wide. On this day of communal rejoicing, the Chinese dockers were all fire-cracking in holiday mood on the Padang, but Japanese prisoners had been rounded up and brought in to clear a quayside passage for the working of the ships. It was our first sight of the enemy. They looked in no way different from other coolie labourers we had known in eastern seaports and worked silently and well, if sullen and dispirited, under the scornful eyes of armed Gurkha guards. . . . In contrast with the enforced activity of the whilom 'masters of Asia', the groups of our intended passengers, standing aside in a cleared quay-space, seemed ghostly and not of the world. Brought down to the embarkation point in army trucks and wagons, many could scarcely summon strength to step down from the cars and take a place in the waiting throng. At first sight, they appeared crippled and mis-shapen—and the semblance was exaggerated by the bamboo 'helping' sticks that many carried, but Major Hafizuddin (the Indian mental specialist) thought that condition due to body wastage—whilst the seemingly large heads had maintained structure and formation. The R.A.P.W.I.'s had already been cleansed and defested at a camp on shore and clothing had there been issued. The day was hot, however, and few wore more than a loin cloth; but each had his little bundle of only belongings and on that he sat or squatted until it was the time for him to straggle on the gangway and take up his ordered place on board.

We sailed for Madras at first daylight in the morning. Routed independently, our progress throughout the long length of the swept and buoyed channel in the straits was unchecked and its only sinister incident the frequent sighting of drifting mines. In other circumstance, we would have opened fire and endeavoured to put them up or hole them, but regard for the state of our passengers prevailed and we had to be content to broadcast their positions by open wireless messages that were now allowed.

The unsettled weather that had marked the failing of the monsoon and the cessation of the rains had given way to steady periods of calm and sunshine when we reached the Bay of Bengal and the benefit of such halcyon days became quickly evident amongst the ailing *pultanis*. The repressions of long captivity appeared to be soon forgotten in the clemency of ship-board routine. The men became interested in the ship's progress. No longer listless and silent, they chattered interminably as they sat or lay about the decks and it could be surmised that forgotten incidents and past experiences would be recalled. With long experience of welfare work, Colonel Nicholson—the O.C. troops—proved himself the ideal commander of our tattered section of the Indian (regular) Army. I thought it strange that, at master's rounds, the sepoys addressed him as 'Nikelsen Sahib' instead of the usual 'Colonel Sahib'. Our contingent of R.A.P.W.I.'s were men of the old regular Indian Army (who had been taken with the gallant rearguard in Burma in 1942), the sons and grandsons and even great-grandsons of professional soldiers. In some way, I was told, rumour had got around amongst them that our colonel was a descendant of the legend-ary John Nicholson of whose exploits they may well have heard at many camp-fires. The colonel disclaimed any knowledge of such a notable connection, but it seemed needless to protest. With me, the men were friendly and respectful. Only, in answer to a word of enquiry perhaps, they had their way of conveying a poor opinion of my halting Hindustani by replying in exactly the sonorous tones my *Munshi* employed at Bombay when he struggled with my faulty efforts as far back as 1900. 'Nick' did not speak Hindustani at all, but that made no differ-ence: he had his way of listening. For him, the *pultanis* would stand wired at attention, their poor weazened knees almost trembling with soldierly intendment. We got on famously together and it was heartening to note the combination of awakened morale and improved physique that only a week of ship-life effected. . . . Below decks, where the badly conditioned men were in the hands of the considerate medical staff, matters were not quite as good. The mental ward was a sad sight, but we were spared the incidence of serious disease. On the 18th of September we arrived at Madras.

If not quite the first transport to return to India with ex-prisoners of the Japanese, *Circassia* was among the early arrivals, and the flags and decorations on the waterfront were still fresh and colourful. As we passed in between the breakwaters, the ship was greeted by a fanfare of steamer whistles from all the vessels in the harbour and flag hoists on every mast and 'trick-stay' kept us busy with the answering pennant. At the quay-berth to which we angled in and made fast, a colourful reception party of state and civic dignitaries was assembled. Speeches of welcome and encouragement were made as the ship hauled alongside. From inboard the ship we could not hear clearly what was said, for the platform party was not expert in the use of what was probably a borrowed loud-hailer. But we could hear the music of the regimental band of a British regiment that had been brought to the breast of the quay. Curiously, the airs they played were un-martial in character. Someone remarked on this. It seemed odd, and I wondered if the bandmaster had his orders. The political situation in India was cloudy at the moment, and it may have been considered inopportune to blare out 'Rule Britannia' on this occasion. But he might, quite properly, have tapped his baton and called 'Hearts of Oak' in compliment to the ferrymen!

Chapter XXXI

OCEAN CHESSBOARD

In October, 1945, the duty of repairing the ravages of the wars in south-east Asia became Britain's task and one that would employ all available shipping in the Far East for a considerable period. Additional to the transport of troops to troubled areas, there was also the need to recover and repatriate Allied prisoners of war and displaced persons, scattered and almost hidden away by the Japanese in Indo-China and Siam and amongst the myriad islands of the eastern archipelago. When I attended naval headquarters at Rangoon to receive sailing orders, I learned from Captain Frame—the Sea Transport Officer—that the ship would be actively employed in eastern waters for a long time. He spoke of obscure ports and islands that were far from the beaten tracks of ocean commerce. As an initial movement, the seasoned Gurkha battalions that we were at the moment embarking in the river, would be taken to Saigon for the reinforcement of the British military mission at Annam. What then, would be anybody's guess. It would depend on the progress of the game: *Circassia* would be a useful pawn on the ocean chessboard for she was stored and fitted as well to attend to the weak and dispossessed, as to transport armed men.

Saigon! I recalled a Company Conference at New York when the employment of the *Transylvania* on a world cruise was under consideration. Saigon had been one of the seaports envisaged, and the passenger department was enthusiastic about a call there for the arresting slogan of 'Visit mysterious Angkor' would look well in the advertising. But we did not go. Saigon is a considerable distance up-river from the sea and its navigation was thought a serious risk for a ship of *Transylvania's* size and length. But *Circassia* was much smaller than my former ship and could be lightened to a navigable draft. We could go there. A sudden thought came and I fumbled in my satchel for the Chart Register. No. It was as I had feared. We held no chart folios and sailing directions for anywhere east of Singapore!

The provision of charts to merchant transports had become an Admiralty obligation on the outbreak of war and so the routeing officer was approached to supply these essentials. He did not have them. The chart depot was not yet re-established at Rangoon and there was word that the stock for such a naval store had been unaccountably held up somewhere. The best he could do for us was to make a signal to Singapore. They would have them there—if not a new issue, then certainly some of those captured in the Japanese ships who still used British Admiralty charts. He would attend to the matter at once; there was no need to worry. It was pointed out that we were not scheduled to call at Singapore. That too, he said, would be attended to. Naval Control there would send the folios off by launch when we were passing Peak Island. Perhaps it would be as well for us previously to send a wireless message giving the time for a rendezvous off that point.

Upon return to the ship I was uneasy. There was no guarantee that Singapore would be able to make good our deficiency and, the more I thought of it, the less it seemed likely that our demands would be met there. But we were now almost fully embarked: the mooring lighter was busy unshackling our cable from the buoys and the pilot stamping with impatience on the bridge; the tide was right for making Elephant Point before darkness came. We sailed as instructed, my only makeshift being a general sheet of the China Seas in which the approaches to Saigon were barely distinguishable, so small was the scale of it. Singapore was apparently as bankrupt as Rangoon, for we were not met at Peak Island, nor was there any reply to our repeated signals. We were committed, and there was nothing for it but to discover the coast of Indo-China ourselves. . . . That proved not too difficult. By taking a longer route, keeping in the deep water the small-scale sheet displayed, passing the islands at a wide berth, we made safe progress. After a few days of steady steaming we raised the prominent wooded island of Pulo Condore where the outflow of the Mekong delta discolours the blue of the sea and sends down floating islands of trees and jungle growth to dismay the mariner. But we had made a good course. With relief, I saw the high promontory of Cap St. Jacques grow up above the horizon and we stood in to the anchorage there, encouraged by the sight of ships—which included the great French battleship *Richelieu*—lying comfortably anchored.

The French pilot who boarded us after arrival was confident that, on our lightened draft, we could safely proceed up-river at a favourable stage of the tide, which would not be until the following morning. He said he required a good flood tide in transit for there were reaches in the river at which he would have to stop engines and drift up-stream. I thought this unusual; but it became quickly fearsome when I learned that there were still acoustic mines, strewn by Allied aircraft, embedded in the thick mud of the channels—mines that could not be swept. There had been many casualties; one, a 'liberty' ship, had been mined on the day before and now lay beached at Nha-Bé with her propeller blown off and the stern-post fractured. From the outer anchorage where we lay there was in sight much evidence of the thoroughness of recent Allied air activity, for shattered wrecks abounded wherever the eye could follow. Nor was this all the hazard of the river passage. There was a state of war in the country. Armed strongly with weapons acquired or stolen from the disordered Japanese and thought to be well led by broken Japanese officers, Viet-Nam rebels were in active revolt. They controlled many points on the river banks from which they had the habit of sniping at the passing ships. We would have to keep our troops and men below on the route of the river passage. . . . That situation was ugly enough, but it was the prospect of entering the most crooked river in the world without a chart that disquieted me the most. Doubtless the pilot thought my insistence on the point a want of confidence and my fears unfounded, but he did take steps to procure a chart from the pilot station on shore. It was an old British Admiralty sheet, considerably out of date, but sufficiently displaying the almost unbelievable maze of snake-like crooks and bends and twists of the Saigon River. But I was glad to have at last something to steer by.

We got under way at noon on the following day with the tide at half flood. The approaches were adequately buoyed and we had no difficulty in crossing the bar, but when, after winding past fishing-stakes and native huts perched high on massive stilts, the ship was swung into an opening in the jungle, I was startled. The pilot's assurance that we were now in the river did little to dispel my anxiety. It did not look like the channel for a large ship. For a few moments we seemed to be heading straight into an impenetrable barrier of tall palms and mangroves; then deftly the helm was put hard over and we slid into another short reach, equally as forbidding. I think the pilot enjoyed my obvious dismay, but he was at pains to trace our progress on the outspread chart. Close study of the river windings displayed on it brought my inspection up to the wharves at Saigon. But the river there did not seem to be of any greater breadth than the reaches we had passed. I could see no proper clearance to turn the ship for heading downstream again on departure. I spoke of this. Would we have tugs, I asked, to cant us in the river off Saigon? 'Rien du tout,' he replied, smiling, his palms upthrown. He told me it was the practice to put the ship's bows ashore in the thick mud of the eastern bank and let the flood tide carry her round! . . . An amazing business, I thought, but I began to borrow confidence from the man's imperturbable aplomb as we swung violently under helm on our way upstream. We did not see the enemy on the river banks and were unsniped. Little villages we passed from time to time—a few bush-covered huts, on stilts beside the fishing-stakes or a clearing in which the countrymen could be seen urging their buffaloes in the paddy fields. But no one seemed to be interested in the passage of a great ship so close to their cooking pots and our progress was only occasionally checked by the stoppage of the engines. Many wrecks, tucked snugly in the mud beside the mangroves, were our road signs for caution. In late afternoon we came slowly to a stop off the wharves of Saigon and I watched, not without apprehension, the measured swing of the ship as her bow was lanced into the river bank. There was a little bamboo jetty there and a woman was dipping her baby into the river from it. She did not even look up to protest this intrusion of an alien shard of grey steel into the deliberation of her domestic pursuits.

Saigon was in a disturbed way when we hauled alongside the Messageries Wharf and made fast. As nearly as sailor understanding could follow it, there was a situation that was criss and cross. If not actually beleaguered by the Annamite rebels, the city's outskirts were at times the scene of vicious guerilla warfare in which strong rebel forces emerged from the jungle at widely separated points to kill and burn and destroy. At night they infiltrated into the city in small bands of incendiaries and the flames of burning structures could be seen at many points throughout the night. Their suppression was a matter for the French authority, but the numbers of reliable fighting men they were able to put in the field—even as now reinforced by the Marines of the *Richelieu*—were pitifully small. It was said that the rebels had no quarrel with the British forces in the area under General Gracie, whose operations were directed to rounding up the Japanese in Indo-China and the recovery of Allied prisoners of war and displaced persons. An extraordinary feature of this knotty problem on the chessboard was that the now defeated Japanese had been co-opted by our forces to aid in the maintenance of peace and order in the district! As we hauled alongside the wharf, it was Japanese naval sailors who took our ropes, positioned the brows and gangways, and settled down to the business of discharging the large cargo of military stores and equipment that we had brought from Rangoon. This amazing situation was further magnified when we observed that the imperial handymen, skilfully turning our lines on the bollards, were belted with full ammunition pouches and their rifles, with bayonets fixed, were stacked in orderly precision within the palisades of the dock area!

To make the river passage at the draft the pilot had stipulated it had been necessary to jettison much of our weighty freshwater supply. On the seaward passage we could be at a deeper draft for there was an anchorage within the river bar at which we could wait for the rising tide. We could water to capacity at the wharf, but the provision of such a quantity presented its difficulty. The only reservoir of potable water was at some distance from the wharf and the flow at the hydrants was weak. British naval command on the waterfront was informed of this and, to 'boost' the feeble pressure, two fire-engines of American design were acquired from somewhere and throbbed alongside for the most part of our stay in port. But at dusk or throughout the night it was common for the hoses to be hastily disconnected, the Japanese naval operators to pick up their rifles from the stacks, mount the engines and scream off towards the city to fight raiders and extinguish fierce fires.

In such a situation the normal periods of leave and liberty could not be granted to the ship's crew. But the British N.O.I.C. concurred that daylight promenade in the main streets and boulevards of this 'Paris of the east' could be allowed. It was in orders that all libertymen must return to their ships before sunset. That assumption of safety in daylight hours was badly shattered on the second day. About an hour before sunset I had an urgent message from the French military hospital in the city. Three of our men had been brought in there by a Japanese patrol. They had been attacked on the outskirts of the town and had been wounded by rifle fire. Two were serious cases and immediate operation for one was necessary: the third was held for lesser attention. . . . It was after dark before the ship's doctor and I could procure transport to take us to the hospital. What young Dr. Weir (the ink scarce dry on his diploma) thought of that eerie flash through sinister and darkened streets and by-ways, I do not know, but I was unhappy. We had been allotted a Japanese armoured truck to take us on and, as its klaxon roared at the crossings and I noted the armed Jap officer on the running-board, I had all the sensation of an appalling nightmare. I had not thought, so soon, to come under the protection of the enemy.

From the slightly wounded man we learned what had happened. They had taken what they thought a brisk walk up-town, but had wandered wrongly into the country at the canal bridge. They had turned back to retrace their route when, from some fields and jungle-growth rifle fire was opened. He saw men running towards them when he was hit and fell, but they paused at sight of the patrol car speeding down the road in their direction. He did not know if the Japs returned the fire and indeed remembered little until he was brought to the hospital. Observing that our men were dressed in civilian shirts and shorts, the kind French interne ruefully suggested that *les Annamites* might have taken them for French civilians. There had been many cases. The doctor thought the flesh wounds of this man could be attended to on board and he could return to the ship with us. *Les autres?* . . . He waved his hand in a gesture of balance. Both had a chance, he said, but it was slender in the more serious case. There would be an operation; the spleen, he added, for they were shot in the back: the surgeon was expected at any moment. Would I like to see the men before he arrived? A brief visit, he said, warningly. Strangely, the man who was due for the operating table was the brighter of the two. He was an old hand and of good character. He was glad to see us and sent messages to his mates in the ship. I told him that everything would be done for him and his home folks would be advised of his plight by cable. As I wrote down the address he gave, I reflected that often there was something on a man's mind in a case like this. I asked if there was anything special I could do for him. I was in expectation of hearing some domestic sentiment, but it was the custody of two Indian carpets he had purchased in Vizag that worried him. He asked if they could be taken from his quarters in the 'Glory Hole' and lodged for safe keeping with the baggage master. When the ship got home, he said, he would come down to claim them. . . . He did too.

Embarked to capacity with Netherlands ex-prisoners of war and civilians who included women and children, we slipped downstream under instruction to proceed to Batavia. The pilot who had conned us up to Saigon was again on the bridge and his smiling confidence was tonic to me after the untoward incidents that had marked our visit to the port. My fears of the river with all its sudden twists and turns had vanished for I was in prospect of reaching the open sea again.

On our passage southward towards the Karimata Strait, we were turned in our track by a wireless signal. The Indonesian outbreak had flared up again in Java and we were routed to Singapore.

★　　★　　★

The naval control officer at Singapore had no apology to offer for letting us pass into the China Seas without charts and books. He had received Rangoon's message and also our repeated signals, but there was nothing he could do about it. Colombo had let them down. Someone there had mislaid the half of a ship's cargo of Admiralty 'stationery' destined to re-equip the fleet and the merchant ships in Far Eastern waters. But all was well again. The consignment had been recovered and I could now take, on signature, all that was necessary for the voyage around Australia. . . . Australia! . . . All my ill-temper and seeming truculence vanished at the word. I called him 'Sir' again, and eagerly examined the folios of charts and the precious books of sailing directions that he put at my disposal. We were to embark Australian units, ex-prisoners from Changi Jail and the purgatory of the Siam railway encampments. As he mentioned our ports of call, I saw myself privileged to visit again the haunts of my youth when I was a prime seaman in square rig.

'Diggers' are mostly tall and lithe. Their faces are often gaunt and their complexion bronzed. Such men do not in general betray in appearance the privations, the indignities, exposures and infirmities they have suffered at the hands of any enemy. There is something too in the rehabilitation brought about by the refreshment of clean clothing, for the men we embarked at Port Keppel had been cleansed from rags and tatters and were again 'kitted' with service uniform which they wore with an air, perhaps even a swagger, they had not forgotten. For the most part, they streamed up the gangways from the quayside without effort but, now and then, a man might stumble, clutch the handrail and pause for a little. He would not look back, shoreward, whence he had come. That was finished and done with. His eyes would rove over the hull and superstructure of the ship, so differing from his late environment. Then, recovered, he would straighten up with a lift of the shoulders and move on towards the sally port. Nor were the civilian repatriates less dignified in taking up again their place in the friendly and civilised atmosphere of shipboard . . . but only the children, who had no memory of freedom other than their own, were gay. The others were grave, quiet. There was no approach to the joy and jubilation the Psalmist records when 'The Lord turned again the prisoners of Zion: then was our mouth filled with laughter, and our tongue with singing'. No. The cup was too full—they were more like 'them that dream'. It is possible that the rigours and restrictions, perhaps punishments, they had so stoically endured for so long had habited them to silence. Within the ship, we made no effusive advances to offset the grave reflective mood; it was well enough to be of service and I noted many kindly and unobtrusive acts. There would be time enough later, on the long sea-passage for the rites of sailor friendship and hospitality to be generously laid on.

Freemantle was not a port I had visited before. It was off-track in my early days at sea. The emigrants we carried in the Loch Line clipper ships were not attracted by the then slender resources of Western Australia. To them the western State was hardly known, and the great openings for their craft and industry in the south and east urged them to Adelaide and Melbourne and Sydney. But it was almost with the enthusiasm of my young sailor days I made the land at Rottnest Island and turned the *Circassia* into harbour. That was on a Sunday and Freemantle with its nearby capital city of Perth had made holiday of the occasion to greet the returning soldiers. The trim little wharf at which we moored was swept and garnished and beflagged. At the upper storey of the dock shed, civic dignitaries and ladies stood assembled and a military band was in position. As we drew in, the band struck up the not very stirring music of 'Advance Australia Fair'. It was apparent at once that this opening number was only barely tolerated by the troops. They had gained high spirits again, brisked and invigorated by the long fine sea days of the voyage since we had dipped Acheen Head on the horizon astern. They were again the boisterous 'diggers' I knew and remembered. 'Waltzing Matilda' was what they roared and shouted for, and 'Waltzing Matilda' it was throughout the periods of the official festivities.

Standing slightly apart from the reception group fronting the position of the gangway that was now run out, I noticed an erect elderly man holding out what I took to be a placard of some sort for the inspection of the landing soldiers. Some paused to speak to him, then moved on with a shake of the head. A turn in my direction showed the placard to be an enlargement of a portrait photograph such as could be on the walls of any modest sitting-room. It was that of a young man in soldier uniform. Mr. Salmon, the Company's agent, who was with me on deck, told me the old man attended the arrival of every troopship from the north. Long after the Freemantle contingent had disembarked, and when the rest of our troops were trickling on shore for the evening's liberty, he was still there . . . in the hope that someone would recognise the picture and tell him where and in what manner his son had died.

On passage from Freemantle to our next port we passed close to Cape Leeuwin that I so well remembered. 'The' Leeuwin was its name then to such as I, a hard-fisted voyaging sailor, sixty-eight days out from the Clyde in 'the fine ship or vessel called the *Loch Ness* whereof, under God, William Martin was master' and I the second mate. But the modest promontory crowned by a trim lighthouse that I saw from my chair on 'Monkey Island' did not accord with my memories, nor the smooth passage of the *Circassia* to seaward of the reefs outlying it resemble the circumstance of my first sight of Australia. Then, we had seen nothing of any land in the many sea days since we had taken our departure from the Tuskar Rock, for 'Bully' Martin was ever the man to seek for the wind, as well he knew where to find it. From the longitude of the Cape we had steered southerly right into the heart of the roaring forties to take spur from the great westerly gales where they storm unchecked around the world.

But the ship was bound to Adelaide and there came the days when we edged northward to make the land. The weather moderated, and on a clear bright day the welcome hail of 'Land-o' came from a lookout aloft. Only a blue ridge above the sea-line and far distant! Whether it was 'the' Leeuwin or not, I did not learn: a humble second mate in square-rig was not often involved with the mysteries of navigation or location. It was enough that he could lead his watch in the sailorising of the day. . . . *Circassia* did not call at Port Adelaide. That was a disappointment, for I had heard the surprising news from Mr. Salmon at Freemantle that the aged *Loch Ness* was still afloat and useful in the harbour at Adelaide. Even although bereft of her graceful masts and spars and with her shapely hull now disfigured to meet the lowly traffic of a coal hulk, I thought I would recognise her again. I had the wish to go aboard, to tread her deck once more, for it was in her I had my sea lessons under one who was probably the finest seaman of his day.

I found Melbourne grown and changed almost beyond recognition. When we arrived, it was necessary for some reason to come to anchor in Hobson's Bay and await instruction, and it was for long I sought some point that I remembered in the appearance of the port. The high modern buildings at tide-line, the dock cranes and structures, factories, gasometers, chimneys and towers, did not resemble the outline I conjured from the past. I did not know the pleasant little seaport suburb of Williamstown in this new guise. Only by diligent canvass through binoculars of the docks and piers did I find traces of the little boat-jetty that was the prominent feature of the shore line there when we clewed up or set sail in the Bay on arrival or departure. The very place. The jetty at whose worn boat-steps we landed the 'Old Man' in the morning for his visit to the agents and where we 'lay off' long into the night awaiting his return. But that would be when the winds were foul southerly in the bay or when sailormen were scarce in the boarding-houses as the lure of shore employment beckoned. Up-street from the boat-steps I could discern between the high new buildings part of the row of low-fronted houses and shops that might have been the waterfront in my day. I recalled its appearance then—the range of sailors' boarding-houses, a tavern or two, shipping offices, bakers' and butchers' shops: particularly I remembered the larger building of the ship-chandler's warehouse in whose smoke-clouded back-room the shipmasters crowded long and hearty in endless reminiscence of winds and freights, passages and landfalls. Of ships too. How the lovely names of *Thessalus, Melpomene, Loch Vennacher, Patriarch* and *Thermopylae* would roll from bearded lips.

I was glad to have these tablets of the memory restored and pondered long. . . . But the flags were up and there was band music at the shining new Municipal Piers. It was time to ring 'stand by' on the telegraphs and take a turn of the steering gear in readiness to haul alongside and land Victoria's warriors returned.

Chapter XXXII

HAULING DOWN

SYDNEY was the terminal port of *Circassia's* Australian voyage. When we had disembarked the last of the repatriates at Dalgetty's Wharf, the next assignment of the ship became the warm subject of conjecture. Former experience of Naval Control could be no guide now that peace had come and, for the most part, we were inclined to indulge in rosy thought of an immediate return to the United Kingdom, perhaps calling again at Singapore to embark 'Pythons' marked for demobilisation. We knew about the disbandment scheme of 'Python' for many of our enlisted shipmates were already in possession of the formal circulars that set forth its priorities. Not all our D.E.M.S. gunners, ship's military staff, signalmen, Radar operatives, and other 'shilling a month' men, were enthusiastic about the return to civilian life that was there laid down for them. Lieutenant Cleare sighed at the thought of going back to schoolmastering in Essex; Colonel Nicholson wondered how he could now stand up to the bleak austerities of northern country life; the S.M.O. commented ruefully on the prospect of cementing up the leakages in his former medical practice: almost daily, my advice was sought by R.A.M.C. orderlies and Maritime R.A.

gunners as to the manners of application for permanent employment in the merchant ships on peace-time occasions. We were keyed to a mood of suspense as we lay there, an empty ship, under the shadow of the great Harbour Bridge.

I should have known better than to busy myself in preparing plans for future voyages. But always it is as well to have an answer ready when 'Capabilities and Condition' of the ship is posed by Sea Transport or Naval Control—or even S.O.U.L.S. again. In thought of a minor triumph at Capteown in 1941 when, by dangling the bait of a bumper cargo, I had gained time and opportunity to put the *Nea Hellas* in seaworthy condition, I had occupied my leisure on the voyage from Malaya in tabling out what must needs be done in loading a great cargo to the exactitude of half an inch in mean draft. My document was formidable. There was first, the business of disencumbering the ship of excess weight, not only of her artillery and war equipment but also of the unprofitable ballast that had lain in her since she was requisitioned by the Admiralty in 1939. I pondered long the page in which I had condemned it. The bulk, required for stability, consisted of sand, now foul-smelling, and —as in the *Nea Hellas*—a large 'deep' tank in which we had, in the years, carried a thousand tons of equally foul Clyde river water over much of the globe. I stressed the need for quick removal of such a content and, as there was space for further argument, went on to include a paragraph on the greatly increased rattage within the ship and the prevalence of weevils and insect pests in the storerooms. (It is a good plan to mention such menaces to health and well-being in a vessel, thus invoking the co-operation of the Port Sanitary Authority.) That done, I covered a new sheet or two in detail of the placement of a suitable cargo in the holds. It required careful consideration and brought up again the almost forgotten rules of good stowage, that we had perhaps lightly regarded in beach-head operations. Certainly, we had carried our share of war stores and munitions, field pieces and bridging irons, barb-wire and tele-poles, but the handling of these was so often governed by late delivery on embarkation and first priorities in unloading that only casual attention could be paid to their seamanlike distribution in the ship's lower holds. Now, it was with due regard to the commercial sea gods of stability and inherent vice, I tabled off the spaces to the decimals of cubic capacity—all shipshape and Bristol fashion.

It was a good memorandum. As I wrote it out, I could pause in its composition to indulge a dream of 'Sailor's Return' after war—a vision of *Circassia*, almost at her load marks, steaming into the Clyde with a lading of essentials to relieve in part the dire austerities of the home kitchen. . . . A good memorandum; but I might have spared myself the effort. The time was not yet. Naval Control and the local Sea Transport Directorate had each its special piegon-hole for such presumptious communications and only the Company's mercantile agent, to whom I gave a copy, gazed hungrily but without hope at its gross tabulation of space for the loading of a profitable cargo.

No. The time was not yet. There were other plans for us. We were to fuel and water to capacity and load food stores at Sydney for a further six months operations. Our insanitary condition was noted and the ship would be fumigated by cyanide: the sand-ballast would be raked and turned over. Arrangement had been made for the Dockyard to dismantle the ship's armament and remove all ammunition. Lieutenant Cleare and the D.E.M.S. gunners would be taken off and re-embarked in an aircraft carrier for passage homeward. But the ship's O.C. Troops and his military staff would remain with us and, as well, the Red Cross auxiliaries. When the last pronouncement was made, I had immediate vision of long extended service in the south and east, but Sea Transport had not yet made up its mind. Only, there was talk of a passage, light ship, to Rabaul in New Guinea and there embark Australian troops for repatriation. Nothing of that engagement was definite. But this much was certain—that our good shipmates of the D.E.M.S. party were to leave us and take passage home in H.M.S. *Illustrious* as soon as the ordnance men from the Dockyard had wrenched away the guns and their fitment that our men had served so well and for so long. We were loath to see our Forces comrades go. We thought it the beginning of some end—the dispersal of a good and loyal ship's company.

It was at this time the ship's Owners re-appeared publicly upon the shipping stage, peeping self-consciously from behind the naval curtain—as though they had not been there all the time prompting us with their help and encouragement and assistance in the many difficult situations that arose under Sea Transport charters. I do not know what other masters thought of it but, to me, it was the complete return to normalcy when I could 'blow in' to the offices of McIlwraith, McEachran and Co.—an ancient sailor firm—and talk of ships and freights and voyages almost as though the war had never been. It was not quite that Naval Control had handed the *Circassia* back to commercial management: rather that they had surrendered a war interest in her pots and pans, her crew embroilments with the port police, her pounds and pennies in meeting the obligations of a stay in port. I thought the war days definitely over when I could draw cash against signature again for ship disbursements. But there was work to do. . . . After ten days of speculation, rumour tidied down to an apparently firm commitment. Being in all respects ready for sea, as then we were, a coastal passage to Brisbane in Queensland was envisaged. There, we were to embark Chinese labourers who had been temporarily imported by the Commonwealth in the war years to aid with manpower. All in readiness, we were held up at the quayside by the Australian Treasury—of all Departments! The Chinese had not paid their Income Tax and could not be allowed to sail for their homeland until they had worked that off! The 'movement' was abandoned. It is possible that this restriction on the part of a financial authority pointed the large cost of holding the ship immobile in port. Whatever the reason, we were sent, light ship, to Manila in the Phillipines to embark Netherlands troops and displaced persons. We sailed on the 20th November, 1945.

There followed a curious Odyssey that had similitude to the wanderings of the Greeks after the fall of Troy. In her early days of landing operations *Circassia* had been referred to as 'an impudent little ship'. No one could call 12,000 tons 'little' and, as for 'impudence', it was possibly her extreme handiness at inshore movements that earned her the not unworthy epithet. Her quality was greatly tested in the months of ocean 'tramping' amongst the islands and peninsulas, the rivers and creeks, of the East Indian Archipelago. Sailing from Sydney, we took the inshore passage through the Great Barrier reefs to Thursday Island—an unbelievable experience of ins and outs in the winding channels that led us on. In my elder years I was finding much to learn in a branch of navigation I had not before undertaken—the arts of timekeeping on a long extended passage. In the Torres Straits pilot who sailed with us, I had a good mentor: he it was who advised the many 'slows' and even 'stops' which, together with bursts of utmost speed, brought the ship to the narrower and more dangerous bends and channels in God's good daylight—a practice that, later, I found good in anxious circumstance when he had gone, for the pilots in the Archipelago were few, and even those who did come off at the beckoning of the 'Jack' at the fore were hesitant and unskilled after long duress. Nor were the coastal lights, the buoys, the seamarks yet re-established to conform with Sailing Directions.

Through the Arafura Sea and by traverse of the Molucca Passage we sailed on to enter Manila Bay on 2nd December. I had seen devastation in a seaport before in war service but nothing comparable with the scale of havoc that had overtaken this modern Troy. It was not perhaps the shattered buildings in the city, the rubble heaps where dwellings had been, the tottering wharves on the waterfront, that held the sailor eye: it was the ship wreckage in the Bay that amazed us by its magnitude. The vast expanse of Manila Bay is free of rock and shoal and sand bank; it is comparatively shallow and has an even bottom. It was doubtless this configuration that exposed the masts and upper works, the riven hulls of the shipping, to view above sea level. In the calm of bright weather, we threaded our way between one mass of disordered iron and another, anchoring where opportunity served us off the shattered city.

The adaptation of existent wreckage to serve a purpose was

long known, but it is undeniable that the Americans were particularly skilled in its operation for wharfage in demolished seaports. When we were ordered alongside to embark passengers, it was sidling on bolted pontoons we lay and with our bows stabbed into the mud of the foreshore. The masts, funnels and part upperworks of a wreck at the quayside had been shorn away somewhat in the manner of a blasting operation on the hillside, and through the gap—clambering on battened staging, the long procession of Dutch personnel filed on board. Adults and children of both sexes, European and Indonesian, Malay and even Chinese, they posed a problem for the ship's berthing staff and the Red Cross, for no detailed lists or plans were available. It seemed enough for the hard-pressed American port directorate to pour on until the bucket was demonstrably full and overflowing. We had perforce, at once to become diplomats and racial discriminators—a dual engagement in which we were not well versed. But one can put up a good face, and the small matters of tolerance and patience won a way for us. A huge Hollander, a brigadier no less—however stiffly he might stand on his rank—could be mollified by the sight of clean sheets again and a smiling steward standing-by, to accept another occupant in his cabin and forget the matters of privilege: a tawny Staats clerk become reconciled to separation from his wife and children by the knowledge that they at least would be well harboured. We had our own ways of resolving all difficulties once we were free of the land.

This was the pattern of *Circassia's* service in the Islands. If a schedule of operations existed, we did not know of it. We were directed here and there, from day to day, from port to port. Creeping in, as always with the lead going seamanlike, to Balikpapaan in Borneo, across the Straits to sleepy Macassar in the Celebes, back to Singapore to embark the ever-valiant Gurkhas and carry them to Soerabaja in Java to 'stand in' for Holland against riot and disorder there. Up north again to Bangkok in Siam, southward to Brunei and Labuan, westward to Swettenham and Penang; a ceaseless round of the Islands where almost daily there was discovery of a new encampment of

prisoners the Japanese had 'parked' awhile—and conveniently
forgotten. . . . The little jack-staff on the stem had pointed to
many degrees of the compass since I had remarked its gradua-
tion of the Garelochside, when, in February of 1946, we found
ourselves at Port Blair in the Andamans and under orders to
steer for home.

★   ★   ★

The Highland hills never looked more lovely than when we
rounded the Cloch on 29th March, 1946, and headed in towards
the Tail of the Bank. It was a brave day with the snap of lingering winter in it and there was snow on the northern peaks, but
the sun shone and there was blue in the sky. I thought of the
many aspects the Clyde anchorage had displayed in the years I
had frequented it. In fog, in storm, in rain, in sun. But this
'Sailor's Return' was special and I looked long, for I would not
see it again as a master sailor on the bridge of his ship. Curiously,
and as I think for the first time in long seafaring, I had become
nervous and uneasy on the last lap. Was there not some un-
imaginable incident awaiting me to break the charmed cycle of
good fortune that had been mine at sea? . . . But the road was
clear and we anchored quietly in my old favoured position off
Princes Pier.

Awaiting the tide! How often had I done that and in exactly
the same place? The first turn of the flood would serve us now,
for *Circassia* was high and light without an ounce of cargo in
the holds, and only the foul old sand and water ballast was still
there to be declared at the Custom House on entry. The ship
looked tired too; whitened and weather-stained by tropic sunshine, salted and rusted on the outer plating by long sea-keeping.
But the flags were hoist and blew out finely with their note of
colour. In ordered groups they fluttered out—the ship's name
and code numbers, the deepest draft of water, the Royal Mail
pennant, flag 'R' for Ritchie, to summons a shore boat for the
purser. All in order, and amongst them my exempt pilot flag
for the lower Firth that, for me, would not again be hoisted. . . .
It was in relief from sober thought I welcomed the coming of a

favoured river pilot and listened to his news of the river and the day.

When we had docked safely and without incident in the King George V Dock at Glasgow I had a last look at the bridge and its sea tools that had been my home and my workshop for so long. The 'scrap log' lay opened on the chartroom desk and I noticed that the final entry had not yet been made. Kindly enough, the Second Officer was waiting for me to do something, as the engines were still at 'Stand-by'. Grasping the handles of the telegraph, I rang off myself, cast an eye aloft at the flags still fluttering, and gave my last command in a ship . . . to 'Haul all down!'

INDEX

INDEX

INDEX

INDEX

INDEX

INDEX

PRINTED IN GREAT BRITAIN BY ROBERT MACLEHOSE AND CO. LTD.
THE UNIVERSITY PRESS, GLASGOW